Tourism in OECD Countries 2008

TRENDS AND POLICIES

OECD

Humber College Library
3199 Lakeshore Blvd. West
Toronto, ON M8V 1K8

ORGANISATION FOR ECONOMIC CO-OPERATION AND DEVELOPMENT

The OECD is a unique forum where the governments of 30 democracies work together to address the economic, social and environmental challenges of globalisation. The OECD is also at the forefront of efforts to understand and to help governments respond to new developments and concerns, such as corporate governance, the information economy and the challenges of an ageing population. The Organisation provides a setting where governments can compare policy experiences, seek answers to common problems, identify good practice and work to co-ordinate domestic and international policies.

The OECD member countries are: Australia, Austria, Belgium, Canada, the Czech Republic, Denmark, Finland, France, Germany, Greece, Hungary, Iceland, Ireland, Italy, Japan, Korea, Luxembourg, Mexico, the Netherlands, New Zealand, Norway, Poland, Portugal, the Slovak Republic, Spain, Sweden, Switzerland, Turkey, the United Kingdom and the United States. The Commission of the European Communities takes part in the work of the OECD.

OECD Publishing disseminates widely the results of the Organisation's statistics gathering and research on economic, social and environmental issues, as well as the conventions, guidelines and standards agreed by its members.

This work is published on the responsibility of the Secretary-General of the OECD. The opinions expressed and arguments employed herein do not necessarily reflect the official views of the Organisation or of the governments of its member countries.

Also available in French under the title:
Le tourisme dans les pays de l'OCDE 2008
TENDANCES ET POLITIQUES

Corrigenda to OECD publications may be found on line at: *www.oecd.org/publishing/corrigenda*.

Photo credit: © Ben Blankenburg/Corbis, © DAJ/Gettyimages®, © David De Lossy/Gettyimages®, © Flying Colours Ltd./Gettyimages®

© OECD 2008

No reproduction, copy, transmission or translation of this publication may be made without written permission. Applications should be sent to OECD Publishing *rights@oecd.org* or by fax 33 1 45 24 99 30. Permission to photocopy a portion of this work should be addressed to the Centre français d'exploitation du droit de copie (CFC), 20, rue des Grands-Augustins, 75006 Paris, France, fax 33 1 46 34 67 19, *contact@cfcopies.com* or (for US only) to Copyright Clearance Center (CCC), 222 Rosewood Drive, Danvers, MA 01923, USA, fax 1 978 646 8600, *info@copyright.com*.

Foreword

This report provides an overview of key trends and tourism policy developments with thematic chapters and country profiles for 30 OECD countries and selected economies. It synthesises thematic work undertaken on a range of topics by the OECD Tourism Committee and within the OECD Centre for Entrepreneurship, SMEs and Local Development and the Trade and Agriculture Directorate.

The OECD Tourism Committee (www.oecd.org/cfe/tourism) was created in 1948 to provide governments with a forum for discussing international tourism policy issues. In the framework of its current Mandate, the Tourism Committee has adopted a programme of work which focuses on key tourism policy challenges in a globalised economy (Box 1.3). This report first reviews some of the key economic challenges faced by developed economies to remain competitive in the global tourism market.

This report then examines the effects of the increasing globalisation of the international travel and tourism industry on small and medium-sized enterprises (SMEs). It analyses in close detail the nature of the global value chains in which tourism SMES now operate. A series of case studies in Australia, Austria, Germany-Jordan, Korea, Spain, Poland and Switzerland are analysed in the report and some of the key challenges and opportunities currently facing the tourism industry are identified. This study shows how governments can accompany SMEs in the tourism sector.

This report also analyses the role that services trade liberalisation could play in fostering tourism growth in developing countries. The study undertakes analysis for Brazil, India and Indonesia, and results show that tourism may be one of the most interconnected services sectors in these economies. Additional case studies for Cambodia, India, Madagascar, Mozambique and South Africa indicate that the growth of the sector may be undermined where the most important service sectors (e.g. transport, infrastructure, electricity, water or education) are lacking or expensive.

This report is the first edition of a new regular publication which aims to make a significant contribution to the international tourism policy debate.

Acknowledgments. This edition was directed and co-ordinated by Alain Dupeyras in co-operation with Hyunhwan Kim and Damian Garnys. Chapter 1 was drafted by Prof. Peter Keller (Swiss State Secretariat for Economic Affairs, Chair of the Tourism Committee). In Chapter 2.A "Enhancing the role of SMEs in the Global Tourism Industry" has contributions by Mariarosa Lunati (OECD Centre for Entrepreneurship, SMEs and Local Development), and Chapter 2.B "Services Trade Liberalisation and Tourism Development" is based on a study prepared by Massimo Geloso Grosso, Molly Lesher and Enrico Pinali (Trade and Agriculture Directorate) for the OECD Trade Committee. The English version of the publication has been edited by Graham Todd.

This book has...

StatLinks

A service that delivers Excel® files from the printed page!

Look for the *StatLinks* at the bottom right-hand corner of the tables or graphs in this book. To download the matching Excel® spreadsheet, just type the link into your Internet browser, starting with the *http://dx.doi.org* prefix.
If you're reading the PDF e-book edition, and your PC is connected to the Internet, simply click on the link. You'll find *StatLinks* appearing in more OECD books.

Table of Contents

Executive Summary 7

Chapter 1. **New Paradigm for International Tourism Policy** 11
    Tourism: A strategic economic sector 12
    Raising competitiveness and productivity in tourism-related industries 15
    Using the potential of the destination 19
    The role of entrepreneurship and innovation 21
    The business environment and competitive tourism destinations 23
    Bibliography 26

Chapter 2. **Globalisation, SMEs and Tourism Development** 27
    2.A. Enhancing the Role of SMEs in the Global Tourism Industry 29
        Introduction 30
        Tourism: A global industry 30
        Global value chains, networks and clusters 32
        SME operating patterns and challenges: case study findings 35
        Conclusions for SMEs 45
        Policy implications 47
        Bibliography 51
        Annex 2.A1. Tourism Industry Case Studies 52

    2.B. Services Trade Liberalisation and Tourism Development 55
        Introduction 56
        Definition and measurement of the tourism sector 56
        Economy-wide effects of tourism 57
        Constraints to tourism development: Case studies from Africa and Asia. 63
        Anticompetitive practices affecting tourism 72
        Policy implications 73
        Conclusion 78
        Notes 79
        Bibliography 79
        Annex 2.A2. Tourism Constraints, Policy Responses and Results
            in the Five Case Study Countries 81

Chapter 3. **Country Profiles: Tourism Policy Developments and Trends** 83
    Synthesis 87
    Country Profiles 95-233
    Annex 3.A1. National tourism administration and related websites 234

ISBN 978-92-64-03967-4
Tourism in OECD Countries 2008
Trends and Policies
© OECD 2008

Executive Summary

This publication looks at global tourism trends and policies. Its main focus is on the 30 OECD member countries. The report also provide analysis and data for several non-member economies.

In 2007, OECD member countries represented 60% of international arrivals. Eight out of ten of the main tourism destinations in the world are OECD member countries. Tourism in OECD member countries accounts for between 2 and 12 per cent of GDP, between 3 and 11 per cent of employment and on average about 30% of service exports.

Tourism is also a key driver of globalisation. Its relevance to countries' economic, services and employment performance is now widely recognised. Governments are also giving increased policy consideration to this industry at national, regional and local levels.

New paradigm for international tourism policy

The globalisation process strengthens worldwide competition and stimulates structural change in the tourism industry. The steady growth of international tourism ensures that this process is not a zero-sum game. It creates new market potential for the OECD member countries, as their unique attractions increase both the willingness to pay and the expenditure of their potential visitors. Conversely, it has to be taken into account that tourism related industries in developed countries are not only under global competitive pressures. They are also competing in factor markets (*e.g.* labour and capital), with other sectors that are more productive. It is necessary therefore, to promote productivity-based growth in tourism in OECD countries. Tourism-related industries must increase their competitiveness in domestic factor markets and use scarce resources in more efficient and innovative ways in order to develop and to market competitive products.

The state can stimulate this process by offering macro-economic stability, a tourism-friendly business environment, attractive public goods and an innovation-oriented tourism policy.

In response to these challenges, the OECD Tourism Committee has developed a new political agenda. A main objective for the committee is to reinforce the global coherence in public policies linked to tourism. Currently, the OECD is working on some of the major issues affecting the globalised economy in the field of tourism including: innovation, productivity and growth; economic and policy impacts of border security measures on travel and tourism; internationalisation of small and medium-sized enterprises (SMEs); economic measurement of tourism services; and, an analysis on the role of tourism and culture in making regions/areas more attractive, not only for visitors but also for residents and for investors.

EXECUTIVE SUMMARY

Enhancing the role of SMEs in the Global Tourism Industry

The effects of the increasing globalisation of the international travel and tourism industry on SMEs are important. The report looks first at the nature of the global value chains in which tourism SMEs are now obliged to operate and then comments on the desirability of greater co-operation between tourism SMEs in the specific context of local networks and clusters.

A series of national case studies carried out on this subject recently – in Australia, Austria, Germany-Jordan, Korea, Spain, Poland and Switzerland – serves to support the analysis and leads to the identification of a range of key issues that present tourism SMEs with both challenges and opportunities. It demonstrates that, for some SMEs at least, the effects of the globalisation of the tourism industry on small businesses are not fully appreciated. In some cases there is a lack of awareness of the importance of global value chains to their businesses. It also follows that many SMEs are unsure how best to tap into the new opportunities presented, either because of a lack of skills or because of a feeling that small businesses are powerless in the face of the power of multinational enterprises.

SMEs can in fact benefit from globalisation by means such as the exploitation of networks and clusters, and by the adoption of new technologies. Strength can be drawn from local clusters and networks, while at the same time SMEs can utilise the digital revolution to their advantage, notably by maximising their use of the Internet for marketing purposes and as a means of getting in touch directly with their client base. Access to the Internet is now indispensable for all tourism enterprises, not least because it has empowered the consumer as never before to do business directly with tourism service suppliers. Case studies reveal that SMEs in many tourism destinations are finding it hard to take full advantage of the power that the Internet gives them to compete on a more level playing field with the major travel companies in their sector.

There are a number of key areas in which SMEs can both benefit from, but also face challenges in exploiting global value chain opportunities. These include the need to boost the technical competence of SME staff, the need to ensure that the quality and standards provided by SMEs reach international best practice, and the ways in which SMEs can act to overcome the inherent problems of small size.

The implications for government policies reflect some of these issues and needs. Government policies can be introduced that are supportive of tourism SMEs without being intrusive. While the case studies revealed an understandable resistance on the part of SME owners and managers to too much direct government intervention in their businesses, the research also highlights a variety of indirect, policy-based interventions that can be helpful to tourism SMEs by the creation of an enabling and supportive environment.

Opportunities for constructive government interventions include taking action where market failures inhibit the ability of SMEs to respond to new market realities, ensuring that SMEs are able to receive support in areas such as training, marketing, financial support and ICT skills, and encouraging and, if necessary, educating SMEs about the advantages of clusters and networks . Governments can assist in raising awareness of the potential of global value chains among SMEs, create effective frameworks for the ICT sector, promote training and skills development, encourage a culture of innovation and establish accreditation standards and quality norms that can be met by SMEs in the tourism sector.

Services Trade Liberalisation and Tourism Development

The report analyses the role that services trade liberalisation could play in fostering tourism development in developing countries, with the aim of contributing to international services negotiations. The focus is on the importance of more liberal trade and investment policies (or lack thereof) in the variety of services and infrastructure that are needed to support tourism.

In many countries the tourism sector has suffered from a lack of political and popular support because its economic importance has often been underestimated. The Tourism Satellite Account is contributing to the rise in worldwide awareness of the role of tourism as a productive activity and its potential to generate significant direct and indirect economic benefits. Tourism is a crucial (and sometimes the leading), source of foreign exchange for many developing countries.

Tourism is also a complex industry. It can generate significant economic activity through linkages with other industries, such as agriculture, manufacturing and services. Backward linkages occur as tourism demands goods and services inputs from other sectors. Forward linkages arise since tourism can also be a supplier of goods and services to other sectors. The study undertakes linkage analysis in three developing economies – India, Brazil and Indonesia – in order to explore their extent. Results show that tourism consistently scores stronger linkages than the average services sector, suggesting that tourism may be one of the most interconnected services sectors in these three economies.

In developing tourism, strong backward linkages can be vital. Where there are constraints to these linkages (i.e. inputs needed for tourism activity are lacking or expensive), the growth of the sector may be undermined. The report presents case studies from developing economies in Africa and Asia – Madagascar, Mozambique, Cambodia, India and South Africa – identifying bottlenecks that need to be addressed to strengthen backward linkages and unleash growth in the sector. Among these, the building of service capacity figures prominently.

Due consideration needs to be given to developing effective regulations to address market failure. Achieving these objectives requires strong public sector management and support. Given the cross-sectoral nature of tourism, governments need to establish a comprehensive policy framework that improves the business environment and addresses the underlying economic relationships and social and physical constraints.

The high level of commitments in the tourism sector indicates that World Trade Organisation members widely recognise the important complementing role that the GATS can play in tourism development, although the complete liberalisation of the industry is far from being achieved. Improved GATS commitments in important related services (e.g. telecommunications) can significantly contribute to the growth of tourism. However, multilateral progress for some services (e.g. energy and education) is more difficult to attain.

Tourism trends and policies

The treatment of tourism within government structures varies considerably. The growing economic and political importance of tourism is reflected by the fact that half of the OECD countries have a Ministry or a Secretariat of State in charge of Tourism. Several countries have their own dedicated tourism ministries (Greece, Mexico and New Zealand), however in most cases, the tourism portfolio is attached to Economy, Industry, Trade or SME ministries (Australia, Austria, Canada, Denmark, Finland, France, Germany, Netherlands, Norway, Portugal, Romania, Slovak Republic, Spain, Sweden, Switzerland and United States). For a few others, the tourism portfolio is linked to Regional Development (Czech Republic and Hungary), Culture and Sports (Ireland, Korea, Poland, Turkey and United Kingdom), Environment (South Africa) or Transportation (Japan).

Tourism budgets are not comparable due to the different approaches to the public funding of tourism support adopted by governments. Readers are referred to the country profiles for details. As a generalisation, however, the largest item in public budgetary support for tourism tends to be the marketing budgets granted to national tourist offices or their equivalents for international marketing purposes. National tourist offices or other public tourism organisations are also taking on more responsibility for the active promotion of tourism opportunities within their own countries to their resident population (domestic tourism).

As an economic activity with the potential to create jobs, add value and earn foreign exchange, tourism is increasingly being seen as a sector in which public investment can be justified, in a number of areas. The most common are:

- Investment programmes in infrastructure which can contribute to facilitating access to the tourism industry for nationals and foreigners alike.
- Programmes supporting the small business sector which, in terms of the number of enterprises engaged, is dominated by SMEs; programmes to enhance quality in tourism most commonly through action of training.
- Programmes aimed at the quality of tourism facilities and services (these often involve the introduction and maintenance of national quality standards and quality accreditation schemes).
- Licensing schemes for personnel engaged in tourism (*e.g.* the licensing of tourism guides).
- The creation of a business and investment climate that is supportive of the tourism sector and which encourages the participation of the private sector as prime investors.

Policy advice and enabling measures are also increasing, led by national governments, to assist tourism industries and especially small businesses to meet the fast-growing competition in global tourism. A notable emphasis is now being seen on maximising the use of on-line technologies to enable tourism businesses to benefit from and cope with the rapid globalisation of tourism marketplaces and of tourism marketing. Information and reservation systems are at the heart of many of these initiatives, as the direct linkages via the Internet between the tourist and the tourism service suppliers.

Detailed statistical profiles on OECD member countries provide up-to-date information on inbound tourism (international arrivals and tourism receipts), outbound tourism (departures and tourism expenditure), employment in tourism and tourism in the economy (*i.e.* tourism as a percentage of GDP, as percentage of total employment, as a percentage of services exports).

Chapter 1

New Paradigm for International Tourism Policy

Tourism: A strategic economic sector

Tourism and globalisation

The process of economic globalisation is unstoppable. Advances in information and communications technology are leading to the virtual integration of mankind. Liberalisation at borders and deregulation within countries are increasing productivity and prosperity. Households in emerging economies are, for the first time, able to put aside a travel budget, as incomes in these countries close the gap with the industrialised world. Also, the increasing division of labour on an international scale is boosting the volume of business travel.

For tourism destinations, spending by foreign visitors is an export, with powerful multiplier effects that can increase a country's level of development. International tourism itself leads to development in destination countries, helping to dismantle economic disparities. Tourism is thus an important market economy mechanism for the redistribution of wealth between rich and poor regions and nations.

Tourism brings together people of different cultures and creates trust between the various actors. It leads to the development of common or shared preferences, modes of behaviour, institutions and norms. In short, tourism accelerates the process of global economic integration.

Global demand – Local production

Globalisation has resulted in the internationalisation of tourism demand. Cross-border travel is on the increase and continental and intercontinental markets are growing fast, while domestic tourism markets in the most open and developed nations are stagnating. Visitors have an increasing number of destinations and an ever-wider range of products and services from which to choose. The traditional OECD tourism countries have lost their monopoly position in the world market. The internationalisation of demand has also increased the intensity of competition. It is now possible, for example, to choose between a winter skiing holiday in the northern hemisphere or sunning on the beach in the southern hemisphere.

However, a corollary of internationalised demand is the decentralisation of supply. While tourism demand is now genuinely global, the supply of tourism-related goods and services still has to be local. The supply of tourism products and services is necessarily bound to a location because tourism is based on the interaction between service providers and visitors, which invariably occurs at the place of consumption. Production depends on local policy environments, and, due to varying local production conditions, the unstoppable process of globalisation has resulted in competition between tourism locations.

The industrialised nations thus find themselves facing a new kind of competition from countries whose resources are still very much intact and which enjoy favourable business conditions in terms of wage levels, prices and currency. In an industry as labour-intensive as tourism, the magnitude of the differences in wage levels between developed and developing countries plays a major role.

Growth and the level of development

In these circumstances, one question that arises is whether the conditions for rapid tourism growth are better in the developing countries than in the developed ones? This argument is supported by the fact that the ratio of value added to gross domestic product (GDP) in the tourism sectors of industrialised nations is in a downward spiral. Other industries and economic sectors are more productive and therefore tend to grow faster. A country's level of development has a considerable influence on tourism growth.

The poorest countries still face significant barriers to market entry, however. The main problem is the high levels of comfort and service quality that visitors all over the world now expect. To meet these expectations requires considerable investment in expensive infrastructure and training. Also, the share of imports in tourism production is generally high, leading to an outflow of currency and raising the risk that poorer countries are obliged to seek foreign loans. On the other hand, poorer countries can also profit from the "relative advantages of backwardness" which are based on resources such as important natural capital, a still vivid traditional culture or a plentiful labour force with a still low level of wages (see also Chapter 2 "*Services Trade Liberalisation and Tourism Development*").

The more developed nations are beginning to put the shock of globalisation behind them, but also suffer from business conditions which can be unfavourable for tourism, such as high wages and hard currency. On the other hand, they benefit from the advantages that go with a high level of development, earning more per visitor and achieving higher added value per employee (Box 1.1).

> **Box 1.1. A new Paradigm for international Tourism in developed countries**
>
> The globalisation process strengthens worldwide competition and stimulates structural change in tourism. The steady growth of international tourism ensures that this process is not a zero-sum game. It creates new market potential for the OECD countries. Their unique attractions increase the willingness to pay and the expenditure of their potential visitors. It has to be taken into account that tourism related industries in developed countries are not only under global competitive pressures. They also have to compete in factor markets (*e.g.* for labour and capital), with other sectors that are more productive. It is therefore necessary to promote productivity-based growth in tourism in OECD countries. Tourism-related industries must increase their competitiveness in domestic factor markets and use scarce resources in more efficient and more innovative ways in order to develop and to market competitive products. The State can stimulate this process by offering macro-economic stability, a tourism-friendly business environment, attractive public goods and an innovation-oriented tourism policy.

Strong international market position of OECD countries

The speed and quality of tourism growth are thus very different in countries with different levels of development. While developments in the world tourism market have strengthened competition and accelerated restructuring in the traditional tourism countries of the industrialised world, it has also led to dynamic and lasting growth in all countries.

The strongest tourism growth in recent years has been in the largest emerging economies, which have attracted about 90% of direct investment and are now enjoying a boom. These countries are in the process of closing the gap with the industrialised world.

While the growth and share of the world tourism market of the poorer developing countries remains very low, today about 40% of international tourism takes place in the emerging and developing countries (Figure 1.1).

Figure 1.1. **Impact of the globalisation process on the world tourism market**

Developed countries: Competition between equals; Similar preferences; Comparable products 60% (OECD countries)

Emerging and developing countries: New competition; Trend; 40%

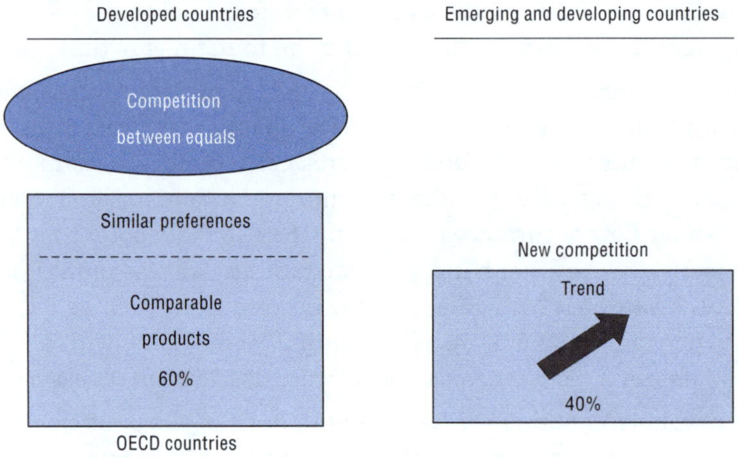

While it is true that the industrialised nations have lost market share, the OECD countries nonetheless continue to occupy a strong position in the world tourism market. This can be explained by the fact that the market itself has grown enormously in the past 50 or so years. In 1948, at the time of the creation of the OECD Tourism Committee (Box 1.2), there were about 25 million international arrivals worldwide. Following more than 50 years of growth averaging 6.5% a year, this number has multiplied to over 800 million. The OECD countries, which have strong domestic markets and a growing market of same-day visitors, still account for 60% of all international arrivals.

The exchange of tourists still mainly involves industrialised countries which have not large differences in their levels of development. The demand preferences of these tourists are similar as are the products and services on offer. Potential visitors look for unique attractions and unforgettable experiences. Their expectations are also similar in terms of comfort and service quality and their demand for leisure travel can be explained by a desire for change and the "love of variety".

Long-run demand potential

The global opening of markets has created the conditions for dynamic tourism growth, with tourism having become a strategic sector of many countries' economies. As an industry, tourism is not limited to a few geographical sites, as in the case of automobile manufacture or the asset management of banks, but is geographically widespread within many countries. Even the poorest countries are able to participate in the world tourism market. By reaching outlying areas, tourism can help to overcome poverty and it also helps emerging countries to earn the hard currency they need to build up their economies.

The macro-economic importance of tourism has also increased for the industrialised nations. Tourism-related exports make a significant contribution to the balance of services (Figure 1.2). In OECD countries, tourism accounts for between 2% and 12% of GNP and between 3% and 11% of employment (see Chapter 3, "*Country Profiles: Tourism Policy Developments and*

> **Box 1.2. OECD Tourism Committee**
>
> The OECD Tourism Committee was created in 1948 with the aim of using tourism as a tool for economic development and co-operation in the context of the Marshall Plan. The OECD Tourism Committee gathers high-level officials from national ministries in charge of tourism and statistical offices. It meets twice a year, and also organises *ad hoc* meetings and conferences.
>
> At the heart of the committee's work is its development of best-practice research and guidance on issues commonly faced by tourism administrations in developed countries. The information produced is highly influential, affecting the way that governments organise and evaluate their support for tourism, encourage innovation in the sector and create the conditions needed to stimulate investment and boost competitiveness.
>
> Its main focus is on economic and tourism policy issues. A more coherent worldwide approach to sustainable development by public tourism policy is another priority. The OECD Mandate 2007-11 for the Tourism Committee indicates the following missions:
>
> - Maximise the economic, social and environmental benefits of tourism through medium and long-term strategic development, soundly-developed tourism policy and greater coherence between tourism and other policies (*e.g.* transport, environment, security, trade, taxation or migration).
> - Promote, in a globalisation and decentralisation context, sustainable tourism development as a source of economic growth, job creation and poverty alleviation in both major centres and regional areas.
> - Improve the infrastructure and image of destinations to make them more attractive to the local population and visitors and more competitive to investors for the benefit of the whole economy.
> - Contribute to the advancement of international co-operation in the tourism sector.
>
> For more information: *www.oecd.org/cfe/tourism*.

Trends"). It enables these countries to use the potential of their existing production apparatus more fully and thus has a positive impact on employment, both in the cities and in rural problem areas.

So it can be demonstrated that the globalisation process is not a zero sum game for tourism. The exponential growth of the world tourism market makes it possible to exploit the remaining growth potential to the full. In the industrialised countries, tourism is still focused mainly on domestic and neighbouring markets. The global growth potential for tourism in the industrialised countries is still far from exhausted. The development of new intercontinental markets has just begun.

Raising competitiveness and productivity in tourism-related industries

A heterogeneous industry structure

Before considering productivity issues in tourism it is necessary to define what is meant by tourism, distinguishing it from other sectors of the economy. In fact tourism can only be defined in terms of demand. The money spent by visitors goes to a variety of different companies and industries, including companies of all sizes in both trade and industry. These offer either labour-intensive services that are in a phase of stagnation, or rationalised services of a progressive nature. Tourism is both a service and a self-service industry.

Figure 1.2. **Share of "travel" account receipts in exports of services, 2005**

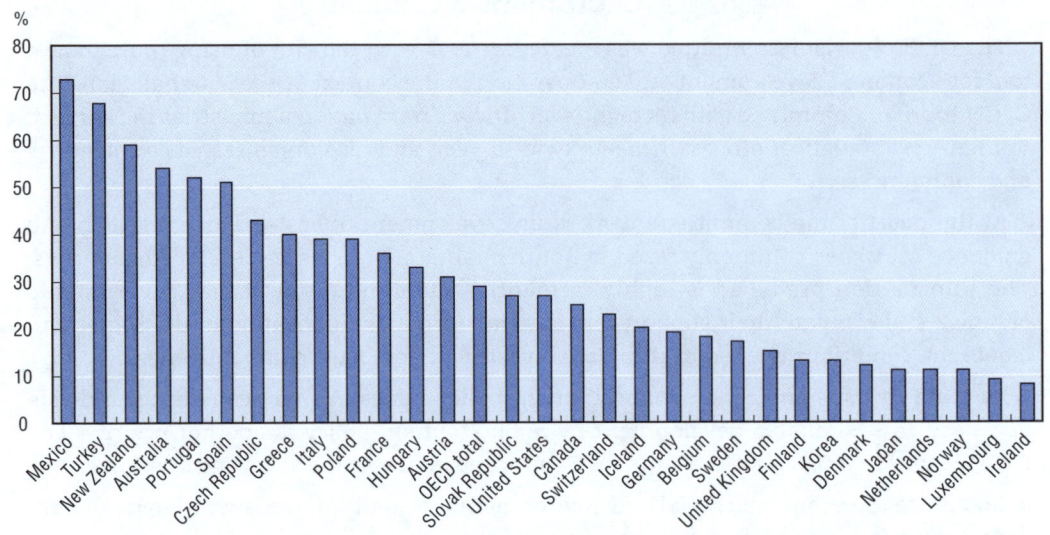

The structures of tourism are constantly evolving. They initially come into being in response to demand for a "package" of tourism services. Here there is an important distinction to be made between demand for tailor-made tourism services and for those tourism services that are produced industrially as a "package" for the mass market. Tourism is, in fact, distinguished by a dual structure (Table 1.1).

Table 1.1. **Dual structure of the tourism related industries**

Characteristics	Travel and Tourism Industry (outgoing)	Destination oriented SME's (Incoming)
Functions	Organisation Information Transport	Welcome Hospitality Leisure
Related industries	Travel agency Airline industry Other	Accommodation Catering Cable cars Other
Corporate Organisation	Large companies	SMEs

In the traditional tourism countries the creation of tourism resorts and destinations resulted in a fragmented sector made up of small-to-medium-sized enterprises (SMEs), devoted to looking after visitors during their stay. However, the increasing popularity and internationalisation of travel also brought about the emergence of an international travel industry, which from the agglomerations in developed nations organised the travel services to the destination of their choice on an industrial basis. These are the tour operators, airline companies, hotel and catering chains, and car rental companies.

Both these ways of organising travel have their strengths and weaknesses. The small business sector is in a position to tailor and personalise its services to the needs of the individual visitor. They are also able to adapt to rapidly changing market requirements. Visitors to destinations have a wide variety of options from which to choose. At the end of the day, however, the prices charged for individual services in destinations can be high, and thus competition between destinations has to be based on quality. Personalised tourism is expensive.

The international travel industry on the other hand applies international strategies to the exploitation of existing local tourism potential. Its products are standardised. Most of the big corporations are able to develop new tourism markets while their very size allows them to cut costs and to offer the customer more for less. Incremental increases in productivity are essential for economic success in the travel industry, where competition on price is increasingly important and costs have to be cut to the bone.

The need for production-based growth

Global competition has given new urgency to the question of productivity in the supply of tourism services in industrialised countries. In these countries, tourism-related industries have to compete with emerging and developing countries, which have plentiful resources to offer and can also produce these services at a lower cost, giving them a competitive advantage. In developing countries, tourism productivity is often higher than in the rest of the economy, not least because tourism is an industry that produces for the world market.

The situation in industrialised countries is quite different. These have industries that are more productive than tourism, and therefore grow faster. The ratio of value added to GNP in tourism tends to fall in the most developed countries. Furthermore natural, landscape and labour resources are increasingly scarce. In conditions of global competition, tourism products and services have to compete at least partially on price.

For these reasons, industrialised countries need to strive for growth based on productivity gains and use the remaining resources sparingly. Production efficiencies in the services sector need to be improved further in order to bring down unit costs. The quality of the experiences offered needs to be assured. Increased productivity will improve the competitiveness of tourism, making it easier to adapt pricing to the competitive environment and will also raise the rewards to labour, making it easier to attract and retain qualified workers.

Tourism – An "experience economy"

Tourism-dependent sectors of the economy are not homogeneous. They are in the business of creating experiences and are part of the new "Experience Economy". A whole package of services is designed, developed and commercialised for visitors to enjoy as experiences. The tourism industry is a kind of "dream factory", with the manufacture of unforgettable experiences requiring high quality levels.

Indeed, productivity in tourism depends on the quality of the experience, reflected in the perceived satisfaction of the visitor which is a subjective judgement. Anything that contributes to the efficient production and marketing of quality experiences helps to promote productivity in tourism.

The productivity of tourism-dependent industries is a complex issue. It can be defined as the inputs in terms of units of human resources, capital and natural resources required for the provision of a service. The magnitude of those inputs measures the efficiency of production. However, the products and services offered also have to be sold efficiently to the markets. The value of a tourism service is thus measured by the price that can be charged, which depends both on the efficient employment of the factors of production and on efficient marketing in tourism markets.

Low labour productivity in core industries

Hotels and catering – two core industries of tourism – offer services which are labour-intensive. The small- and medium-sized enterprises (SMEs) in these sectors have no room for further rationalisation, and thus suffer from a "cost disease". Compared to other economic sectors in industrialised countries, their productivity is low.

SMEs in tourism have to compensate for their lack of productivity through increased prices. This weakens them in two ways. Their services become more expensive, and efforts to procure land, human resources and financial capital become more difficult, because they must compete in those factor markets with enterprises that are more productive.

A whole series of measures is required to improve the productivity of labour in tourism-dependent SMEs, both at the company level and in general. SMEs are already able to take advantage of the network externalities of information and communication technology. For example, hotels can now advertise themselves and take direct bookings via the Internet, offering the potential to achieve higher occupancy rates. SMEs can grow internally or externally. By extending their capacities they can achieve greater size and thus bring down their fixed costs. They can take advantage of co-operation or mergers to offer customers more. By consistently improving quality, they will be able to charge higher prices.

Key factors in tourism competitiveness

It has been argued that increased productivity is one way to improve the competitiveness of the tourism industry. Productivity gains in tourism-dependent industries and SMEs in developed countries are important for their economic survival. As productivity rises, higher wages can be paid, improving the industry's competitiveness in labour, capital and real estate markets. This is also a way to offset the effects of hard currency. Finally, by making possible a higher return on investment, increased productivity also helps to attract more investment in tourism installations and equipment.

Competitiveness in tourism depends above all on the firms themselves, which can be said to be "productive" when they manage to sell their services and earn income. The ability of poorer countries to sell and earn is based on an abundance of low-cost resources. In emerging economies this is driven by a high volume of investment. In industrialised nations, productivity gains at corporate level increasingly require entrepreneurship and innovation, making it possible to operate cost-effectively and to develop markets more intelligently with the help of new products and marketing approaches.

Competitiveness at the corporate level is not, however, sufficient in itself to ensure success in today's hotly-contested tourism markets. The real key to success is a favourable macro-economic business environment. To be truly productive, tourism enterprises need qualified staff, better information and greater know-how, attractive infrastructure, top-quality suppliers, the removal of administrative obstacles, low taxes, plenty of competition and highly qualified research facilities.

Using the potential of the destination

Attractions as destination goods

Demand in tourism is driven by two fundamental motives which make people want to travel: the need to escape the pressures of daily life and relax, and the desire to see and experience something new and different. Here the role of attractions is fundamental.

Attractions are the "raw materials" of tourism, and are location-specific. Perhaps only agriculture is as dependent as tourism on a given location. The geographic location of attractions leaves tourism-dependent industries, beginning with hotels and restaurants, no choice but to locate themselves as near as possible to the attraction that draws the visitor. Thus, it is in the vicinity of these raw materials that tourism industries take root and flourish.

Chief among these attractions are natural resources, landscapes and the "magic" of a certain place. All of these are free goods. The increasing development of tourism makes them into public goods, which must be protected and cared for with government help. They can also be marketed and become economic goods, once access is controlled and carrying capacity restricted. What are known as "destination goods" include social resources and mixed goods, i.e. goods which are both private and public – beaches and ski slopes, for example. Positive externalities – for example, flower displays on the balconies and windows of local homes that increase the attractiveness of a locality – are also destination goods.

Building a destination

Attractions are given an economic value by the visitor market. Potential visitors choose their travel destination on the basis of something special and unique about its attractions. This also determines their willingness to pay. The more famous the destination the higher the price visitors are ready to pay for the services they will need (Figure 1.3). Tourism-dependent businesses in the vicinity of these attractions can take advantage of this. A famous attraction has the same characteristics as an established consumer good brand name. It generates profit for individual companies, enabling them to demand prices that are significantly higher than their production costs ("value based pricing"). Unlike the international travel and tourism industry, price-based competition hardly exists between destinations. They compete for visitors with their uniqueness.

Attractions play an important role in the creation and growth of destinations. The more important the attraction, the greater will be its endogenous growth potential. Really big attractions draw large numbers of visitors, generating increased returns and raising the possibility of internal growth for local firms. There will also be growth in the number of firms, bringing new agglomeration advantages such as the creation of airports, motorways or the development of attractive shopping streets. Local companies can internalise these agglomeration advantages in their products, offering customers more for their money, and can benefit from economies of scale and lower production costs as a result.

Decentralisation of supply and the hierarchy of destinations

Attractions are found all over the world, hence the decentralisation of supply in the world tourism market. Virtually all countries have tourism attractions, and the most important tourism countries are generally those with the greatest number of major attractions (Table 1.2).

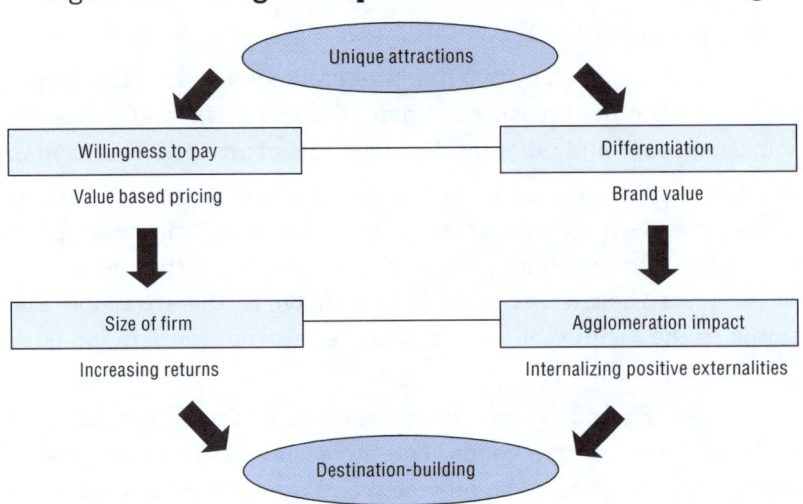

Figure 1.3. **Endogenous process of destination building**

Table 1.2. **The decentralisation of the tourism offer**
Examples by country (millions tourist arrivals, 2006)

Highly developed countries		"Catching up" developing countries		Raw material producer countries		Less developed countries		Countries with isolated economies	
France	79.0	Malaysia	17.5	Russia	19.9	Peru	1.6	Azerbaijan	1.2
USA	51.1	Turkey	20.3	Bahrain	4.5	Madagascar	0.3	Uzbekistan	0.3

StatLink http://dx.doi.org/10.1787/153400042865

Source: Adapted from J. Sachs, 2007.

There is in any case a hierarchy of destinations. The market for the most attractive destinations is truly global. Generally, less attractive places or less well-known attractions appeal mainly to domestic markets. Tourism resorts also cast a shadow on the development of tourism in the hinterland. The big five star hotels are all present in the major tourism centres, but, in the neighbourhood of these centres, the hinterland is often restricted to niche products of the "bed and breakfast" variety. There is naturally a concentration of demand on the best locations when a destination life cycle tends to maturity.

Imperfect competition between destinations

Local attractions are catalysts for the economic development of a location, but can only realise their economic value by investment in installations, equipment, products and services. It will then be possible to attract tourists, whose spending will help to increase local employment and income. Tourism makes use of natural, cultural and man-made attractions, and in so doing enhances the overall attractiveness of a destination.

Places which are interesting from the cultural and leisure points of view as well as for the quality of life will also be able to attract direct investment. Moreover, they are ideal locations for companies and strengthen the local production brands in export markets.

The unique nature of attractions in one sense diminishes competition between destinations. When destinations are neither comparable nor interchangeable, there can be no perfect competition. Attractions differentiate destinations in tourism. When it comes to differentiation strategies, the producers of tourism products benefit at least temporarily from a monopoly position.

The role of entrepreneurship and innovation

"Creative destruction" and the improvement of tourism structures

The advantages of a given location in terms of attractions have a considerable influence on the travel decisions of potential visitors. There is first a competition between destinations. It is only after the client has decided on a destination that the question of products and services arises. In view of the constantly changing requirements of visitors, suppliers of tourism products and services must update them regularly.

Over time tourism products come to the end of their life cycle, as can be seen from the saturated markets for seaside holidays and skiing. Destinations can go out of fashion and fall into oblivion without warning. To avoid this danger they need to reinvent themselves constantly, explore new markets, develop new products, and invest in new installations and equipment, while improving production structures and constantly seeking to innovate.

In conditions of global competition between destinations, industrialised countries need to question themselves constantly, and be ready to adapt to changing conditions in tourism markets. This process of "creative destruction" or the improvement of existing structures requires the most open kind of competition.

Entrepreneurship as a scarce resource

Innovation means making a conscious effort to develop products that are new and more profitable, which is one of the main tasks of the entrepreneur. In a market economy, investors and capitalists are free to seek the most profitable opportunities for making their businesses grow. Innovation is a must, and is by definition unique. Innovation is based on truly original thinking, creating more or less revolutionary products to bring to the market. Such products are usually the work of independent innovators, who stand apart from the mainstream of increasingly technocratic or bureaucratic managers.

These independent innovators are pioneers in the true sense of "entrepreneurship", able to anticipate new social trends for which they will develop new products, processes and forms of organisation. The tourism structures of today are above all the result of entrepreneurs who were not afraid to take risks in the Schumpeter sense and who, with total commitment and at great personal risk, changed the way people do business. It is to such people that we owe today's outstanding luxury hotels, leisure parks, hotel chains and "low cost carriers".

In many cases, the innovators in tourism originated in small family businesses. Hilton and Marriott in the USA, for example, developed the most successful standardised hotel chains mainly to meet the needs of business travellers. An attack on the monopolies of traditional national and network carriers was first launched by two pilots from Southwest Airlines and has led to an explosion in low cost airlines in all continents.

In tourism, an industry dominated by SMEs, the barriers to entry for would-be entrepreneurs are not always particularly high. The various branches of this sector of the economy offer many opportunities for the independent operator. What is lacking in many cases, however, are explicit business models. Entrepreneurs are a rare breed in everyday tourism.

Characteristics of the innovation process in tourism

In tourism, the transition from individual and corporate learning processes to innovations is a fluid one. Learning by doing is extremely important. When an activity is constantly repeated, productivity is bound to increase eventually. No special resources are required for this learning effect. Change and technical progress is in that case a side-effect of productive activity. The tricks can be learned by a second and third firm and so on until they become generalised in a process of "creative imitation" that requires no investment in research and development (Figure 1.4).

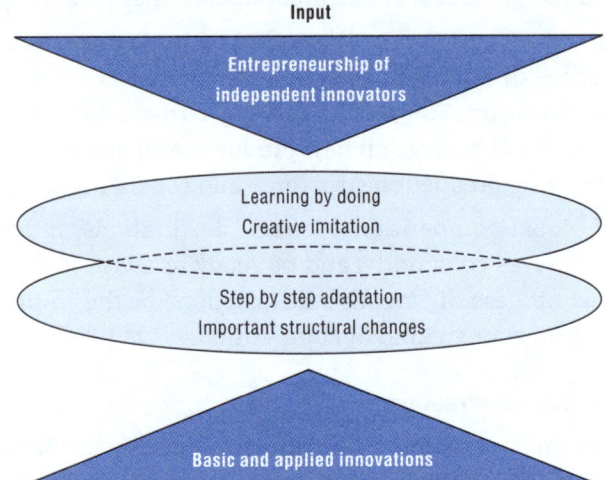

Figure 1.4. **Characteristics of the innovation process in tourism**

Tourism also depends to a great extent on fundamental socio-economic innovations which cannot be foreseen, and over which it can have no influence. These often lead to major market transformations. Such a fundamental social innovation was the introduction of the paid holiday which popularised tourism for the mass market. Basic innovations in the transport sector also resulted in unexpectedly radical changes in tourism. First the railways, then the automobile and finally the airplane caused distances to shrink rapidly, dramatically reducing the time needed for, and the cost of travel. Conditions were then ripe for the growth of large tourism resorts, the spread of tourism across the world and the development of remote markets. Today, tourism is in the throes of a new revolution under the influence of information and communication technologies, which is making production far more efficient.

Tourism is also an activity that very gradually absorbs a great many adaptive innovations, many of which have had a major impact on tourism production and marketing processes. The introduction of the credit card, for example, has made payments much easier, reducing the cost of transactions and currency exchanges.

Innovation-creation mechanisms

The level of development is less important for industrialised countries than the so-called innovation-creation mechanisms. These help to dismantle barriers to innovation in the areas of education as well as the production and dissemination of knowledge, in turn improving labour productivity in tourism. Creative entrepreneurs, well trained managers and specialised, sector-specific know-how together with inputs from research and development combine to create a business climate that leads to the improvement of existing structures and the ability to take full advantage of a destination's potential for endogenous growth.

Education creates personalised knowledge in the form of human capital. It takes effect only in the long term and is just another variable in the field of tourism, together with personal commitment and diligence, all of which help to improve the productivity of labour. "Learning on the job and by using" in tourism, as a sector very much identified with newcomers to the labour market, is as useful as the nearness of the learner to the market. Learning is optimal at the level of the destination, where there is "face to face" communication between the customer, management and the "pupil".

Innovation-creation mechanisms include the production of knowledge, which is to be found outside the company. Productivity increases when a company is able to participate in knowledge pools in its own sector or at the level of the national economy. The dissemination of knowledge promotes innovation and ensures its implementation by means of a series of gradual steps. In this context, innovation soon leads to the improvement of products in tourism, a sector numerically dominated by small businesses.

Efforts in the area of education and the dissemination of knowledge help to make innovation a matter of routine, at least at the level of the destination. Tourism associations and organisations have an important role to play here, as the catalysts of innovation and above all as platforms for co-operation. Without co-operation between the various service providers, it is much more difficult to improve tourism structures (see also Chapter 2, "*Enhancing the role of SME's in the Global Tourism Industry*").

The business environment and competitive tourism destinations

Liberalisation and deregulation

Tourism is an industry that has been widely internationalised. It has been subject to extensive liberalisation at borders. On the demand side, barriers to travel such as currency restrictions and departure taxes need to be dismantled, while customs and immigration controls tend to be carried out in a more efficient and "visitor friendly" manner than previously. On the supply side, it is the rules of the General Agreement on Trade in Services (GATS) of the World Trade Organisation that matter.

In fact, world tourism market liberalisation is well-advanced on the demand side. The principle upheld by the OECD Tourism Committee, that "tourism must go both ways", is widely observed. Currency restrictions between OECD countries have been lifted. Tighter security regulations and procedures, introduced in the face of international terrorism threats, are a problem nonetheless when it comes to the efficient operation of border controls, and are costly both in terms of time and money.

On the supply side, the closer integration of those countries that make up the bulk of the world tourism market is being encouraged through increasing co-operation within various intergovernmental bodies. In line with the OECD decisions, the Global Relations Strategy of the OECD's Tourism Committee (Box 1.3) is a case in point, building ties with selected emerging economies in an effort to make the world tourism market more homogeneous.

Macro-economic stability and the business environment

Stable macro-economic conditions do much for the development of tourism. A booming economy stimulates demand for tourism, which is very much dependent on the business cycle. Sustained growth makes it possible to invest in the necessary infrastructure and superstructure. Both effects help to take fuller advantage of the

> **Box 1.3. A new political agenda for the OECD Tourism Committee**
>
> In response to global challenges, the OECD Tourism Committee has developed a new political agenda. A main objective for the Tourism Committee is to reinforce the global coherence in public policies linked to tourism. Currently, the OECD is therefore working on some of the major issues affecting the globalised economy in the field of tourism:
>
> - Innovation, productivity and growth in the field of tourism.
> - Review of economic and policy impacts of border security measures on travel and tourism with a view to enhancing coherent strategies and policies that can help to mitigate the negative impacts of the security measures on travellers, on the travel and tourism industry and on national economies.
> - Analysis of climate Change and Tourism issues (OECD publication on *Climate change in the European Alps*).
> - Internationalisation of SMEs and Services Trade Liberalisation and Tourism Development (see Chapter 2).
> - Economic measurement of tourism services: best-practice research on the use of data from Tourism Satellite Accounts to inform tourism policy and support business in the framework of the broad economic agenda.
> - Analysis and case studies on the role of tourism and culture in making regions/areas more attractive, not only for visitors but also for residents and for investors.
>
> A focus point for the OECD will be the 2008 high-level Tourism Committee which will discuss key topics related to the governance of tourism in the globalised economy. In support of these actions, the Tourism Committee has also significantly broadened its links with non-member economies, the private sector and other international organisations active in tourism.
>
> For more information: *www.oecd.org/cfe/tourism*.

potential of tourism installations and facilities, ultimately leading to full employment. Keeping inflation at bay helps to contain the price of tourism services.

While good macro-economic relations are important prerequisites for the successful development of tourism, they are not sufficient in themselves. A business environment favourable to companies in the tourism sector is also necessary. As explained above, this includes a full range of economic, financial and location policy measures.

The state as co-producer of destination goods

The state normally makes available a substantial supply of destination goods, including protected and carefully-maintained natural sites and landscapes, cultural monuments and museums. The state is also mainly responsible for the development of the means of transport that ensure that destinations are accessible.

The state is thus a co-producer in tourism (Figure 1.5). It creates the policy environment necessary for potential growth in tourism while its services contribute substantially to making destinations attractive to potential visitors. A country's competitiveness in tourism is defined largely on the basis of the services provided by the state. Of course, tapping the existing tourism potential can only be done in a second step by the providers of services since the state is rarely engaged in filling airline seats or hotel beds.

Figure 1.5. **Main areas of state intervention in the field of tourism**

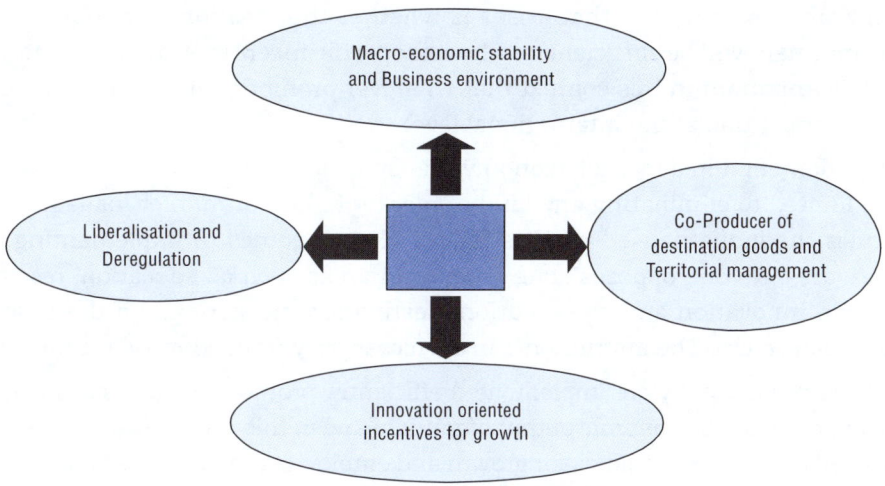

Territorial management and environmental protection

A successful tourism sector means that more people will use existing transport, accommodation and protected areas' facilities. Indeed, visitors are above all interested in beautiful landscapes and an uncontaminated environment. In the case of the suppliers of tourism products and services on the other hand, it is the utilisation of these resources that is of prime concern. This leads to conflicts of interest between the need for protection and the need for development. Therefore regional planning and environmental protection policies both have a direct bearing on tourism.

At the local level, careful planning is necessary to achieve an optimal balance between the need for development and the need for preservation, so as to prevent the squandering of resources and keep environmental pollution to a minimum. It is also important to ensure that natural and cultural landscapes that have remained intact continue to be protected and preserved over the long term.

Some of the environmental problems affecting tourism are global in nature and can only be resolved by the international community acting in concert. An obvious example is the issue of climate change, which is now having a direct impact on the essential resources of tourism. For example, melting glaciers and the lack of snow in lower parts of the mountains are a threat to skiing in the Alps, an important and lucrative area of recreation for world tourism. Climate change is forcing tourism-dependent sectors of the economy to adopt expensive adaptation measures. There is increasing political pressure to tackle the problem by introducing measures to limit growth in certain tourism related industries by measures such as the taxation of flights or even the imposition of travel restrictions. The main target for reductions is the industrialised world.

From the point of view of simple efficiency, general measures affecting all areas of life are preferable to sectoral measures. Climate protection is in fact going to be much more expensive in the industrialised countries, where the level of protection is already high, than in the poorer countries. From the point of view of tourism policy, preference should be given to measures such as technology transfer and compensation payments to the less developed countries, in the framework of the so-called flexible mechanisms of the Kyoto Protocol.

Innovation-oriented incentives for tourism growth

Finally, another question that arises is whether the creation of a tourism-friendly policy environment will be sufficient or whether specific incentives are needed to promote tourism. It is important in this context that whatever promotional measures are taken do not distort competition at the international level.

It is fundamental in a market economy that specific measures taken in a given sector should be limited to eliminating any kind of market failure or market inadequacy. These are the rules the industrialised nations follow when it comes to implementing tourism policy measures. No one opposes state support in areas such as education, research and development, innovation and co-operation, destination marketing and the financing of tourism infrastructure. The instruments in each case vary from country to country.

To the extent that they are implemented efficiently, promotional measures can make a contribution to the socio-economic output of tourism and in this way considerably strengthen the associated positive externalities for growth and employment in given territories.

Bibliography

Baumol, W. (1991), *Productivity and American Leadership*, MIT Press, Boston.

Commission of the European Communities, OECD, United Nations, World Tourism Organisation (2001), *Tourism Satellite Account: Recommended Methodological Framework*, Luxembourg, Madrid, New York, Paris.

Keller, P. and T. Bieger (2007), "Productivity in Tourism, Fundamentals and Concepts for Achieving Growth and Competitiveness", AIEST, 2 International Tourism Research and Concepts, ESV, Berlin.

Keller, P. (2006), "Competition Between Destination: Will Natural and Cultural Attractions Play a Role in the Future", *Management of Attractions*, Linde, Wien.

Keller, P. (2000), "Globalisation and Tourism", *Trends in Outdoor Recreation, Leisure and Tourism*, CABI Publishing, New York, pp. 287-297.

OECD (forthcoming), *Entrepreneurship and Innovation in Tourism*, OECD Publishing, Paris.

OECD (2007), *Climate Change in the European Alps: Adapting Winter Tourism and Natural Hazards Management*, OECD Publishing, Paris.

OECD (2006), *Innovation and Growth in Tourism*, OECD Publishing, Paris.

OECD (2003), *Challenges and Policies regarding Human Resources in Tourism*, OECD Publishing, Paris.

OECD (2000), *Measuring the Role of Tourism in OECD Economies, The Manual on Tourism Satellite Account and Employment*, OECD Publishing, Paris.

Porter, M. (2006), "Building the Microeconomic Foundations of Prosperity: Findings from the Business Competitiveness Index", WEF, *The Global Competitiveness Report 2006-07, Creating an Improved Business Environment*, Geneva, pp. 43-73.

Sachs, J. (2000), "Globalisation and Patterns of Economic Development", *Review of World Economics*, Vol. 136(4), Kiel.

Chapter 2

Globalisation, SMEs and Tourism Development

ISBN 978-92-64-03967-4
Tourism in OECD Countries 2008
Trends and Policies
© OECD 2008

2.A. Enhancing the Role of SMEs in the Global Tourism Industry

Introduction

The main objective of this chapter is to examine how the globalisation of tourism is affecting the role of Small and Medium-Sized Enterprises (SMEs) in the industry's supply and distribution value chains and networks. It examines how SMEs can best operate in a global market place, even though their theatre of activities is local, how small companies can best compete with both local suppliers and with major international tourism companies and multi-national enterprises (MNEs), and how recent developments in technology, especially in the area of Internet-based information and reservations systems, can best be embraced by SMEs. The report draws on previous work by the OECD and on a series of case studies carried out on this subject by a number of member States.

The chapter also seeks to identify strategies and policies that will strengthen the position of SMEs in those value chains. Seven countries, Australia, Austria, Germany-Jordan, Korea, Spain (Andalusia and the Balearic Islands), Poland and Switzerland have carried out case studies on related tourism-sector issues (Annex 2.A1), the results of which have been taken into account in preparing this report. The primary focus of these case studies is on SME tour operators, travel agencies and hotels.

Tourism: A global industry

Tourism is one of the world economy's growth sectors. Despite crisis-induced slumps the long-term growth trend appears to be stable. The tourism industry has benefited from the process of globalisation. The trend to a better division of labour on a worldwide basis has been particularly favourable to tourism, resulting in increased productivity and prosperity in many countries. The introduction of a market economy and the development of democracy in many emerging and transition economies have provided real incentives for the development of business and leisure tourism in these regions.

As a result, tourism today is one of the most internationalised sectors of the world economy. The world tourism market has been substantially extended, adding considerably to the potential for further growth and at the same time bringing about greater competition between tourism destination countries.

The dual structure of the tourism industry

Tourism has developed a dual economic structure over the years. To generalise, in most of the leading tourism origin markets, especially in Europe and Asia, the international travel and tourism industry is composed mainly of large companies that organise tourism to various destinations on an industrial basis. They offer standardised products, and develop global strategies that enable them to make the best worldwide use of local potential. While large companies are supported by a network of smaller specialists, these specialists generally serve only a small proportion of the overall market.

To a large extent, these large enterprises are based on innovation. In civil aviation, charter flights were invented as a way of dealing with seasonal peaks in tourism demand.

Hotel chains such as Hilton and Marriott grew from family companies, and were based on a desire to satisfy the needs of business travellers, and on the concept of brand reliability and the application of established standards across the chain. The giant car rental sector now allows visitors to have the same mobility abroad as they do at home. Credit cards have made international money transfers much easier while at the same time reducing the risks involved in foreign exchange operations. Equally, general access to ATMs (automatic teller machines) for cash withdrawals is increasingly important in tourism destinations.

However, in many tourism destinations, the story is very different. Here, it is SMEs that primarily offer tourism services (*e.g.* accommodation, catering, excursions and leisure activities). SMEs (notably micro and small enterprises), in tourism destinations are often numerically dominant in terms of enterprise numbers, number of employees and profit. The available figures indicate that the number of SMEs in tourism is, on average, continuing to increase.

Here, a distinction should be made between some major tourism destinations, such as Spain, where vertical integration within the tourism industry often means that hotels and ground tour operators are linked to and often owned by the major tourism groups based in leading origin markets. In developing countries and less "industrialised" tourism destinations on the other hand, SMEs still predominate in the supply of tourism services and facilities.

Statistical evidence suggests that, while the number of large companies is relatively small in the tourism industry of the more developed tourism destinations, they can nonetheless account for more than half of total turnover in the sector and for a significant proportion of employment. On the other hand, 60-90% of all enterprises in the hotel sector, a leading branch of tourism, or in the travel agency sector, are micro companies, *i.e.* firms that employ fewer than nine persons (in Austria, for example, 99% of tourism establishments are SMEs and 90% of them employ fewer than ten people, while in Andalusia in Spain, 89% of travel agents and 81% of hotels also employ fewer than ten people)

Large companies, which benefit from standardisation and economies of scale, are in a position to offer their clients more attractive services at very competitive prices. They are able to develop new tourism markets and offer new products. This helps them to increase the "customer value" and to reduce their operating costs. Small enterprises find this harder to achieve, and yet offer the opportunity to address one of the key, emerging demands of the market – the personalisation of the tourism product.

In the modern and increasingly experienced major tourism origin markets, many tourists no longer want standardised products, preferring to tailor their holiday experience to their own specific needs and tastes, and insisting on personalised services. It is here that an opportunity arises for SMEs, since they are an important part of a destination's ability to adapt to the ever-changing requirements of the individual tourist, and are often more fleet of foot than larger companies in adapting to consumers' changing tastes and preferences.

Thus, tourism enterprises, especially in destinations, operate in a global market place but, for a large majority, remain actors at the local level. Rising international competition is forcing all enterprises to look at innovative ways of improving the quality and market orientation of their products, their profitability and competitiveness. This situation confronts SMEs with many challenges in the framework of globalisation.

The case studies illustrated in this report demonstrate that value chains, networks and co-operation among SMEs, multi-national enterprises (MNEs) and destinations are important drivers of SME growth. For example, the participation of SMEs in value chains and networks is an incentive for entrepreneurs to take a more managerial approach to business and for SMEs to increase their capacity, thus leading to economies of scale and cost reductions. To remain competitive, SMEs need to co-operate. In tourism, the success of an individual business often depends upon the success of a destination, a network or a global value chain. That being said, very often SMEs are unable to utilise the maximum potential of the value chains and networks due to their lack of capital, time, human resources or experience. It is in this area that supportive public policies can help.

Global value chains, networks and clusters

Global value chains

A value chain describes the full range of activities and actors required to bring a particular set of products to market (Sturgeon, 2001). These include design and product development, production, marketing, distribution, and support to get the product to the final user and for its disposal after use. Typically, the concept of a value chain is applied to manufacturing industries, where value is added throughout the process in a linear fashion which links the initial product development and its manufacture and distribution to the consumer.

In the tourism sector, the relationships are more complex, given that tourism services are supplied by many different suppliers. Figure 2.1 illustrates the concept. This represents a simplified version of the value chain in the context of international tourism markets. At one end of the chain, tourism product suppliers are identified as "Principal". The "Principal" produces products and services for the consumer/tourist who is represented at the other end of the value chain. The "Intermediary" is in charge of bundling, packaging and promoting the tourism product and making it available to the consumer. With the adoption of information and communication technologies (ICT), the "Principal" is now able to distribute its products directly to the consumer/tourist, cutting out the intermediary ("disintermediation").

Figure 2.1. **A simplified version of the value chain of the tourism-related Industries**

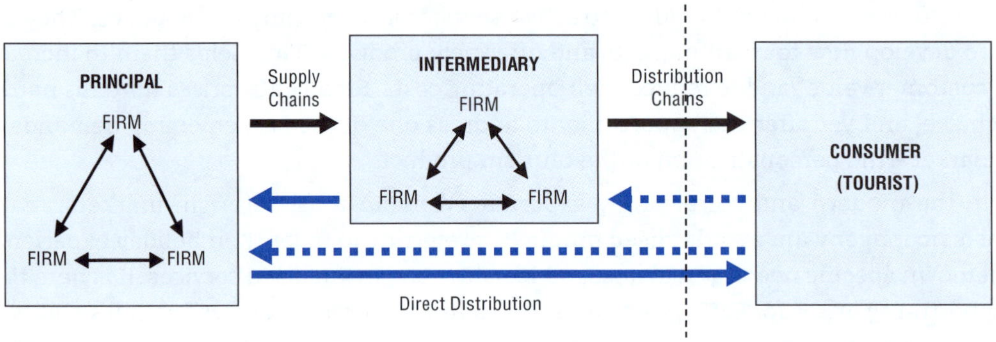

Source: OECD, adapted from Paraskevas, 2005.

The notion of value chains highlights one specific aspect of the links between firms, which is the economic linkage of "value addition" in the full range of activities that are required to bring a product from its conception to its end use. "Value addition" is indeed key. It is the pursuit of those productive activities with the highest returns that makes lead firms in the value chain decide on which activities to keep in-house and which to outsource.

It is important also to emphasise that tourism is perhaps one of the most global of economic activities. The consumer is usually geographically far removed from the "product" to be consumed (*e.g.* the holiday). The suppliers are located in the destination, the sellers/ bundlers are usually located in the country of the tourist's origin, while the corporation with which the consumer deals can be either national or, often the case in Europe at least, part of a multi-national corporation that may only operate through a national subsidiary in the tourist's country of origin. For this reason, the concept of "global" value chains is especially appropriate when considering the international tourism industry.

Networks and clusters: The central role of the destination

There are important differences between value chains and networks. A "chain" maps the vertical sequence of events leading to the delivery, consumption, and maintenance of goods and services, while a "network" highlights the nature and extent of the inter-firm relationships that bind sets of firms into larger economic groups.

The concepts of networks and clusters, notably for SMEs, are as relevant for tourism SMEs as for any other economic sector. In a nutshell, a network represents circumstances where a group of SMEs voluntarily co-operate with each other in order to gain some of the competitive advantages that larger-scale companies can achieve through economies of scale.

A cluster on the other hand represents a group of SMEs that, usually due to a similar geographic location, serve broadly the same market and thereby create a physically close group of companies that may either compete and/or co-operate with each other. In horizontal clustering, tourism operators are co-located in a particular geographic area, share an industrial or technological base, operate within a common market and use a common purchasing and/or distribution channel.

In tourism, the key element in both networks and clusters is the tourism destination itself. This creates by its very nature a geographical concentration of service providers in the same place, creating in turn the conditions for network and/or cluster development. The differences between value chains, networks and clusters are summarised in Table 2.1.

Over the last decade there has been considerable interest and dynamism in developing clustering and networking among destinations and tourism-related SMEs to strengthen their competitive advantage. Research demonstrates that belonging to a cluster or a network can:

- Enhance productivity and the rate of technological innovation.
- Help to build a common industry view to lobby local authorities.
- Overcome some of the disadvantages of small size by undertaking co-operative actions (*e.g.* in marketing).
- Pool resources for human resource development.
- Enhance growth and the competitive performance of firms.

Clusters and networks can thus allow SMEs to combine the advantages of small scale with the benefits of large scale.

The growing role of the consumer in the governance of tourism value chains

The Internet has fundamentally changed the international tourism industry. In essence, this change has two dimensions. First, all categories of firms, large and small, from anywhere in the value chain, can now communicate directly with their end customers. Second, whereas the consumer used to be outside the value chain, he/she is now at the heart of it. Just as suppliers can reach the consumer directly, by-passing

Table 2.1. **Value chains, networks and clusters**

	Value chains	Networks	Clusters
Definitions	The sequence of productive (*i.e.* value-added) activities leading to and supporting end use	A set of inter-firm relationships that bind a group of firms into a larger economic unit	A group of SMEs, co-located and serving similar markets in competition and/or collaboration
Modalities	The bundles of activities that various actors do or do not engage in	The character and extent of inter-firm relationships	The process of collaborative actions based on co-location
Alternative names	• Supply chain • Commodity chain • Production chain • Activities chain • Product pipeline	• Value network • Supply-base	
Characteristics	• In linear (*e.g.* manufacturing) chains, the process of adding value in the various stages between initial design and product delivery • In non-linear (*e.g.* tourism sector) service industries, the process of adding value between the assembly of travel products by the wholesaler and delivery to the custorm in tourism destinations	• Allows firms access to specialised services at lower costs based on contractual agreement • Restricted membership based on co-operation makes it easier for firms to make complex products and supply complex services • Has common business goals	• Attracts much needed specialised services to a region • Based on social values that foster trust and encourage reciprocity • Open membership • Involves both co-operation and competition at the same time • Generates demand for other fims with a variety of similar and related capacities • Has collective vision

Source: OECD, adapted from Sturgeon, 2001 and Rosenfield, 2001.

industry intermediaries, so the consumer now has direct access to the supply-side. Indeed, it is no exaggeration to say that the Internet has brought one step nearer the realisation of perfect competition in travel and tourism markets – where all suppliers and all consumers are aware of the range of services and prices offered for a given product and can make their choices and adjust their supplies accordingly.

Consequently, it is now the consumer who governs the tourism value chain. Consumers have several different paths available when purchasing the end product, unlike in other industries (Figure 2.2). They have a wide range of ways to identify the product of their choice, they can surf from website to website and use different types of search engines, they can move from direct to indirect travel distribution channels, benefit from a relative online cost transparency, make informed comparisons and sometimes even name their price for the tourism product they want. If information is power, then consumers have an infinite number of tools to gather this information and are able both to dictate their "value" terms in the chain and often co-create it as well.

Perhaps the most important of all issues now facing SMEs in the tourism sector is therefore to ensure that the quality of the information provided to the consumer is fully competitive with the consumer's next best option. The actors who will be able to position themselves best in the value chain will be those best able to manage the flow of information to and from the consumer as well as to and from all the actors involved in the bundle of the tourism product on offer.

Figure 2.2. **Australia: Consumers and the tourism value network**

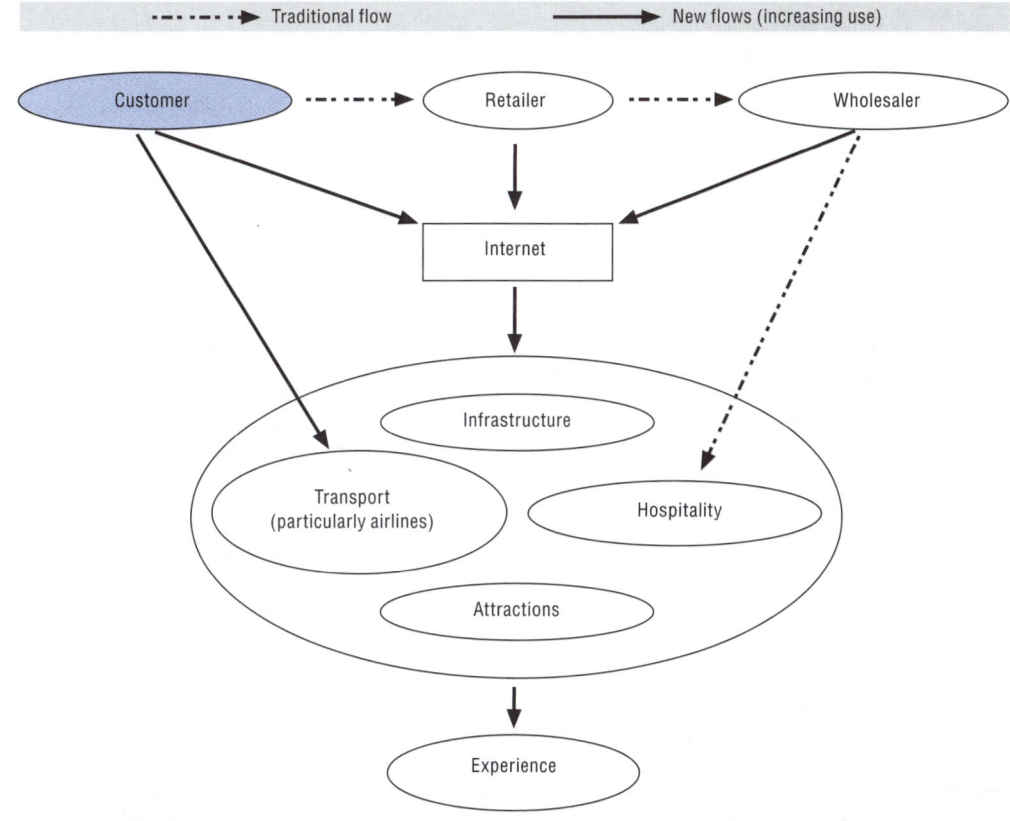

SME operating patterns and challenges: case study findings

This section identifies the main issues faced by tourism SMEs and presents case study evidence on how some of these have been tackled.

How significant are value chains for tourism SMEs?

The case studies demonstrate (Table 2.2) that tourism SMEs often have limited knowledge of their role in global value chains (GVCs). Given the complex nature of the industry, value chains involving tourism businesses are generally highly fragmented and SMEs are not able to identify their competitive advantage through a value chain analysis. For SMEs in tourism, the idea of greater participation in GVCs is therefore not necessarily a high priority. SMEs do not always have a clear understanding of the significance of the multiple linkages that occur along the tourism value chains.

Case studies also indicate, however, that the concept of GVCs has been gaining significance recently. A majority of enterprises are increasingly (and mostly intuitively) aware of the significance of a value chain in creating a product for the customer. The impact of globalisation on the structure of tourism supply is evident. Globalisation is undoubtedly creating a range of opportunities and opening up many new foreign markets for the international tourism industry. These large industry players tend to occupy a dominant position, often controlling access to key resources such as finance, information/market research and technology. SMEs, however, often lack the time and skills to be able to

Table 2.2. **SMEs' awareness and understanding of the tourism value chain**

Case study / Question	Tourism value chain(s) structure, the market/price structure/ competitors	SMEs' key assets or weaknesses in the chain
Australia	SMEs do not find the concept of GVCs very pertinent to their activities.	Branding and well-trained staff are recognised assets. Strategic alliances and geographic clusters allow organisations to work together to increase their market share. High potential of SMEs for further development of high yield markets.
Austria	SME hotels participating in co-operative schemes have a good understanding of the service value chain.	For SMEs, professional co-operation management is key in creating added value that is both measurable and sustainable. Only a few SME alliances have undertaken international co-operation.
Germany/Jordan	Jordanian SMEs recognise the German tour operators – the producers of the package tours – as the main agents of the value chain.	The high costs of establishing a branch office in the country of destination are an obstacle for SME tour operators.
Korea	Most companies in the tourism sector have a low level of awareness of GVCs, although they try to establish new business models to generate more revenues.	Lack of finance, knowledge and technical know-how, brand management and marketing skills are important barriers for the participation of SMEs in GVCs.
Poland	Many SMEs have limited knowledge of their role in tourism GVCs. They consider travel agents and tour operators, as well as large international or domestic hotel chains, as the key players.	SMEs identify costs, service quality and coverage as key factors in their competitiveness. Competition at the local, regional and international level drives cost reduction and training of personnel.
Spain (Andalusia)	For SME hotels, the main partners within the tourism value chain are the large, vertically-integrated tour operators that create high dependency on tour operators and low customer loyalty. Travel agencies acknowledge their role of intermediation and identify the large vertical groups and transport companies as the main agents of the value chains.	Small independent hotels try to differentiate themselves from establishments belonging to the large hotel chains by dealing in a more direct and familiar manner, seeking to avoid the more impersonal environment of the large chains.
Spain (Balearic Islands)	Balearic enterprises see themselves as producers within the structure of the value chain, which they believe should always be focused on the customer.	The most important business attributes remain the brand name, the real estate, the surrounding environment, information systems and know-how. Product diversification is seen as an important strategy to reduce dependence on a specific market and also to counteract seasonality.
Switzerland	Travel agencies and tour operators have a better knowledge and understanding of the value chain than SME hotels.	For SMEs, personalised service and advice to their customers is key.

understand the global context or to analyse strategic issues, thereby reinforcing their competitiveness.

How SMEs can create added value through GVCs and networks?

Case studies underline the various benefits that SMEs can gain by diversifying and expanding their activities through greater participation in GVCs and networks (Box 2.1 and Table 2.3). SMEs' participation in value chains and networks contributes to innovation by a process of continual improvement to satisfy customers' expectations and by allowing SMEs to reach new markets and customers. It also enables companies (such as travel agencies) to specialise in specific, often niche, markets, to increase their expertise and raise the quality of their advice to their clients. The tailor-made services that they can deliver can raise the value they add for their clients who, in return, will be ready to pay more. By knowing and meeting their customers' requirements, they can raise their customers' loyalty and hence raise their profits.

The case studies also underline the fact that those SMEs which are privately-owned and which do not co-operate with others face the severest difficulties in these areas.

> **Box 2.1. Poland: Benefits for SMEs from participating in GVCs**
>
> - Enhanced brand image by being able to use the logo of a well-known international brand.
> - Significant fixed cost reductions, resulting from economies of scale.
> - Reaching more markets due to joint marketing and promotion, and participation in various global online reservation systems.
> - Greater numbers of foreign tourists and tourist groups organized by travel agents or tourism operators co-operating with a chain.
> - Access to major databases on customers and market trends, enabling service quality to be matched more closely to the customer, and the adoption of better company operating strategies.
> - Access to the latest technologies and proven solutions.
> - Access to professional training for all personnel, including management.
> - Promotion and implementation of innovative practices at the enterprise.

Table 2.3. **Estimated benefits to tourism SMEs' from participation in GVCs**

Case study / Question	Benefits of being part of a supply/value chain
Australia	The idea of greater participation in GVCs is not necessarily a high priority for most tourism operators in Australia. Although there is strong awareness of the immediate, first-hand interactions that connect particular businesses, there is little understanding of the importance of the multiple linkages that occur along the entire length of these chains.
Germany/Jordan	Jordanian travel agency SMEs can get access to foreign markets.
Korea	At both industry and company level, SMEs are becoming aware of the importance of the value chain system for their competitiveness in the currently highly competitive business environment. Value chain participation allows SMEs to take advantage of interactivity, customer and quality management.
Poland	Lack of knowledge about the potential benefits hinders SME participation in value chains and co-operation with large companies. While value chains have a small impact on SMEs, very positive examples exist of SMEs benefiting from co-operative networks.
Spain (Andalusia)	To deal with competitive pressures, travel agencies estimate that they should focus on offering a better quality product, with greater added value, in order to increase customer loyalty.
Spain (Balearic Islands)	Value chains contribute to niche market development, improved know-how and innovation, expansion prospects (*e.g.* in markets and customers) and specialisation. Enterprises believe they are in a leading position as a result of their specialisation, the quality of their service and their accumulated experience, and therefore do not intend to increase their role in the value chain. However, most admit that they are experiencing a loss of competitiveness due to increasing competition.
Switzerland	Travel agencies can increase their profitability through more focused participation in GVCs. Hotels can reach a critical mass in marketing/branding, organise their reservation systems and streamline their purchases.

Co-operation within the value chain

The globalisation of the tourism industry has prompted numerous SMEs in tourism to initiate or join a co-operative scheme in order to increase their performance and profitability (Table 2.4). Given the importance of small businesses in tourism, personal relationships, networks and clusters are considered crucial elements in tourism value chains.

The Austrian case study, for example, identified three main co-operative schemes: "horizontal", "vertical" and "lateral" (Table 2.5). This approach is illustrative of the range of co-operative ventures open to SMEs and of their likely impact on the firms concerned.

Several case studies indicate that those SMEs that exclude themselves from tourism networks are disadvantaged. The consumer is looking for a comprehensive tourism

Table 2.4. **Co-operation within the tourism value chain**

Case study / Question	Level of co-operation with contractor(s), suppliers and/or partners	Degree of SMEs' dependence on main contractor(s)
Australia	SMEs tend to be loyal to their traditional partners, with whom they have long-standing alliances. Relationships tend to be more prevalent at the domestic than at the international level. However, an increasing number of SMEs are affiliating themselves with MNEs, either as individual suppliers or as local franchisees.	Most tourism providers continue to see themselves as largely self-sufficient and independent entities. They develop their own strategies, identify and meet the needs of particular segments of the tourism market in their own unique ways, and generally rely on a finite set of partners to bring their products and services to market. However, even the most "independent" travel agent now feels compelled to join a franchise in order to extend its market power.
Austria	Inter-firm co-operation includes co-operation between companies of the same sector (*e.g.* family hotels) or with partners in a different sector (*e.g.* hotels and cable car companies).	Local hotels choose to co-operate to maintain their independence at the same time as reaching critical mass. A co-operative venture in the tourism sector without a clear legal basis or a specific co-operation agreement just does not work.
Germany/Jordan	The co-operation between tour operators and incoming agencies is central to the operational management of the value chain from the market to the destination.	Incoming agencies (IAs) play a central role as co-ordinators and controllers of package holidays in Jordan due to regulations which force every foreign tour operator (TO) to work in partnership with a Jordanian IA. However, in attracting foreign tourists, they are dependent on the foreign TO as they have no direct access to markets. IAs are highly fragmented and have little scope to negotiate with foreign TOs.
Korea	About 50% of the medium-sized hotels surveyed are in a partnership with companies in other industries – most frequently credit card companies. Small hotels partner with travel agencies, to receive support in reservation systems.	Most SMEs hotel (generally those with less than four stars) are operated as independent hotels.
Poland	Most SMEs are affiliated with trade organisations (*i.e.* tourism organisations, chambers of commerce). However, it is felt that affiliation does not bring clear benefits.	More than half of the SMEs interviewed are independent of any hotel chain, and they only envisage co-operation for joint advertising or, more rarely, to share reservation systems. Some SMEs have franchise contracts.
Spain (Andalusia)	The hotels consulted have signed many individual contracts with different tour operators, booking centres, and virtual or traditional agencies. Prices and quotas tend to be set, with strong pressure on prices. A high percentage of hotel establishments belong to chains which allows them to increase their negotiating power with others in the tourism value chain. Co-operative networks in the hotel industry are particularly active between innovative firms and are contributing to product upgrading and better quality services.	All SME hotels and travel agencies interviewed are independent. However, both small hotels and travel agencies depend on tour operators for most of their reservations and turnover. In particular, "sun and sand" destinations typically see the subordination of hotel establishments to the interests of tour operators. SME hotels' dependency is especially high with respect to attracting foreign tourists.
Spain (Balearic Islands)	Co-operation occurs within associations of tourism enterprises at the local level, and with employer organisations at a regional, national and international level, mainly for joint promotion. SMEs also associate with tour operators through guaranteed contracts or co-operation agreements for joint promotion. The big hotel chains also establish joint venture agreements with suppliers and partners for the joint development of their activities or to benefit from the brand name of specific international enterprises.	Only the big hotel groups are able to belong to several value chains, since their activities are both horizontally and vertically integrated.
Switzerland	Tour operators develop close partnerships with hoteliers and other partners in order to strengthen their connections with different products, respond quickly to the customer and achieve scale economies. Travel agencies tend to work with a limited number of tour operators to optimise their revenues. Hoteliers co-operate with colleagues for marketing purposes or to optimise their supply chain. Hoteliers also develop new forms of co-operation with ski lifts and cable car companies.	Some independent travel agencies choose to join the brand of a tour operator to increase their revenues. Due to their small size, however, many hotels cannot work with tour operators.

Table 2.5. **Co-operative models in Austria**

	Horizontal	Vertical	Lateral
Co-operative schemes	Co-operation between partners belonging to the same sector and offering the same type of service	Co-operation between partners belonging to the same sector or belonging to two neighbouring sectors and offering different types of services	Co-operation between partners belonging to completely different sectors
Impacts	Economies of scale	Optimisation of the service chain	Exploration of new market segments
Examples	Co-operation between several hotels	Co-operation between a hotel and a cable car company	Co-operation between a hotel and a company of the automotive industry
Keywords	Intra-sectoral co-operation	Service chain	Distribution partnership

experience which includes all the products and services (transport, accommodation, catering, entertainments, etc.). Such an experience often cannot be provided by a single small business. However, while tourism is by nature a "connecting business", co-operation within a network is not always viewed as positive. Weak co-operation can generate additional costs or conflicts of interests among the partners/competitors without yielding any measurable benefits. A number of key factors can be identified for successful co-operation models (based on the Austrian case study – Box 2.2).

> **Box 2.2. Austria: Key factors for successful alliances in the tourism sector**
>
> - *The legal form of the venture or the type of co-operative agreement*: A co-operative venture in the tourism sector without a clear legal basis or a specific co-operation agreement just does not work.
> - *The intensity of the co-operation*: Commonly agreed and clear priorities for the co-operative venture have to be set.
> - *The size of the venture*: Very tight co-operation between establishments in the tourism sector will inevitably bring about equally intensive personal contacts and presupposes a readiness among all stakeholders to develop a feeling of togetherness.
> - *The spirit of co-operation: a)* for target group-oriented co-operative ventures, partners are characterised by the similarity of their mission statement and their product offer as well as by a largely homogeneous level of quality; *b)* the partners in a destination-oriented co-operative model share common territorial roots.
> - *The internal organisational structures*: Essential ingredients for success are: leadership qualities at company management level, excellent internal communications, a systematic approach to co-operation and the presence of certain characteristics such as trust, integrity and commitment to the co-operative project.

Research has shown (Braun, 2005) that successful tourism clustering requires a high level of cohesion, professionalism and industry knowledge, underpinned by SMEs networking and knowledge sharing. Instinctively, SMEs rarely act proactively in network development, however, and often need encouragement to do so. Natural resources have long provided small tourism firms with a clustering incentive, although it is also the case that many regions have insufficient firms, physical, financial or human infrastructure for the successful development and growth of clusters. In such cases, enabling policies can make all the difference (see policy implications below).

How SMEs compete and are structured in tourism destinations

Competition in tourism is primarily between destinations, and only secondarily between individual service providers within destinations. It is a destination's natural and cultural attractions that attract tourists; each country, region and location has a unique character. Differentiation is the market strategy of destinations.

As shown in some case studies, tourism companies profit from the uniqueness of destinations and SMEs operating in those destinations have considerable strength. They can gain from the destination's brand image without having to incur high marketing costs themselves, are able to meet the customer's changing requirements flexibly, can offer a wide range of services and can use their local knowledge to exploit the locality's potential to the maximum. Moreover, smaller enterprises, such as a family operated business, can personalise the tourism experience to differentiate themselves from other, higher volume operators.

Despite these advantages, however, the case studies have shown that the SMEs themselves have to invest time and effort in their own success. Brand quality has to be maintained through constant investment in product improvements, quality assurance systems and human resources development.

The impact of information technology

Travel and tourism services are information-intensive, highly amenable to digital delivery, and targeted towards customers who are typically not local. Digital delivery brings opportunities and challenges for travel and tourism services, and mediation and disintermediation are central to these opportunities and challenges. All case studies emphasise that the travel and tourism value chains have been profoundly and fundamentally affected by information and communications technology (ICT) (Box 2.3). Consumer services can be delivered directly to the consumer (*e.g.* the purchase of an online airline ticket) or mediated by a services supplier.

Box 2.3. Australia: The Internet – opportunity, or barrier?

The Internet has had an enormous impact on the tourism industry, from computerised reservation systems to last minute Internet accommodation booking companies. It has also changed the way many customers and suppliers interact and navigate through the global value chain.

An inbound tour wholesaler who was interviewed speculated that he would be out of business within the next five years as a direct result of customers and retailers dealing directly with suppliers, owing to the effectiveness of the Internet in by-passing the "middle man".

In contrast to this, another travel agent interviewed believed that his competitive advantage centred on his ability to add value in the area of service, industry knowledge and organisational simplicity, as opposed to the Internet, which they speculated created more work and uncertainty for prospective consumers.

The impact of the Internet on the tourism industry provides an example of the importance for companies large and small to adapt to changes in technology if they are to remain competitive. Therefore from a global perspective the Internet is as much a threat as it is an opportunity, and those companies that adapt to the ever changing market place will be rewarded with increased competitiveness.

Level of adoption of ICT in travel and tourism services

On the demand side the uptake of digital delivery will depend on factors such as price, flexibility, bandwidth, ease of access, and the use of online interfaces. The rapid development of access to the Internet, its affordability and the inclination of users to search for information and purchase online have been important factors explaining the recent development of e-tourism by consumers (Box 2.4).

> **Box 2.4. Consumers' preference: E-tourism websites *versus* traditional agents in the United States**
>
> 66% of American users believe that e-Tourism websites provide better services than travel agents. These figures come from a study that surveyed 1 351 leisure and 1 200 business travellers on 30 April 2002, carried out by Yesawich, Pepperdine and Brown/Yankelovich Partners. According to the study, 39% of American leisure travellers (whether they use the Internet or not) think that the Internet is easier and faster to use for travel planning than a travel agent. This is extremely important, both for the future of the e-Tourism sector and for consumers' behaviour.
>
> The survey indicates how positively e-Tourism websites have been developing, such as the improvement of their interfaces as well as their very rich content and offers which now allows more than a third of American leisure travellers to use the Internet rather than a travel agent. Since 59% of the American population use the Internet, this means that 66% of American Internet now prefer e-Tourism websites to services provided by their travel agent. Put another way, only a third of Internet users prefer dealing with a travel agent than a website – a major worry for this segment of the travel trade.
>
> *Source: www.etourismnewsletter.com.*

From the perspective of the enterprise, e-tourism is developing at a steady rate. For example, in Europe, online travel sales increased by 44% during 2003 to reach EUR 11.7 billion (5.4% of the total market). Growth in the European online travel market is expected to slow, but its value was predicted to increase to more than EUR 20 billion by 2006 – an expected 8.6% of the total travel market (Marcussen, 2004) (Figure 2.3). There are notable differences in the levels of e-commerce and e-business activity among European countries. For example, in 2003, more than 50% of tourism enterprises in Austria were doing e-business, compared to fewer than 20% in France and Poland. At that time, only 20% of enterprises in Poland, Greece, France and Ireland were purchasing online (E-business Watch).

Further developments on the supply side will depend on the relative cost per transaction of online *versus* face-to-face alternatives, as well as the development and availability of new delivery systems and of course the quality of the infrastructure.

ICT and tourism

Case studies indicate that whereas the tour operators and airlines have adopted ICT relatively early, SME hotels have been relatively slow in embracing ICT in their business, due mainly to the lack of a clear strategy, expertise and available financial resources (Table 2.6). In contrast, large hotel chains have been playing a leading role.

2. GLOBALISATION, SMES AND TOURISM DEVELOPMENT

Figure 2.3. **The western European online travel market, 1998–2006**
EUR billlions

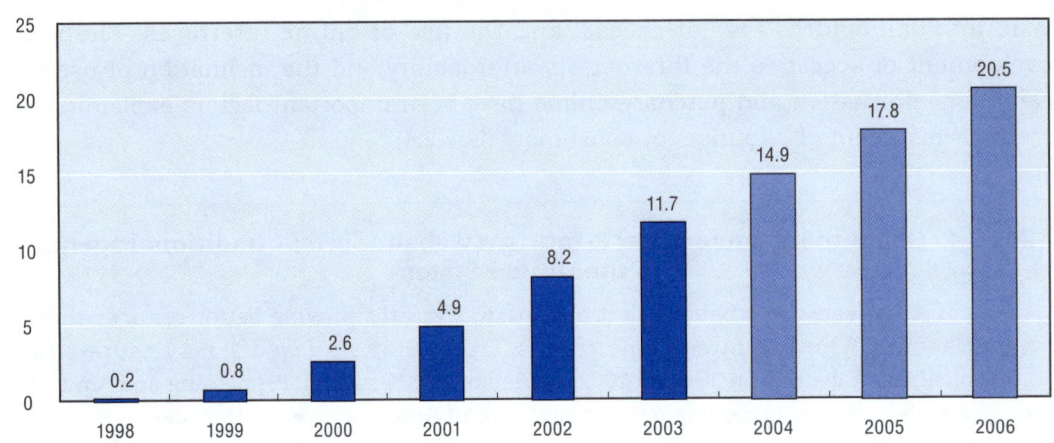

Note: 2004 through 2006 forecasted.
Source: Marcussen, C.H. (2004), "Trends in European Internet Distribution of Travel and Tourism Services", Centre for Regional and Tourism Research, Denmark.

StatLink http://dx.doi.org/10.1787/153067554010

Table 2.6. **Technology and standards within tourism**

Case study / Question	Technology (including ICT)/Ability to cope with required standards
Australia	Operators of small accommodation units see the Internet as a complex opportunity which is currently being only partially utilised. Tour operators and travel agents are much more likely to view the Internet as a barrier to increasing their role within the GVC. The Internet boosts the power of consumers to by-pass intermediaries and deal directly with suppliers.
Korea	ICT uptake by SMEs is gradual and is seen as a tool to strengthen competitiveness.
Poland	The majority of hotel SMEs make insufficient use of ICT, due to the high costs of implementing new IT solutions and buying licences. As a consequence, such SMEs tend to use only basic IT tools.
Spain (Andalusia)	The use of new technologies is imposed, more in travel agencies than in hotel establishments, by large tourism intermediaries or suppliers. However, set-up costs are paid exclusively by the agencies, involving considerable effort on their part. They all work with Amadeus which pays the maintenance costs for its IT application.
Spain (Balearic Islands)	The travel agency sector sees the Internet as a very serious competitor. Innovation is intended in the form of expanding and improving the offer. Information systems and the Internet are making this process easier.
Switzerland	For tour operators and SME travel agencies, the use of ICT for connecting the various providers of services is essential to give the consumer accurate price information and to validate reservations in real time. Many SME hotels are still not connected to networks or reservation systems, but would like to do so to increase profitability.

Table 2.7 highlights ICT-related opportunities and challenges for travel and tourism service providers, including SMEs. ICT has created new opportunities for hotels to streamline internal management, *e.g.* reservation and yield management systems, guest accounting, call centres, and to a lesser extent employee management (e-training, labour scheduling) (Box 2.5). Large hotel players have created dedicated career websites. ICT has enabled hotels to manage their customers, their needs and sometimes their complaints more effectively. Quality management and performance measurement have been enhanced. ICT has, however also brought concerns to hotel managers in regard to negative impacts on prices and to the commoditisation/standardisation of hotel products.

Concerning the external value chain, technology has resulted in a streamlining of the supply chain management. Online connectivity using extranet and Internet technologies has allowed data synchronisation with suppliers (product availability and prices) and improved

Table 2.7. **ICT-related opportunities, challenges, enablers and obstacles for tourism SMEs, 2003**

Opportunities	Challenges
Direct access to potential customers	Minimising setup costs by developing systems and applications more suitable for SMEs
Cutting marketing and sales costs	Creating standard ICT and e-business applications for SMEs
Optimising lead-time and instant adjustments of supply according to demand	Employing multi-channel strategies
Enablers	**Obstacles**
The formation of network relations among SMEs	SME reluctance to invest in ICT and e-business
Customer-driven demand for e-business products and services	The business case for SMEs to grasp the potential of implementing e-business
Large enterprises leading the way for SMEs	Lifestyle SMEs and management motivations

Source: Adapted from E-business Watch (2004), Electronic Business in Tourism, Report 07-II, August 2004, European Commission, Brussels.

> **Box 2.5. Marriott: Impact of Internet reservation system on revenue**
>
> Increasing use of Internet reservation services may adversely impact the revenues of hotels. Some of our hotel rooms are booked through Internet travel intermediaries serving both the leisure, and increasingly, the corporate travel sectors. While Marriott's Look No Further Best Rate Guarantee has greatly reduced the ability of these Internet travel intermediaries to undercut the published rates of Marriott hotels, these Internet travel intermediaries continue their attempts to commoditize hotel rooms, by aggressively marketing to price-sensitive travellers and corporate accounts and increasing the importance of general indicators of quality at the expense of brand identification. These agencies hope that consumers will eventually develop brand loyalties to their travel services rather than to our lodging brands. Although we expect to continue to maintain and even increase the strength of our brands in the online marketplace, if the amount of sales made through Internet intermediaries increases significantly, our business and profitability may be harmed.
>
> *Source: Annual Report,* Marriott, 2005.

---

communication and information sharing on issues such as demand changes and product modifications. The global players are increasingly looking for local SME hotels that can join in their strategic alliances to strengthen and stabilise their own value chains (Box 2.6).

With the Internet, service companies, and in particular travel agencies, have come under pressure from other actors such as airlines and accommodation suppliers, who are reducing or eliminating commission payments. As a result, travel agencies have had to seek other sources of revenue, such as charging customer service fees to replace lost commissions. The case studies show that many travel agents have joined co-operative agreements with other partners in the value chain, notably the tour operators (Box 2.7). Nonetheless, the number of travel intermediaries has been declining in many countries.

The Internet has encouraged the emergence of new online intermediaries. These have built successful businesses by placing e-commerce technology at the centre of their operation to ensure the widest distribution with the lowest cost base (Box 2.8). These new Internet intermediaries can typically be either new participants or consortia of existing

> **Box 2.6. TUI: Technology adding value for money while increasing customer choice**
>
> The TUI Group is employing advanced IT solutions to respond to changing demand in the tourism sector, where customers require more value for less money and are increasingly moving away from package holidays to independently constructed itineraries.
>
> The Apollo system, a group-wide and web-based platform interfacing with all existing systems, will improve communication between tour operators and hoteliers in the TUI group. The sharing of information on destination and accommodation capacities across the group will allow faster and better reaction to supply and demand factors, thus offering customers a better quality of service while keeping costs low.
>
> Through the TUI Hotel Portal, selected hoteliers will be able to enter and manage their own information via the web where it will be administered and sorted by TUI and retailed via relevant Internet pages. The portal will facilitate a rapid and easy handling of the mass volume sale of hotel capacities providing customers with a cost efficient, personalised service. For a more detailed description of The Apollo system and TUI Hotel Portal visit *www.tui.de*.
>
> *Source:* World Travel and Tourism Council, 2005.

> **Box 2.7. Germany: Retail agents**
>
> Germany currently has approximately 18 200 travel agencies which sell travel as their main source of income. Of these, around 4 461 are IATA agencies.
>
> Consolidation in the retail sector is making it increasingly difficult for travel agencies to remain independent. Between 1985 and 2003 the share of truly independent travel agents is estimated to have fallen from 71.2% to about 5%. This means that agents are either consortia-controlled, belong to chains, franchise organisations or co-operatives.
>
> Training retail agents is a key factor for success in this market, and agencies such as Tourism Australia focus on agent training in conjunction with wholesale partners and tour operators.
>
> *Source:* Deloitte Touche Tohmatsu, Reaching Travel Services To Consumers, 2005.

> **Box 2.8. Online travel agents in Spain**
>
> 2004 was the year of consolidation of online travel agents in Spain. Parallel to the birth of a multitude of web pages and tourist websites, a process of concentration in the distribution sector has taken place. This has led to the consolidation of four large virtual travel agencies (Rumbo, Viajar.com, eDreams and Lastminute.com) which were leaders in a market exhibiting exponential growth since its inception.
>
> Online travel sales in Spain represented about EUR 1.2 billlion in 2004 (135% up on 2003). This strong growth is due to a combination of factors: *a)* the growing use of the Internet for hotel reservations through online travel agencies; *b)* the strategy of disintermediation by airline companies and hotel chains, which increasingly choose their own channels of e-distribution rather than conventional agencies; and *c)* the growing level of adoption of ICT and e-commerce by the Spanish. As a result, the Internet has become both the first search option when planning a trip, and one of the main purchase channels.

participants. In some cases therefore, new segments within the travel and tourism industry are created by combining existing participants into new entities. Travel comparison websites, offering easy comparisons of travel prices and product features, represent another kind of intermediary striving to upgrade their position in the chain; these are growing in importance.

Whereas industry computer reservation systems or global distribution systems were highly complex, proprietary systems requiring access agreements and significant investment in ICT infrastructure and the skills needed to use them, the Internet is a "free", open network that can be used by anyone at a modest cost. The costs of adopting Internet-based technology are therefore low, and can bring many benefits to SMEs (Box 2.9).

> **Box 2.9. Korea: A successful example of IT application in the tour operator industry**
>
> Hanatour has become one of the biggest tour operators in Korea by the extensive introduction of ICT throughout its business, and by integrating external businesses into its value chain. Hanatour started in 1993 as a small travel agency. Based on a clear strategic plan, it developed a strong IT infrastructure in 1997 and also became a wholesaler. In 2001, Hanatour became the first tourism company listed in KOSDAQ (Korea Securities Dealers Automated Quotation). The value of the company has increased tenfold in a decade, and has seen rapid growth in its workforce since 2000. As a result, it has moved beyond its initial status as an SME.
>
> Hanatour has signed co-operation agreements with 4 500 Korean travel agencies (more than 50% of the total). These agencies sell Hanatour products and provide all the company's services to customers on its behalf. It made a "General Sales Agency" agreement with eleven foreign companies including Trek America, Amtrek, Star Cruise, Royal Caribbean Cruise, Eurailpass, JR pass, and Alamo Rent-a-Car, and also entered into strategic partnerships with 30 domestic companies, including BC Card, Samsung Card, Hana Bank, LG Eshop and Emart.
>
> Hanatour invested heavily in its network infrastructure ten years ago and has prepared its own "Enterprise Resource Planning" system as well as real time reservations services. This very innovative approach for Korea has resulted in strong internal growth.

Conclusions for SMEs

Globalisation is changing the structure of supply and distribution chains in the tourism industry, creating numerous challenges and opportunities for SMEs. Consequently, tourism SMEs have more opportunities to reach international markets, especially through wider use of ICT and lower transport costs. The tourism case studies highlight the potential of niche and especially of high yield markets. GVCs and networks encourage SMEs to make permanent improvements in know-how, innovation and product quality. ICT developments place the consumer at the centre of the chain, providing SMEs with an important opportunity to fulfil consumers' expectations and provide them with individual treatment. Efficient and well-designed co-operative ventures can increase SMEs' profitability.

The challenges are also numerous, however. The participation of tourism SMEs in GVCs has increased their responsibilities in the value chains. They need to do more in training and skills development. They need to cope with new products and process standards. Many SMEs in the hotel or travel agency sectors are dependent on global/regional players and compete fiercely with other SMEs, sharpening the price battle and often reducing profitability. Many tourism SMEs do not understand how to benefit from greater participation in GVCs and therefore do not co-operate with large players. Some of the most important issues for SMEs to deal with are as follows:

Key issues

Human and financial resources, and technical competence

All the case studies underline the fact that small businesses find it difficult to develop their human resources in order to participate fully in the industry's value chains. Even where the role of SMEs in GVCs is significant, they are not always ready to co-operate with other partners in the chain or in competitive business models, due to their limited capacities in areas such as entrepreneurial and business skills, and financing.

Unbalanced market power and internal tensions

SMEs interviewed for the case study research also underline some of the perceived negative effects of globalisation. Interviews highlighted that globalisation increases uncertainty and sometimes leads to a real "price war". SME hotels, for example, note that in recent years profit margins have been reduced by the continuous price pressure applied by large tourism operators and new online intermediaries. However, they also note the positive effects of globalisation, such as the reduction in air transport prices, especially since the appearance of the "low cost" carriers and the new markets they have created.

A survey by a private Greek consultancy on the market influence of tour operators on resort hotels shows their high degree of dependency (for about 60% of their total business) on tour operators. It underlines the fact that the enormous market power of the major UK and German tour operators affects the way these hotels conduct their business. According to this study, the main advantages of working with tour operators (as seen by Greek resort hotels) include: a) high volume of business; b) significant business outside the high season; c) getting paid on time and d) satisfactory room rates. The main disadvantages are a) pressure to lower prices, often implying a reduction in quality; b) diverting clients to other destinations; and c) some late payment problems.

Quality and standards

The tourism case studies, as with some other sectors, have shown that meeting product and process standards is essential for SMEs to be able to participate fully in either value chains or networks. Tourism enterprises have to adjust to new standards quickly to remain in the chain or network. The costs of accreditation can be very high for small firms; (Box 2.10 illustrates Australian governmental action in this area).

Several case studies show that SMEs working with value chains and networks, while meeting new standards, should also avoid compromising their authenticity. In a service industry like tourism, success in co-operative ventures requires that the SME provides a unique and authentic experience for the visitor.

Overcoming the problem of small size

The research carried out for this study has established that the fragmented small business sector that dominates tourism at the destination level finds it difficult to remain competitive in the international market. Tourism SMEs (of which typically 65-95% are micro enterprises), are disadvantaged because of their small size. Their capacity is often

> **Box 2.10. Australia: Accreditation and quality in the tourism industry**
>
> The tourism industry has recognised the impact that poor quality can have on repeat business. The task of meeting industry accreditation standards can be difficult for SMEs, and minimising the administrative burden while maintaining standards is a challenge.
>
> The Australian Government is providing support towards the development of a tourism business and accreditation portal. The portal (*www.qualitytourism.com.au*) is designed with two toolkits. One helps the industry to develop and market tourism accreditation and relevant products through a single, accessible, user-friendly site. It also helps to raise awareness of accredited products available in the marketplace.
>
> The second provides information and assistance to enable operators to improve their business management skills and includes links to key industry and Government websites that provide information on business and tourism accreditation. The portal is a voluntary self-sustaining tourism accreditation system that provides a national set of business improvement mechanisms. High levels of service and product quality are becoming key issues for Australia in terms of its reputation as a tourism destination. Tourists now have a greater capacity to research (and to discern between) the tourism experiences they are seeking. The creation of the portal is aimed at capturing benefits from this development by encouraging Australian tourism operators to align the products and experiences they offer more closely with the expectations and perceptions of travellers.

under-utilised (*e.g.* through the impact of seasonality) and their earning power is limited. They often have little know-how in marketing, technology and market trends and only limited access to distribution channels. A way forward for these micro-enterprises is to take far greater advantage of the potential for internal growth. For example, small firms can reduce their average costs by increasing their size (*e.g.* by adding more rooms in hotels or more seats in restaurants).

However, external growth is also urgently needed to overcome such size disadvantages. In tourism destinations, the development and marketing of tourism products and services needs to be increasingly based on partnerships and clusters which enable SMEs to position themselves better in the markets they serve. Provided that a cost advantage can be demonstrated over unilateral action, co-operation is one way of achieving this. Several case studies have shown that SMEs can take advantage of value chains to overcome their size disadvantages and sustain their competitiveness in the global tourism market.

Policy implications

Government policy should focus on areas where the market may not sufficiently provide what is needed to improve the performance of the tourism industry, especially for small enterprises. While the extent to which governments can help businesses to become more innovative and competitive may be limited, it is nonetheless the task of governments to create favourable policy environments to encourage tourism enterprises, both large and small, to adopt best practices in global value chains and networks, and to embrace innovation. There are in practice many areas in which governments could assist tourism SMEs to participate more effectively in GVCs and co-operative networks through policy initiatives in specific areas.

The role of governments

While the private sector plays the central role in creating and enhancing successful value chains, the public authorities also have a responsibility to promote better co-operation and networks by promoting permanent dialogue between the public and private sectors. These actions can enhance collaboration among enterprises and improve the quality of policy for inter-firm and inter-regional networks and clusters.

Most case studies identified policy issues and roles for national/regional/local public authorities (Table 2.8). According to the SMEs interviewed, the main objective should be to facilitate the participation of SMEs in GVCs or networks and/or to help them upgrade their position in the system.

Table 2.8. **Policy issues identified in the tourism industry case studies**

Case study / Question	Policy issues — Tourism
Austria	• When clear market failures occur, it might be worthwhile for national/local public authorities to accompany SMEs in planning their co-operative strategies with a view to optimising the service chain on both the supply and demand sides, or to upgrade co-operation to an international level.
Germany/Jordan	• To protect the established value chain relationships between Jordanian and German SMEs from unexpected structural changes and political shocks. • To help SMEs in developing new value chains in new international markets. • To develop a policy in Jordan for upgrading the destination to attract new investors (*e.g.* vocational training, investment regulation, infrastructure development, quality and standards). • To increase the coherence of tourism with other policies.

Korea	• To strengthen the global competitiveness of the travel industry by:
	  – Focusing on support rather than regulation policies.
	  – Providing support through fiscal incentives rather than grants.
	  – Seeking a policy of indirect rather than direct support.
	• To strengthen consumers' rights by:
	  – Developing an efficient complaint system for tourists.
	  – Organising an effective system of redress.
	  – Paying more attention to safety issues for both inbound and outbound travellers.

Poland	• To improve knowledge and disseminate good practice among SMEs (*e.g.* ICT, marketing, financial support, education and professional training).
	• To support pro-development activities, through:
	  – Education programmes.
	  – The inclusion of SMEs in development strategies.
	  – Evaluation of public programmes for SMEs.
	  – The identification and transfer of good practice.
	  – Financing a website addressed to SMEs.
	  – The provision of market information.
	  – Raising awareness among SMEs about existing financing programmes and how to use them.
	  – Harmonizing taxes.

Spain (Andalusia)	• SMEs would like to see less bureaucracy. • An SME group would like to receive direct public support for ICT development, rejuvenating infrastructure and the promotion of co-operation. • Another SME group sees the role of public authorities more in designing the appropriate policy framework (standards, infrastructure) or in creating an industry advisory board.
Spain (Balearic Islands)	• A group of SMEs would like to see more public support in terms of promotion or improvement of infrastructure to improve their role in the value chains. • Half the enterprises interviewed receive support for training programmes, implementation of quality and environmental management systems. • Larger enterprises tend to say that the less public intervention the better. • Small business can be supported if aid does not interfere with the independence of the firm.

Table 2.8. **Policy issues identified in the tourism industry case studies** (cont.)

Case study / Question	Policy issues
Switzerland	• Tour operators consider that airport taxes are too high while at the same time recognising that this may be the price to be paid for good infrastructure and security. Travel agents are in need of support for vocational training. Hoteliers point out the necessity if increasing their added value through innovation and infrastructure development, although it is difficult for them to undertake action themselves due to a lack of finance.
Australian research paper on clusters presented at the 2005 OECD Conference (Dr. Patrice Braun)	• Tourism policies directed towards SMEs should always include clustering aspects. While such policies cannot compel SMEs to network, they can help augment the destination, provide infrastructure, promote leadership, and benefit the overall clustering processes. • Mapping assets at the destination end of the service chain will provide knowledge on local and regionally-embedded networks, while a strategic analysis of the local/regional value chain will help destinations to match local attributes with established and emerging visitor profiles. • Reassessing the role of SME clusters *vis-à-vis* global distribution systems will advance the adoption of ICT by individual tourism firms and contribute to new destination management partnerships.
OECD study on Digital Delivery of travel and tourism services	• Governments can provide a framework and business environment to enable the adoption and diffusion of ICT services, and enhance transition and adjustment in some of these areas. These include: – ensuring the availability of network infrastructure and enhancing the skills base to foster innovation; – increasing diffusion and use through information, demonstration and standardisation; – helping to establish an environment of online trust; and – ensuring that the business environment is both competitive and conducive to the take up of innovations (OECD, 2005a).

Two groups of SMEs have been identified. The first argues that governments should play a direct role in supporting SMEs, while the second advocates an indirect public sector role in strengthening the overall policy framework. The case studies tend to indicate that there is actually little or no support for facilitating the role of tourism SMEs in GVCs or networks directly – reflecting typical SME independence and suspicion of direct government intervention in their businesses.

In summary, some of the principle roles for public policy and government intervention may be summarised as follows:

Raising awareness of the potential of GVCs

Although the diffusion of ICT has made market intelligence easier for SMEs, their limited resources still hamper accurate information about the opportunities and challenges facing them. Many SMEs that are used to serving local markets may find it difficult to gain a good understanding of the potential advantages of co-operation with other enterprises or different business areas. Raising awareness of opportunities through public initiatives can encourage SMEs in tourism to participate in GVCs (OECD, 2006).

Creating an effective framework for ICT use

Information technology is crucial to improving performance in the tourism industry. Regulatory reform and investment in information technology are among the main reasons why productivity has improved in diverse sectors of tourism business. To create an effective framework for IT use by tourism services, governments need to address regulatory reform to bring down ICT costs and to develop standards and an international regulatory framework for electronic commerce. They also need to pay attention to ICT skills in education and training policy. Governments also play a role in developing the generic technologies and technological infrastructure related to ICT use, since the business sector may not always engage in long-term research on these aspects itself (OECD, 2005a).

Promoting training and skills development

Tourism is first and foremost a service industry. A primary role for governments is to support training and skills development and increase the entrepreneurial/management capacity of SMEs through appropriate small business support and training programmes. In order for SMEs to operate effectively in global value chains, it is essential to ensure and enhance the capacity of managers and employees to cope with new technologies, understand customers' needs, improve product quality and capture the potential of new (niche) markets. Strong leadership in management can play a crucial role in making a co-operative venture successful and in developing customer loyalty and quality management.

Promoting a culture of innovation

Tourism SMEs need to make more intensive use of innovations (mainly driven by large players) in view of their increased participation in GVCs and their relationships with larger companies. The sharing of innovative practices in terms of organisation, entrepreneurship or process development can be instrumental in strengthening the role and importance of SMEs in GVCs. Innovation-oriented tourism policies can contribute to a better spreading of innovation in tourism (*e.g.* for the rejuvenation of tourism supply). Government policies and programmes geared to the dissemination of information to the SME community and to the provision of support services to SMEs in this area can be very helpful. More specifically, where issues such as electronic banking and the availability of ATMs inhibit the development of a full range of tourism services, governments should examine the operating environment of the banking sector with a view to opening up their financial markets to greater competition and to the modernisation of the financial infrastructure. In the same vein, liberalisation of the telecommunications sector can reduce the costs of Internet provision to SMEs.

Facilitating accreditation standards and quality

A difficult task for SMEs, especially for the smaller ones, is to maintain and adopt the standards required for a high quality, dynamic and sustainable tourism industry, at local, regional, national and international levels. Adequate supporting policies that provide information on business and tourism accreditations and encourage SMEs to align their offer with the expectations of consumers can enhance the participation of SMEs in GVCs and networks. As demonstrated by the Australian example in Box 2.10, government programmes can be created to facilitate this process and provide support to SMEs lacking in the skills and experience required to meet standards and gain the appropriate accreditation.

Facilitating co-operation and networks in the tourism industry

There is great potential for the development of alliances, networks and clusters in travel and tourism. Because of the cross-sectoral complexity of the tourism industry, such alliances involve a wide variety of industry activities (*e.g.* transport, accommodation, food, entertainment, etc.) as well as many small businesses. Co-operation is important for achieving economies of scale and added value in the industry. Travel and tourism SMEs are likely to be based around a specific geographic location and could be supported through existing or new destination marketing/management organisations. Governments can play a major role, through their involvement in national and regional tourism organisations, in encouraging collaborative activities, supporting the development of networks of SMEs and in promoting their connections with large enterprises.

Bibliography

Braun, P. (2005), "Creating Value to Tourism Products through Tourism Networks and Clusters: Uncovering Destination Value Chains", OECD-Korea International Tourism Conference, 6-7 September.

Carroll, B. and J. Siguaw (2003), "The Evolution of Electronic Distribution", *Cornell Hotel and Restaurant Administration Quarterly*, August.

Hagenhoff, L. (2003), "The Role of the Travel Agent in the New Travel Marketplace", *Anite Travel Systems*, March.

Johnson, C. (2005), "Global Enhancing the Role of SMEs in Global Value Chains: Draft Conceptual Background and Research Framework", Keynote Address, OECD-Korea International Tourism Conference, 6-7 September.

Keller, P. (2005), "Global Tourism Growth: A Challenge for SMEs, A Few Thoughts by Way of an Introduction", Keynote Address, OECD-Korea International Tourism Conference, 6-7 September.

Kim, C. (2005), "Enhancing the Role of SMEs in Global Value Chain: A Case Analysis on Travel Agencies and Tour Operators in Korea", OECD-Korea International Tourism Conference, 6-7 September.

Kim, H. (2005), "Enhancing the Role of SMEs in Global Value Chain: A Case Study of Korean Hotel Industries", OECD-Korea International Tourism Conference, 6-7 September.

Lafferty, G and van Fossen, A. (2001), "Integrating the Tourism Industry: Problems and Strategies", *Tourism Management*, 22(2001) 11-19.

OECD (2006), "Digital Delivery of Travel and Tourism Services", internal working document, Directorate for Science, Technology and Industry, OECD, Paris.

OECD (2006a), *Innovation and Growth in Tourism*, OECD Publishing, Paris.

Paraskevas, A. and K. Kontoyiannis (2005), "Travel Comparison Websites: An Old Friend with New Clothes", In A.J. Frew (ed.), Information and Communication Technologies in Tourism 2005, Proceedings of the ENTER 2005 Conference, Vienna, Springer-Verlag, pp. 486-496.

Paraskevas, A. (2005b), "The impact of Technological Innovation in Managing Global Value Chains in the Tourism Industry", OECD-Korea International Tourism Conference, 6-7 September.

Rosenfeld, S.A. (2001), "Backing into Clusters: Retrofitting Public Policies, Integrating Pressures: Lessons from Around the World", Paper presented at the John F. Kennedy School Symposium.

Strugeon, T.J. (2001), "How Do We Define Value Chains and Production Networks", Published in IDS Bulletin, Vol. 32, No. 3.

UNWTO (2005), *Statistical Yearbook*, UNWTO, Madrid.

ANNEX 2.A1

Tourism Industry Case Studies

Australia	
Research team:	Australian Government Department of Industry, Tourism and Resources (DITR).
Coverage:	The study focuses primarily on three distinct types of hotel accommodation (chain hotels, boutique hotels, and other accommodation, including hostels and bed and breakfasts), in four areas of the Gold Coast (Gold Coast Airport and surrounds; the Lamington and Springbrook National Parks and surrounds; Surfers Paradise and surrounds; and the theme parks of Sea World, Warner Bros Movie World, Wet "n" Wild, Dreamworld and surrounds).
Main findings:	Large MNCs, foremost hotels and airlines, are significant investors in Australian tourism and have raised the profile, appeal and accessibility of specific locations. These large firms are not well connected to SMEs. Australia's tourism industry is dominated by SMEs, and for these firms local and international personal networks drive activity more than business relationships across national borders. Co-operation in marketing is working reasonably well at national, state and local levels. Potential exists for SMEs to further develop high yield markets. There is a need for small and large firms to work together on training and skills development. Internet is seen as an opportunity and threat.

Austria	
Research team:	Austrian Bank for Tourism Development.
Coverage:	The study is based on: an analysis of the co-operation projects funded in the framework of a Tourism Promoting Scheme made available by the Austrian Federal Ministry of Economics and Labour; the results of a questionnaire addressed to the managers of active co-operation ventures within the Austrian Tourism sector; and structured interviews of industry experts as well as on the results of an analysis of the annual accounts of already active co-operation ventures.
Main findings:	Successful co-operation ventures show a number of specific characteristics, such as the legal form, the intensity of the co-operation and the internal organisational structure. A large majority of these ventures represent the classic pattern of horizontal co-operation. Co-operation schemes may increase profitability of SMEs.

Germany/Jordan	
Research team:	A co-operative research project between German and Jordanian research teams from the University of Jordan and the University of Frankfort am Main, funded by the German Research Council (DFG) and the German Federal Ministry of Co-operation and Development.
Coverage:	In-depth personal interviews were carried out with a total of 43 Tour operators, six of these in Austria, mostly independent medium-sized and small operators of regular Jordan packages as well as some occasional providers. Structured interviews were carried out with incoming agencies in Jordan, with hotel managers, airline managers and representatives of Jordanian tourist authorities.
Main findings:	The study identifies the key factors to ensure that the firms operating in the specific market niche of package tours from Germany to Jordan maintain their competitive advantage. Trust is a significant factor in ensuring the continuation of co-operation and lowering transaction costs. Inbound travel agencies in Jordan play a central role as co-ordinator and controller of package holidays. The branding of Jordan should be encouraged to enable the country to explore new niche markets.

Korea	
Research team:	Kyunghee University, Sejong University and Ministry of Culture and Tourism, Korea.
Coverage:	The survey of 16 hotels was conducted through in-depth interviews over a two week period during July 2005, with general managers and department heads, which included seven large hotels and nine 1st-3rd class tourist hotels. The survey for travel agencies and tour operators was conducted through in-depth interview during a four month period from 1 December 2005 to 30 March 2006, with managers and CEOs of 11 travel agencies and tour operators.

Main findings:	The wider adoption of ICT is a major concern for competitiveness among SMEs. There is an important participation of SMEs in global brands; value chain strategies allow SMEs to take advantage of interactivity, customer and quality management.

Poland

Research team:	*Instytut Turystyki w Krakowie* (the Cracow Tourism Institute), Ministry of Economy, Department of Tourism.
Coverage:	21 hotel enterprises and five entities (2 travel agents, 1 SPA and 2 local governments) from the domestic hotel industry and its environment were selected for interviews, usually with top level executives. All the hotels that participated in the survey were SMEs.
Main findings:	Lack of knowledge about the potential benefits hinders SME participation in value chains and co-operation with large companies. International, regional and local competition is going to force actions, especially in personnel training and cost reduction. Networks created for the promotion of particular products have a chance to develop on a local or regional scale. The necessary co-operation is not developing since there is suspicion in participating in networks together with competitors. SMEs are practically invisible in innovation networks, associations of producers of various tourism products, tourism clubs, and Internet networks. There is a small impact of value chains on SMEs, but some very positive examples of SMEs participation in co-operation networks.

Spain (Andalusia)

Research team:	Research team from the University of Seville.
Coverage:	Four hotel establishments and three travel agencies, located in the provinces of Malaga and Seville. Interviews took place with the owners and/or directors of the hotels and travel agencies. The study also benefited from the collaboration of the President of the Andalusian Travel Agencies (FEAVV) and the Seville Entrepreneur Association of Travel Agencies (AEVISE), as well as the Vice-President of the Seville and Province Hotel Association (AHS) – they presented the view of their respective subsectors and complemented the individual contributions from the firms.
Main findings:	Intermediaries such as tour operators, booking centres, and traditional or virtual travel agencies exert a high pressure on hotel prices, although intermediaries usually do not fulfil the quota reserved to hotels in the individualised contracts they signed with them. To reduce uncertainty, some hotels are part of a hotel association, which increase their commercial potential in exchange for quota and commission per room. Travel agencies estimate that they should focus on offering a better quality product, with greater added value in order to increase clients' fidelity. Globalisation increases uncertainty for SMEs and often results in a real "price war" and a reduction in profitability. Co-operation networks in the hotel industry are particularly active between innovative firms. They are contributing to product upgrading, and better quality and services. There is a need for small and large firms to work together on training and skills development.

Spain (Balearic Islands)

Research team:	Centre of Tourism Research and Technologies of Balearic Islands (CITTIB) in co-operation with the Balearic Ministry of Tourism.
Coverage:	The sample comprised of 25 enterprises, of which 18 enterprises responded to the survey including 4 large, 8 medium and 6 small enterprises. Members of the enterprises' Board of Directors were interviewed in every case.
Main findings:	In terms of products, a large number of Balearic enterprises are involved in different lines of business. For example, travel agencies which are engaged in incoming *and* outgoing activities, or some of the large hotel chains which are also involved in the property market. This includes the addition of spa, wellness or sporting centres in hotels. Tourism value chains contribute to niche market development, improvement in know-how and innovation, expansion prospects (*e.g.* in markets and customers), and specialisation (*e.g.* the value chain has enable travel agencies to focus their services). The most important business attributes of the firm are location, facilities, service quality and excellence, brand, know-how, customer satisfaction and individual treatment.

Switzerland

Research team:	Hospitality Research Department of the "École hôtelière de Lausanne".
Coverage:	The sample comprised of 20 enterprises from tour operators (multinationals, whose products cover among others, the Swiss holiday destination), travel agencies (major establishments, which distribute and sell products covering among others, the Swiss holiday destination) and hotels (small and medium-sized hotels covering different existing products in Switzerland proposed in holiday packages).
Main findings:	The main structural changes linked to the participation of SMEs in global value chains occurs in the outgoing branch of the tourism industry. There is a potential for SME travel agencies to further develop high-yield specialised niche markets. SME hotels prefer to strengthen their competitiveness through internal value creation. There is a need however for small hotels to co-operate and network to increase their participation in tourism value chains.

Note: Most of the case studies mentioned are available at *www.oecd.org/cfe/tourism*.

ISBN 978-92-64-03967-4
Tourism in OECD Countries 2008
Trends and Policies
© OECD 2008

2.B. Services Trade Liberalisation and Tourism Development

Introduction

The key objective of this chapter is to examine the role that services trade liberalisation could play in tourism development in developing countries, with the aim of contributing to international services negotiations. The focus is on the potential offered by the adoption of more liberal trade and investment policies in the variety of services and infrastructure that support tourism.

The importance of tourism for economic development is widely acknowledged. A critical feature of tourism is the movement of consumers – the consumer typically goes to the supplier instead of the other way around as in many other services. Sustainable tourism development[1] can thus play a key role in poverty alleviation. Tourism has the potential to employ unskilled or semi-skilled workers in the main centres and in outlying areas, and also stimulates further job creation in supply industries.

The significance of the sector is reflected in the relatively liberal environment currently in place in most countries and in the Uruguay Round commitments of World Trade Organisation (WTO) members. Nearly 130 WTO members, greater than for any other sector, have made GATS commitments under the category "Tourism and Travel Related Services" as defined in the GATS classification (W/120). This underlines the desire of most members to expand their tourism sectors and to attract foreign direct investment.

Developing countries' tourism potential and the opportunities it offers for socio-economic development could be significantly expanded. A prominent constraint to tourism development is the lack of adequate services and infrastructure needed to support the sector. This includes transport services and infrastructure, telecommunications and financial services, as well as electric power and sewage treatment facilities. Adequate consideration also needs to be given to construction, advertising and education services. Enhanced services trade and investment liberalisation, including at the regional and multilateral levels, could substantially contribute to the development of tourism. Liberalisation, however, needs to be appropriately designed and effectively implemented, giving due consideration to social and environmental impacts.

Definition and measurement of the tourism sector

The United Nations in 1994 defined tourism as "the activities of persons travelling to and staying in places outside their usual environment for not more than one consecutive year for leisure, business and other purposes not related to the exercise of an activity remunerated within the place visited". Although there is now a growing recognition of the role of tourism as a productive activity and of its potential to generate significant direct and indirect economic benefits, the sector has suffered in many countries from a lack of political and popular support. This is because tourism's economic importance has often been underestimated.

Tourism is difficult to define and measure since it comprises sellers of many heterogeneous products and services. National accounts and industry statistics fail to present tourism as a specifically-defined sector, nor does tourism appear explicitly in typical economic input-output (I-O) tables. The category "Tourism and Travel Related Services", as defined in W/120 comprises hotels and restaurants, travel agencies and tour operators, and tourist guide services (and an "Other" sub-category).[2] Numerous other tourism services – computer reservation systems, cruise ships and many other transport services, hotel construction, etc. – are placed in other W/120 sectoral categories.

In an effort to improve understanding of the industry, the OECD, the World Tourism Organisation (UNWTO) and Eurostat developed the so-called *Tourism Satellite Account: Recommended Methodological Framework (TSA)* in 2000. The TSA attempts to provide a credible measure of the true contribution of tourism to a national economy by analysing those aspects of demand for goods and services that are associated with tourism, observing the interface between demand and supply of such goods and services, and describing how supply interacts with other economic activities. TSAs are already in place or under development in a significant number of OECD countries, and in an increasing number of developing countries.

Economy-wide effects of tourism

Broadly defined, tourism could be regarded as one of the world's largest and fastest growing industries. According to the World Travel and Tourism Council (WTTC), an organisation made up of executives from the travel and tourism industries, the contribution of travel and tourism to worldwide GDP will rise from 10.3% (USD 4 963.8 billion) to 10.9% (USD 8 971.6 billion) between 2006 and 2016. Employment is estimated at 234.3 million jobs in 2006, 8.7% of total worldwide employment, or 1 in every 11.5 jobs (WTTC). Direct employment growth in 2005 was estimated at 2.1 million new jobs, 6.5 million counting indirect job creation. The countries expected to increase the most in terms of employment between 2006 and 2015 are China, the US, Mexico, Indonesia, India and Brazil (WTTC).

According to the UNWTO, worldwide earnings from international tourism in 2006 reached a record of USD 735 billion, an increase of about 8% over 2005. Europe earned more than half of worldwide receipts (51%), followed by the Asia Pacific and the Americas (21% each), the Middle East (4%) and Africa (3%). Tourism is a crucial source of foreign exchange for developing countries. By 1998, tourism became the main source of foreign exchange revenue for the 49 LDCs, not counting the oil industry. Tourism also accounted for more than a sixth of their non-petroleum exports, far more than raw cotton and textiles, their second and third largest export earners. As a whole, tourism is the main export for a third of developing countries.

Tourism is a complex industry, generating significant economic activity with other industries, through two kinds of linkages – backward and forward linkages. Backward linkages relate to the importance of tourism as a demander of inputs from other industries, including a wide range of agricultural and manufacturing goods, and a variety of services, *e.g.* construction, telecommunications, energy and water and sanitation. Forward linkages relate to the importance of tourism as a supplier (or input) to other industries. As pointed out by Cai *et al.* (2005), while visitor expenditures (final demand) *per se* do not have forward linkages, the tourism industries that sell goods and services to tourists may have forward linkages by selling their products to businesses in other industries.

At the same time, the degree to which tourism will act as a key driver of economic growth in a country or region will depend on the extent of so-called tourism leakages.

These are defined as the amounts subtracted from tourist expenditures, and can take the form of profits and revenue paid abroad to international tour operators, interest payments on debt and the cost of imported goods and services. Leakages may also arise from the non-sustainability of environmental, cultural or other tourism assets over time.

Minimising leakages requires proactive processes that strengthen internal linkages and improve the tourism value-chain, notably by building domestic capacity rather than protecting domestic markets. In the early stages of development, as infrastructure and service investment takes place, leakages are likely to be high and desirable. Thereafter, they may diminish in parallel with the country's rising ability to meet its investment, services and goods needs domestically, and by developing appropriate policies to strengthen local capacities (see Gollub *et al.*, 2002, for a detailed discussion of these policies along the tourism value chain).

Tourism linkage analysis in selected developing and emerging economies

In this section, tourism linkage analysis has been carried out for three developing countries – India, Brazil and Indonesia. Linkage analysis recognises that changes in demand have both a direct and an indirect effect on the economy. For example, tourists spend money in certain sectors (direct effect) and these sectors in turn purchase goods and services from other sectors (indirect effect). Thus, a change in tourist demand affects an economy in ways that may be less than, equal to, or greater than the initial value of the change in demand. Linkage values exceeding one, indicate important multiplier effects and facilitate technology transfer within an economy.

An important issue in conducting linkage analysis for tourism is that the definition of the industry is not straightforward. As noted, tourism is not a category characteristically included in an I-O table, which is one of the necessary inputs to undertake linkage analysis. To abstract from these problems, the analysis presented here generally follows the methodology of Cai *et al.* (2005). This implies using a country's TSA to create a composite "tourism" industry and analyse the backward and forward linkages between "tourism" (as a whole) and the other I-O industries.

The three countries studied below exhibit a similar pattern in their tourism linkages. Backward linkages are about average or slightly above one, and forward linkages well above average. Linkages in the tourism sector appear to be strongest in Indonesia and the least strong in Brazil, with India falling somewhere in between. Given the level of economic development of the countries under study, and the structure of production across sectors, it is not surprising that linkages are generally strongest in the manufacturing sector. However, the tourism sector consistently scores stronger linkages (both backward and forward) than the average for the services sector, suggesting that tourism may be one of the most interconnected services sectors in these three economies.

India

Demand for tourism services in India was expected to increase by 8.4% in 2006 and to continue to rise steadily in the next decade (WTTC). The tourism sector in India, as in many countries, is made up of a diverse set of different sectors. As defined by the Indian TSA, Table 2.9 shows the share of the tourism characteristic industries (*i.e.*, the primary sectors that satisfy tourism demand) that can be attributed to tourism consumption.

Table 2.9. **Tourism industry ratios, India, 2002/03**

Industry	Total tourism consumption (%)
Accommodation services	92
Food and beverage serving services	18
Passenger transport services:	
• Railway	29
• Road	
– Buses	63
– Other mechanised vehicles	3
– Non-mechanised vehicles	90
• Water	2
• Air	94
Transport equipment rental	75
Travel agencies and similar	96
Other recreational and entertainment activities	49

StatLink ⟶ http://dx.doi.org/10.1787/153405122182

Source: Reproduced from India's TSA for 2002-03.

The tourism sector is even more diverse when tourism-related sectors are included (i.e., the secondary sectors that satisfy tourism demand). India's TSA identifies the following sectors as tourism-related sectors: clothing and garments, processed food, tobacco products, alcohol, travel related consumer goods, footwear, toiletries, gems and jewellery, medicines and health related items, and printing and publishing. However, because of issues of data availability in the TSA and aggregation in the input-output table, these sectors could not be included in the composite tourism sector for India. As a result, the linkages presented in this paper probably underestimate slightly the tourism sector as a whole.

India's backward and forward linkages for total inputs are shown in Figures 2.4 and 2.5. The composite tourism sector has an average backward linkage of about 1. Thus, an increase in final demand implies an about average effect on the sectors that supply inputs to the tourism sector. Using a slightly different method of creating a composite tourism sector, Cai et al. (2005) report similar findings for Hawaii's tourism sector in 1997. It is interesting to note that the backward linkage for tourism (1.01) is above a simple average of all of the other services sectors included in Figures 2.4 and 2.5 (0.87).

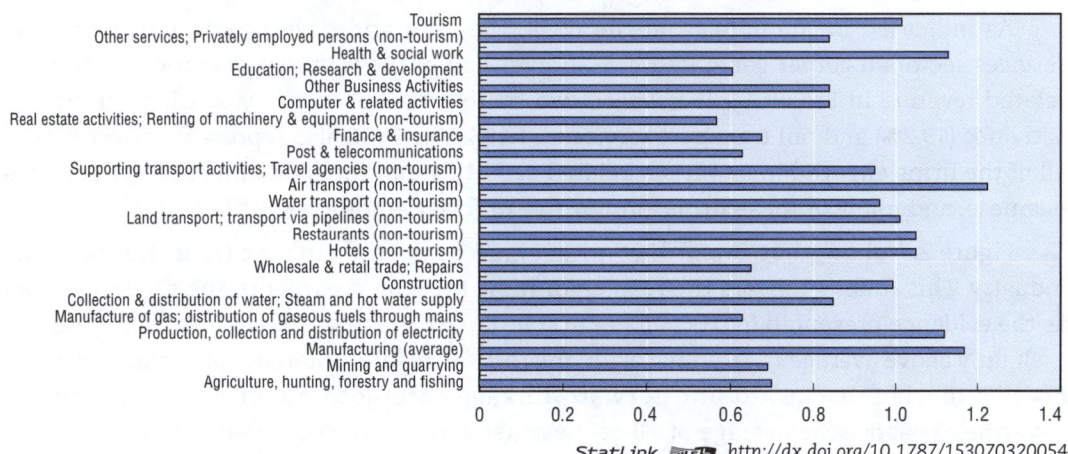

Figure 2.4. **India's backward linkages**

StatLink ⟶ http://dx.doi.org/10.1787/153070320054

Figure 2.5. **India's forward linkages**

Sector	Value
Tourism	~1.16
Other services; Privately employed persons (non-tourism)	~1.0
Health & social work	~0.5
Education; Research & development	~0.5
Other Business Activities	~0.6
Computer & related activities	~0.7
Real estate activities; Renting of machinery & equipment (non-tourism)	~0.7
Finance & insurance	~1.8
Post & telecommunications	~0.7
Supporting transport activities; Travel agencies (non-tourism)	~0.5
Air transport (non-tourism)	~0.5
Water transport (non-tourism)	~0.5
Land transport; transport via pipelines (non-tourism)	~1.4
Restaurants (non-tourism)	~0.5
Hotels (non-tourism)	~0.5
Wholesale & retail trade; Repairs	~2.2
Construction	~0.9
Collection & distribution of water; Steam and hot water supply	~0.5
Manufacture of gas; distribution of gaseous fuels through mains	~0.5
Production, collection and distribution of electricity	~2.5
Manufacturing (average)	~1.0
Mining and quarrying	~1.4
Agriculture, hunting, forestry and fishing	~2.0

StatLink http://dx.doi.org/10.1787/153076318462

Note: The input-output table for India comes from the OECD as of June 2006 and relates to the period 1998-99. India's TSA was compiled by the Indian Ministry of Tourism as of January 2006 and represents the period 2002-03. Using data on real growth in travel and tourism demand from the WTTC, the data in India's TSA was converted to 1998-99 to ensure comparability with the most recent input-output table available for the country.

Similarly, tourism forward linkage is above average, with only six sectors having a higher forward linkage. This finding differs from the results obtained by Cai *et al.* (2005), who observe a below average forward linkage for the tourism sector in Hawaii in 1997. However, this difference could be accounted for either in the divergence in methodology or by the different level of economic development between Hawaii and India. In addition, the average forward linkage for the tourism sector (1.16) is greater than a simple average of the other services sectors (0.91). Coupled with the findings for the tourism sector's backward linkage, one can conclude that tourism may be one of the most interconnected services sectors in the Indian economy.

Brazil

Analysts at the WTTC estimate that demand for tourism services in Brazil grew by 5.3% to approximately USD 70.4 billion in 2006, which represents about 1% of the total global market for tourism services (WTTC). Similar to India, the Brazilian tourism sector is made up of many different sectors. Figure 2.6 shows the relative importance in terms of revenue of each of the "primary" sectors characteristic of the Brazilian tourism industry in 2003.

As indicated in the data from the IBGE, the food and beverage and air transport services sectors together generated in 2003 over half of the total net operational tourism-related revenue in Brazil (56.2%). These two sectors are followed by auxiliary transport activities (13.2%) and rail transport services (11.1%). The IBGE also reports that over 80% of all of the firms engaged in a tourism-related activity are in the food and beverage services business, and many of these firms employ five or fewer employees.

Figure 2.7 show that Brazil has an average backward linkage (1) in the tourism industry. This finding mirrors the results for India presented earlier in the section as well as the evidence presented for Hawaii in Cai *et al.* (2005). Brazil's forward linkage (Figure 2.8) is slightly above average (1.1), which again mirrors the results obtained for India. And while Brazil's tourism backward and forward linkages are both about average, they are nevertheless above the average of all of the other services sectors analysed. So while one might expect stronger linkages in the manufacturing sector – which is indeed what

Figure 2.6. **Per cent of net operational revenue of Brazilian firms in tourism-characteristic activities, 2003**

StatLink http://dx.doi.org/10.1787/153145630404

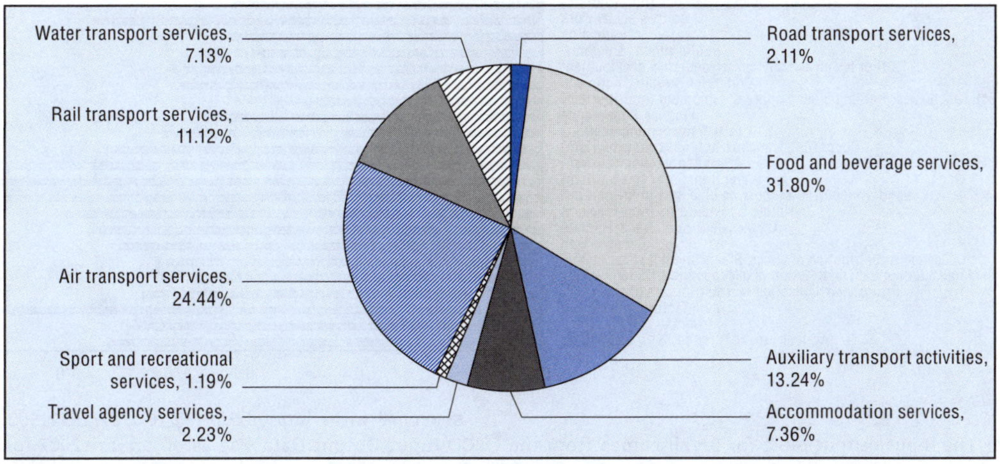

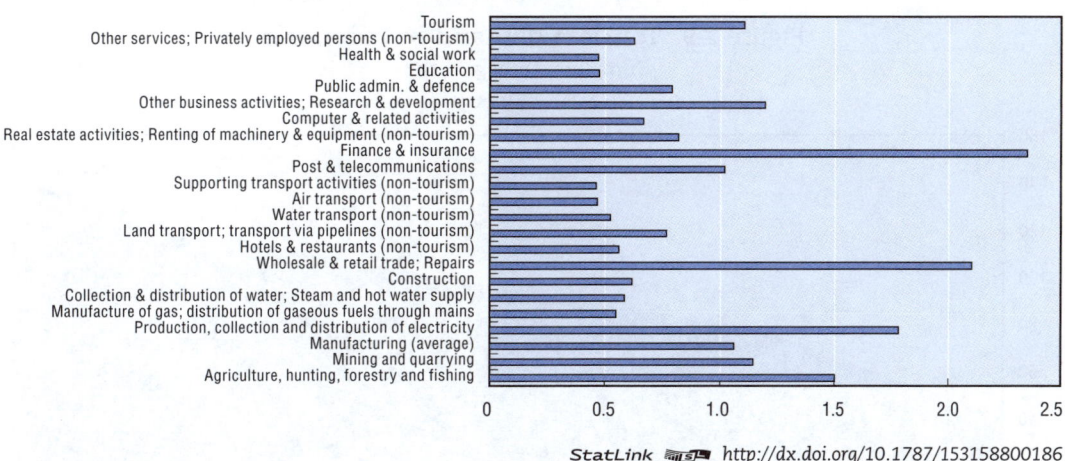

Source: Brazilian Institute of Geography and Statistics (IBGE), 2003.

Figure 2.7. **Brazil's backward linkages**

StatLink http://dx.doi.org/10.1787/153158800186

emerges in this analysis – tourism can be viewed as having relatively more linkages than the average services sector in Brazil.

Indonesia

Indonesia is also characterised by a growing tourism sector. For example, demand for tourism services in Indonesia is estimated to have increased 5.5% to approximately USD 37.3 billion in 2006, which represents about 0.6% of the total global market for tourism services (WTTC). Moreover, Indonesia is experiencing solid cumulative real growth in tourism demand (Figure 2.9).

While tourism demand in Indonesia has indeed been steadily increasing, Indonesia's market share of total world tourism demand has showed a more volatile pattern. Data from the WTTC show a steep dip in Indonesia's share of world tourism demand around 1997. Since then, its share of global tourism demand has been steadily increasing, but Indonesia has yet to get back to the highs experienced in the mid-1990s (WTTC).

2. GLOBALISATION, SMES AND TOURISM DEVELOPMENT

Figure 2.8. **Brazil's forward linkages**

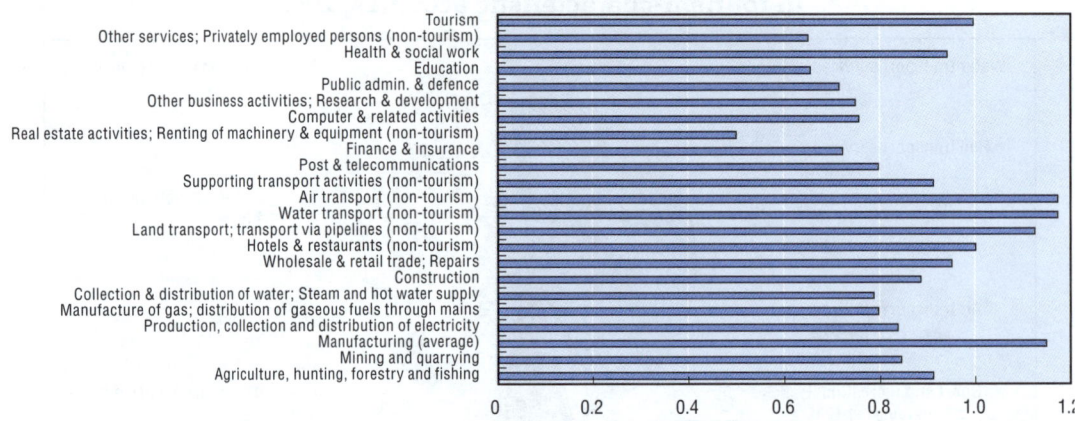

Note: The input-output table for Brazil comes from the OECD Input-Output Database as of January 2007 for the year 2000. Because Brazil has not yet completed its first TSA, data on output by sector is unavailable. Thus, the study assumed that the tourism share in each primary tourism-related sector is constant across all of the countries analysed (*i.e.* the shares calculated for India are applied to Brazil's input-output table to create a tourism composite sector). While this assumption means that the results presented for Brazil are estimates, it does not alter the structure of production across sectors, which is critical to linkage analysis.

Figure 2.9. **Tourism demand in Indonesia**
Cumulative real growth

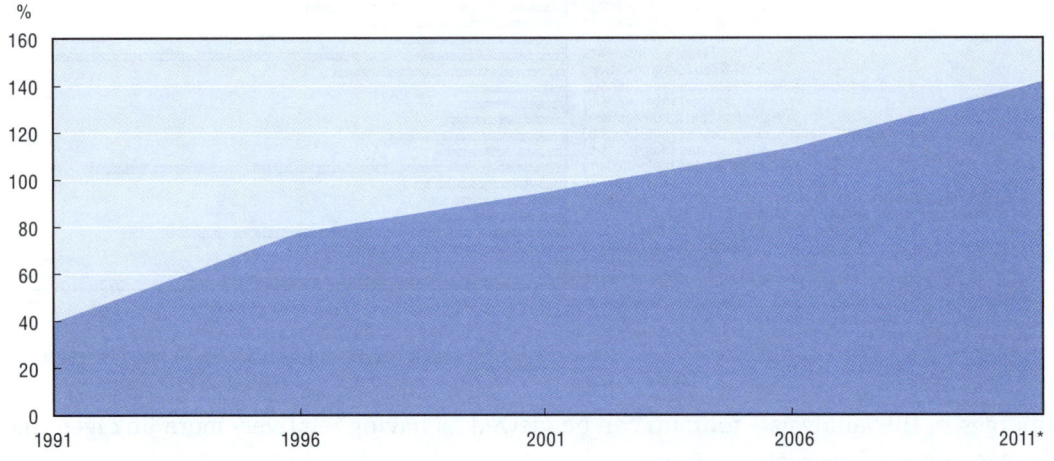

* Projected.
Source: Adapted from WTTC, 2006.

Figures 2.10 and 2.11 indicate that the backward linkage for tourism in Indonesia, at 1.05, is the strongest backward linkage for tourism in the three countries studied. In fact, only four other sectors have a higher backward linkage in the Indonesian economy. Indonesia's forward linkage is also more markedly above one than the other two countries (1.44). Both the backward and forward linkages for the tourism sector in Indonesia are also well above the average services sector in the economy, with the forward linkage being particularly strong when compared to the average service sector (0.84).

Figure 2.10. **Indonesia's backward linkages**

StatLink http://dx.doi.org/10.1787/153334516548

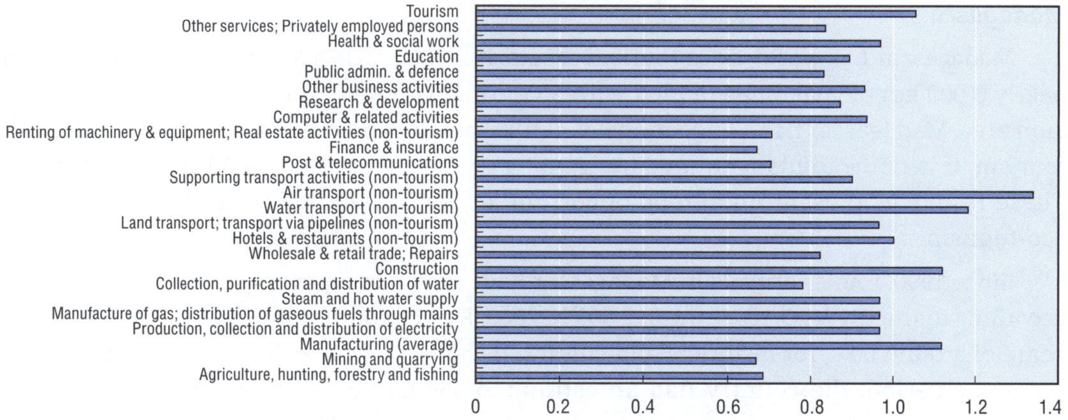

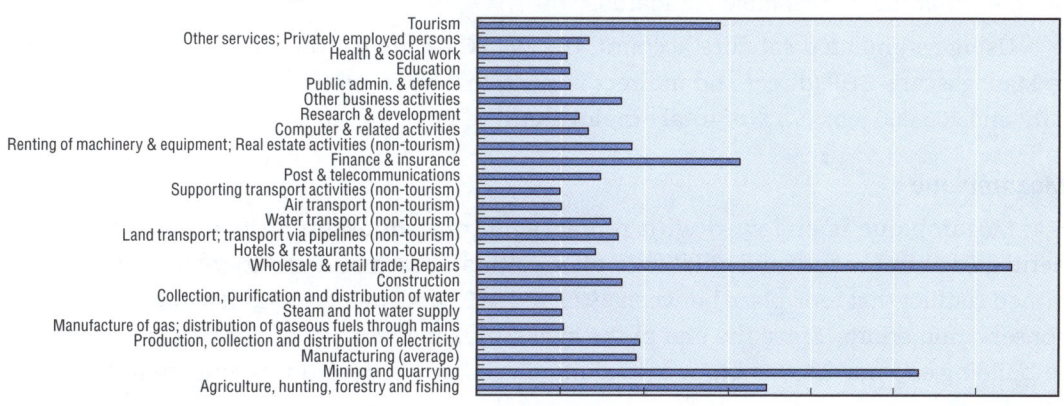

Figure 2.11. **Indonesia's forward linkages**

StatLink http://dx.doi.org/10.1787/153378253061

Note: The input-output table for Indonesia comes from the OECD Input-Output Database as of January 2007 for the year 2000. As noted, the study assumed that the tourism share in each primary tourism-related sector is constant across all of the countries analysed (*i.e.*, the shares calculated for India are applied to Indonesia's input-output table to create a tourism composite sector). This assumption should not affect the inter-linkages among sectors.

Constraints to tourism development: Case studies from Africa and Asia

From the point of view of tourism development, strong backward linkages can be vital. If there are constraints to these linkages, *i.e.* inputs needed for tourism activity are lacking or expensive, the growth of the sector may be undermined. In particular, the ability of a country to deliver tourism effectively depends critically on how well its services and infrastructure are capable of sustaining the sector. Against this backdrop, this section presents case studies from developing economies in Africa and Asia – Madagascar, Mozambique, Cambodia, India and South Africa. The case studies review the key constraints to tourism development and discuss the steps taken by the relevant governments to address them.

Key tourism features of the case study countries

Madagascar

Madagascar has world-class tourism assets. It is the world's fourth largest island, with nearly 5 000 km of coastline coupled with a continental shelf equal to 20% of the island's land area. Madagascar has a wide range of natural beauty and cultural resources to support tourism. It is home to many unique indigenous species, among them 30 species of lemur. These resources present numerous opportunities for developing both resort-based and eco-tourism.

Since 1990, tourist arrivals in Madagascar have grown at an average annual rate of 11% according to the UNWTO, reaching 312 000 in 2006. French tourists dominate arrivals, with a share of around 60%, for historical and cultural reasons, as well as flight itineraries. During the same period, the country had an estimated 556 hotels, of which around 111 were classified as meeting international standards and another 109 met local standards. The remaining hotels were unclassified, with many containing no more than 5 rooms. Operators have stated that this leads them to compete with each other for rooms in the small number of hotels that meet acceptable standards.

Using a simulated satellite account, the WTTC estimates that tourism's contribution to Madagascar's GDP (direct and indirect impact) in 2007 is expected to account for 6.3% of GDP and 206 000 jobs (5.1% of total employment).

Mozambique

Mozambique is endowed with remarkable tourism assets. It combines historical heritage, natural beauty and wildlife to offer cultural, beach and eco-tourism. However, the armed conflict that took place between 1973 and 1992 decimated tourism as well as wild-life conservation efforts. Since the end of the civil strife, operators' confidence has been slowly re-building and now Mozambique is in a unique position to revamp its tourism industry.

International tourist arrivals in Mozambique have risen significantly from the first measurable point in 1999 when they amounted to 240 000. UNWTO figures suggest that 578 000 tourists arrived in 2005, 23% up on 2004. Most visitors are intra-regional, with about one third coming from South Africa. Tourism receipts in 2005 totalled USD 130 million, 103% up from USD 64 million earned in 2001, an average annual rate of increase of about 15%. Currently available data for accommodation establishments estimate an availability of around 7 700 hotel beds in Mozambique, with an approximate occupancy rate of just below 40%. The capital, Maputo, generates about half the hotel nights.

In 2003, tourism only accounted for around 1.2% of GDP well below the Sub-Saharan Africa average of 6.9%. However, in 2005 the industry grew by 37%, which was the fastest growth rate in the world and also registered positive trends in attracting foreign investment, reaching about USD 84 million, the largest for any sector of the economy. The sector employs 32 000 people, an increase from 19 600 reported in 1990. Despite these encouraging signs, there remains much scope for the further development of Mozambique's tourism.

Cambodia

Cambodia is often mentioned as one of the top emerging tourism destinations in the world. Phnom Penh with its distinctive cultures and heritage and the legendary Khmer temples near Siem Reap, especially Angkor Wat, give Cambodia its reputation as a tourism destination worldwide. The Khmer temples date from the IXth and XVth centuries and form one of the most important and largest archaeological parks in the world, recognised as a World Heritage site by UNESCO. Other prominent tourist attractions include outstanding rain forest vegetation, the Mekong River and the Elephant Mountains along the southern coast.

The number of tourists in Cambodia has continuously increased to reach 1.4 million in 2005, a 35% rise on the previous year. The tourism sector is perceived as one of the most promising and as a primary source of foreign exchange. International tourism receipts in 2005 were estimated at USD 840 million, 39% up from 2004. WTTC estimates that 20% of GDP is accounted for by the tourism sector (direct and indirect impact) and that tourism employs one person in six. However, most of the growth has been concentrated in Siem Reap, which has raised issues of sustainability.

India

India has spectacular natural and cultural tourist attractions, with a cultural heritage of over 5 000 years. It is home to thousands of monuments and archaeological remains, including the Indus Valley Civilisation, one of the world's most ancient river valley civilisations. The natural resources and climate are very diverse, ranging from mountainous regions to valleys, plains and deserts. The country also has some of the best beaches in the world, many still unexplored, and many wildlife areas with a large variety of flora and fauna. Its visitor-friendly traditions, varied lifestyles and religions, and colourful fairs and festivals are strong attractions for tourists.

It is estimated that tourist arrivals in India grew from 1.8 million in 1992 to 4.4 million in 2006. The average annual rate of increase in tourist arrivals between 1990 and 2004 was 5.2%, although the rate accelerated to 9.2% between 2000 and 2006. According to the government, tourism has become an important employment generator and an instrument of poverty alleviation and sustainable human development. In 2004, employment generation through tourism is estimated at over 24 million, or 5.5% of total employment. Tourism receipts in 2006 were estimated at USD 8.9 billion, 18.7% up from USD 7.5 billion in 2005. Tourism is the third largest net foreign exchange earner for the country.

South Africa

South Africa's immense tourism potential went unrealised prior to 1990 during the Apartheid era. Given the inherent destination assets, since 1990 the tourism economy in South Africa has experienced strong and steady growth. The country's resource base is enormous and highly diverse, including accessible wildlife, spectacular sceneries, unspoilt wilderness areas, and cultural and historical attractions. There are numerous opportunities for special interest activities, including whale watching, sailing, fishing, volunteering, backpacking, hiking, eco-tourism and golf. South Africa also has international class hotels and resorts for business, and the quality of infrastructure and health services is generally good.

The number of international tourist arrivals visiting South Africa more than doubled between 1994 and 2004. Tourist arrivals continued to increase, reaching 8.4 million in 2006. Regional source markets contribute for almost 6.3 million tourist arrivals, while Europe accounts for around 16% of foreign arrivals, with the UK, Germany and the Netherlands being some of the key markets. In the Americas (4.3% of market share), the US, Canada and Brazil dominate; the Asia Australasian region (3.6% of market share) is represented by Australia, India and China. South Africa has about 8 500 tourist accommodation establishments with over

160 000 rooms. Camping and caravan sites account for the highest share (28% of the total), followed by hotels (25%), and holiday apartments and resorts (11% each).

Using a simulated satellite account, the WTTC estimates that tourism's contribution to South Africa's GDP (direct and indirect impact) was ZAR 141.86 billion (or 8.3%) in 2006, up from ZAR 122.49 billion in 2005. It is estimated that 425 930 jobs are directly supported by tourism, and an additional 521 600 jobs in indirect and induced activities.

Constraints to tourism development

Research in these five countries reveals a wide measure of commonality in the constraints faced in developing the tourism sector (Annex 2.A2). The most common constraints fall into five categories: transport services and infrastructure, accommodation, utilities and IT infrastructure, marketing and promotion, and education and training. Limited financial services also create bottlenecks in some of the countries studied. Some of these concerns are, of course, not limited to the tourism industry but reflect wider development issues affecting both residents and visitors.

Madagascar

In Madagascar, international air access is both restricted and expensive, due mainly to dominance by just two airlines – Air France and Air Madagascar. A lack of competition forces up fares (Paris-Antananarivo return is of the order of USD 2 200), there are only five services a week and virtually no other links to extra-regional destinations. Airport infrastructure requires upgrading, with only a few of the country's 133 airports having a paved runway. Domestic air services are also in the hands of Air Madagascar which further controls ground handling.

Roads throughout the country are in poor condition, with only 5 000 km paved out of 33 000 km nationally. Railways are limited to a few main routes and require further development, while ports infrastructure lacks the facilities required to profit from the country's location between two cruise ship poles in Mombasa and South Africa.

Hotel capacities are limited with mainly small units unable to accommodate larger groups and few establishments meeting international standards. A lack of bandwidth throughout the country prevents the provision of reliable Internet connections and thus shuts the tourism industry out of the key area of on-line bookings and the provision of information services direct to the traveller. Electricity supply is unreliable outside the main centres, as is water supply. Sewage disposal is widely inadequate with uncontrolled dumping actually damaging marine and other environments.

Madagascar's budget for marketing and promotion in 2002 was just USD 150 000, compared with USD 10 million in Kenya and USD 23 million in South Africa. In the key area of training, the country lacks skills and training in all tourism-related sectors, including language skills other than French. This hampers both the provision of information to tourists and the extent to which investors can obtain information on the country.

Mozambique

The situation in Mozambique to some extent mirrors that in Madagascar. Air access is very limited, with only one connection (to Portugal) other than regional services to Johannesburg, Nairobi, Harare and Dar es Salaam. The bilateral air service agreement with Portugal makes no provision for charter flights. Low service frequencies are also reflected in high fares. Domestic air transport is very limited as well, although fares are falling as a result of the arrival of some new, small carriers. The impact of such factors is illustrated in Box 2.11, which shows that international and domestic air fares account for 40% of a short holiday package.

> Box 2.11. **Packaging a complete tourist experience in Mozambique**
>
> OECD/Foreign Investment Advisory Service (FIAS) provides an analysis of the value chain of a typical tourist experience packaged for Portuguese travellers. The study maps the main economic agents that influence the cost and value of the itinerary Lisbon to Bazaruto. As shown below, domestic and international transport account for 40% of the total cost, while accommodation reaches 19%, tour operator commissions 15.5%, ancillary services 15% and airport's fees and taxes 10.5%.
>
> **Value chain map for Lisbon-Bazaruto travel package**
>
>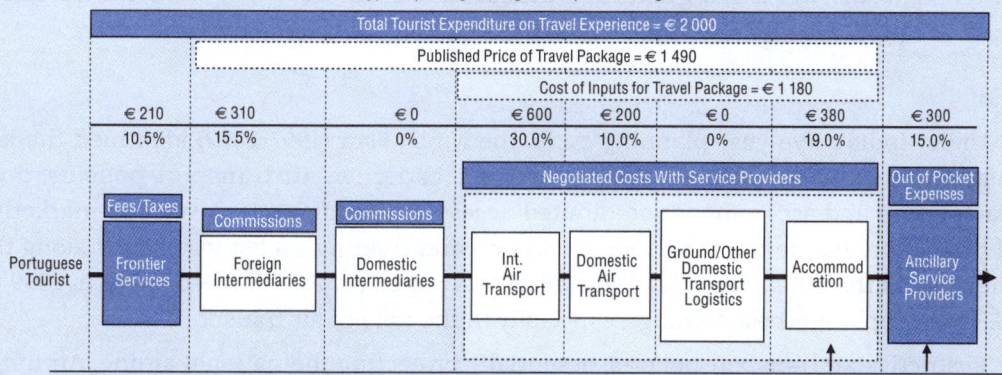
>
> The package is assembled wholly by the Portuguese tour operator, which procures the international flight, the local connecting flight as well as accommodation and transfers. The tourist pays a commission of EUR 310 to the tour operator and about EUR 600 for the discounted airfare. The domestic ticket amounts to about EUR 200 and accommodation totals EUR 380 including transport, some food and entertainment. The 7-nights itinerary is priced at EUR 1 490 and its main competitors are on the lower end of holidays to Cape Verde (price range EUR 369-EUR 1 389), and on the higher end of holidays to Mauritius (EUR 1 222-EUR 4 849) and Seychelles (EUR 1 256-EUR 4 410). However, Bazaruto cannot compete on price terms with Cape Verde and other similar destinations as its cost structure remains quite high. At the same time, it faces challenges competing with Mauritius and Seychelles as its tourism offer is not yet of a quality comparable to those competitors in the high end markets.
>
> *Source:* OECD/FIAS, 2006.

Accommodation is in short supply, and there is no ability to accommodate groups of more than 30 people in the same establishment. The process of accessing land for new hotel development is slow, complex and expensive. Utilities are very costly and supply has been unreliable. Many tourist operators supply their own power, achieving supply reliability at a premium of some 240% above public tariffs. As in Madagascar, inadequate marketing budgets inhibit tourism's development, and a lack of tour operators also limits the sector's growth. There is a critical need for better trained personnel in an industry which is just at the beginning of realising its considerable long-term potential.

Cambodia

Cambodia's tourism sector suffers from the same general constraints as the other countries cited here. Basic infrastructure is lacking, trained tourism sector workers are in short supply, and limited resources allocated to marketing and promotion have led to a loss of market shares in parts of the country other than Siem Reap. The country's financial system is underdeveloped and the supply of foreign banking services is limited by government controls. Credit card acceptance in hotels and other tourist establishments remains limited, and so is ATM availability, exposing foreigners to the risks and impracticalities of bringing cash.

In addition, extreme pressure has been exerted on Siem Riep, the location of the country's internationally iconic attraction of the Khmer temples, to the extent that serious environmental damage is being done in the most sensitive areas. Water and sewage systems are not adequate even for residents, while electricity supply is unreliable and costly.

India

Under India's five-year planning cycle, the Ninth Plan (1997-2002) identified the key constraints to the development of tourism as restrictive air transport policies, poor infrastructure and accommodation, limited access to capital, underdeveloped marketing and promotion and deficient tourism education and training – a list very much along the same lines as the other countries featured in this paper. A more detailed study in 1999 by UNESCAP supported these findings, especially in the field of air transport.

Restrictive air transport policies, essentially protecting the national airline, Air India, which also suffered from capacity constraints, slowed until recently the development of reasonably-priced international access to the country. Only 10 out of India's 250 airports had runways over 10 000 feet and none possessed up-to-date automatic landings systems.

In the early years of this decade there was a national deficit of the order of 30 000 hotel rooms. Promotion and marketing was limited especially in the light of the rapid progress being made in this area by some of India's Asian neighbours. Indian banks and financing institutions, including the Tourism Finance Corporation, provided inadequate access to investment capital, while taxation on the tourism sector was regarded as excessive by some. Training and education in the hospitality and catering services, and more generally in the tourism industry, was seen as inadequate, with a national training capacity only one third of what the industry required.

South Africa

While South Africa is way ahead of the other countries featured here in terms of its tourism infrastructure, there remain nonetheless some important constraints. These were identified in an EU-assisted "*White Paper for the Development and Promotion of Tourism in South Africa*" of 1996, where education and training was identified as a key bottleneck. At that time, the country was able to satisfy only 10% of its training needs.

Although South Africa's air transport system compared well with countries in the region, with respect to both domestic and international traffic, efforts were needed to fully liberalise the industry. Deficiencies in infrastructure were also identified, notably regarding the inadequacies of the transport network to open the country's rural areas to tourism and thus spread the sector's benefits widely among the population. Accommodation continued to be highly concentrated in Cape Town, Durban and Gauteng, accounting for approximately 40% of total room stock. Marketing efforts and the lack of an appropriate supporting institutional structure at regional level also hampered the industry's wider regional development.

Addressing the bottlenecks

In the face of broadly similar challenges, each of the five governments have sought to address these issues by establishing a variety of policy responses. As shown in Annex 2.A2, the essence of these policies has been to seek to improve the functioning of the markets that serve the tourism industry. It is in these areas that national, regional and multilateral actions can be most effective.

Air transport liberalisation

All five countries reviewed have taken steps to liberalise their air transport sectors, albeit with different degrees. South Africa has liberalised domestic air travel allowing the operation of low-cost carriers, with the result that fares have fallen and passenger numbers have sharply increased on key domestic routes. Similar gains have been made by liberalising international routes (for example, the Nairobi-Johannesburg route was liberalised between 2000 and 2003, leading to a 69% rise in passenger traffic in a five year period). South Africa has a well developed airport infrastructure, resulting from a successful privatisation in the 1990s. The Airports Company South Africa is a globally competitive company which operates the country's 10 principal airports.

India has introduced a range of liberalising measures in air transport, including steps to privatise Air India and opening domestic routes to new carriers. Open skies agreements are being pursued and have been signed with Australia and the US. These measures have resulted in an increase in the number of airlines operating both domestically and internationally, greater private sector participation in airport operations and a boost in demand. In Madagascar, steps have been taken to end Air Madagascar's domestic monopoly and to introduce more open skies policies. The first open skies agreement was signed with the US in 2004. Airport reforms have also been introduced, with concessions granted for the management of the 12 largest airports.

In Mozambique, some liberalisation of domestic air services has been undertaken by allowing new carriers to compete with the national airline, LAM, internally. The government has also attempted to privatise the national airline, although thus far without success. Despite positive signs, a more difficult task seems to be liberalising at the international level. Mozambique signed the 1988 Yamoussoukro Declaration and SADC Protocol on Transport Communication and Meteorology, both of which in principle significantly liberalise traffic between signatories. These initiatives, though, still need to be implemented. In Cambodia, a 1998 open skies agreement with Myanmar, Vietnam and Laos has boosted services and passenger carryings in the region. Efforts to liberalise traffic beyond the region have not yet been made.

Utilities and IT infrastructure

While the supply of utilities is clearly also a general development issue that affects more than the tourism sector, the international tourism industry is very dependent on efficient basic infrastructure and IT services. This has been recognised by the countries reviewed here; in South Africa, for example, the White Paper stressed the importance of upgrading the existing infrastructure, including telecommunications, and improve accessibility in rural areas. Cambodia has received assistance by the Japanese International Co-operation Agency (JICA) to address infrastructural and environmental issues affecting Siem Reap. A new water supply system has been constructed as well as new electricity supply facilities to meet increasing demand for reliable power.

Concrete steps have also been taken to liberalise these services to increase efficiency and expand access. In Madagascar, for example, introduction of competition in the telecommunications sector was completed in 2004. The reforms have led to significant telecommunications service improvements compared to five years ago with the widespread use of cellular phones and the Internet. Mozambique has also embarked on an ambitious telecommunications reform, introducing competition and private sector participation in both fixed and mobile services, which has substantially expanded connectivity.

Furthermore, the government has committed to reform in the energy sector, by gradually introducing private sector participation through concessions coupled with new regulatory instruments to enhance efficiency and service access. This approach was piloted in mid-2004 in the Inhambane Province, where a contract to provide electricity was awarded to an international consortium. The Inhambane Province includes the Bazaruto archipelago, where it is expected that growing international tourism will generate high demand of electricity from hotels and other tourism establishments. There are early indications of success with the concession arrangement.

Hotel accommodation

Adequate hotel accommodation is central to a successful tourism sector. In India, the government is taking steps to improve land availability, one of the key limiting factors. In 2005, the Ministry of Tourism has proposed to the state governments to identify hotel sites and make them available to entrepreneurs on suitable terms, such as long-term lease. A number of fiscal incentives and other concessions have also been granted in order to encourage the expansion of available accommodation. Privatisation has also taken place in Madagascar's hotel sector; accommodation still requires action in Mozambique, although the problem has been recognised. The *National Tourism Policy and Implementation Strategy* includes a call to promote access to land for tourism growth.

In 2006, South Africa established a tourism programme within the Deputy-President's Accelerated and Shared Growth Initiative (AsgiSA). The AsgiSA programme identifies several areas for attention in an effort to take forward the bottlenecks and priorities identified in the White Paper. These include a proposal around the design of a cash rebate for tourism investments that create employment outside the main metropolitan areas.

Financial services

Although a strong financial services sector also represents a broader development issue, the need for appropriate access to capital for tourism establishments and to financial services for visitors has been highlighted in some of the countries studied here.

India, for example, has taken steps to expand the presence of foreign banks to provide for a wider and more competitively priced range of financing products, including for the tourism industry. In 2005, as part of the continuing process of financial market liberalisation, the Reserve Bank of India (RBI) initiated several banking reforms. It established a three-phase road map (to be concluded in March 2009), which will allow foreign banks satisfying the RBI's eligibility criteria to establish a wholly owned banking subsidiary (WOS) or to convert their existing branches into a WOS. Furthermore, the RBI is considering a further opening of foreign acquisition of shares in Indian private sector banks.

Education and training

The development of adequate education and training for tourism has been identified as a key challenge in all the case study countries. In Madagascar, a comprehensive tourism policy framework is under development, which includes a determination of how to fund expansion of education services building on the relative strengths of the public and private sectors and the establishment of a conducive framework for domestic and foreign investors. Similar national policies and action programmes are under development in Mozambique and Cambodia.

The AsgiSA programme established a national tourism skills development forum to guide the work needed to improve tourism human resources in South Africa. This forum was put in place after a national skills conference held in 2006, at which government, business, labour and community interests committed themselves to accelerating work targeting tourism skills. Critical to this are public-private partnerships to ensure that education and training are in line with the needs of the industry.

In India, the government's plans have progressively strengthened the institutional set-up in human resource development, including by creating the Advisory Board of Tourism and Trade charged with providing policy guidelines in the area of tourism training. Altogether, 21 government-run Hotel Management and Catering Technology Institutes and 14 Food Craft Institutes were also established under the Ninth Plan for imparting specialised training in these areas, with 15 more Craft Institutes to be set up in the Tenth Plan. The government also noted that more remains to be done in this area, including by promoting partnerships with the private sector to further strengthen capacity.

Promotion and marketing

The promotion of a country's tourism sector internationally remains mainly a public sector function. The comprehensive tourism policy framework put in place in Madagascar is intended to address this issue, as is the strategic planning process in Mozambique. In South Africa, the marketing efforts are spearheaded by South African Tourism, the country's national tourism organisation, which receives considerable financial support from the fiscus. The government of India, recognising the fierce competition in neighbouring tourist generating markets, significantly increased promotional expenditure since 1999-2000.

At the same time, the countries reviewed here recognise that, to be performed effectively, promotion and marketing of tourism destinations requires a co-ordinated approach developed jointly with the private sector. In South Africa, for example, a partnership between the government and the private sector led to the establishment of a Business Trust, which co-finances several services including marketing activities. Cambodia has recently been considering the establishment of a Tourism Marketing and

Promotion Board to step up co-operation between the public and private sectors in this area and enhance the country's image as a worldwide tourist destination. The importance of fostering public-private partnerships in tourism marketing has also been acknowledged by the Indian government.

Anticompetitive practices affecting tourism

Anticompetitive practices in tourism and related sectors can also be a bottleneck to the development of the industry and can arise at different stages of the tourism value-added chain according to the type of service supplied. Preliminary research has identified some key anticompetitive measures affecting trade in tourism, including cartels, abuse of dominant position and of buying power, and attempts to monopolise. These practices tend to minimise the impact of multiplier and other positive effects inherent in tourism, and exacerbate leakages in developing countries.

The vertical relationship between holiday package providers, retailers and tourism service suppliers can be an important source of anticompetitive behaviour. International tour operators act as the wholesalers of tourism products, such as transport, accommodation or organised excursions, provided in destination countries by local suppliers. Travel agents in origin markets act as the retailers. The tour operators' segment of the industry is dominated by a few large international firms and has featured increasing vertical integration in recent years (Meyer, 2003). Other segments of the industry, especially local suppliers such as independent hotels, restaurants and tourist guides, are characterised by a large number of SMEs.

In this context, anticompetitive practices can arise from the unbalanced market power of tour operators compared to that of independent suppliers. The power of large international tour operators (and increasingly of their allied agencies) can be used to bid down the margins of suppliers in destination countries. These suppliers, particularly in developing countries, have a weak bargaining position and lack negotiating skills, often resulting in unfavourable contractual conditions (Barbados Private Sector Trade Team, 2004). Similarly, destination management operators acting as intermediaries for international tour operators may abuse their dominant position to the detriment of small local service providers (Box 2.12).

The operating patterns of tour operators and travel agents differ among industrialised countries. For example, in Europe all-in-one package holidays are widespread, while in the US there is more reliance on direct airline use and associated bookings. Thus, competition and regulatory issues are likely to be different. In particular, for the unbundled travel package, computer reservation systems (CRS) and global distribution systems (GDS) can be of central importance.[3] Despite their major contribution to tourism development, a number of anticompetitive practices associated with their use have been identified. These include unfavourable access to competitors, prohibitively high user fees and restrictions on information display (UNCTAD, 2002).

Scope for anticompetitive practices may also arise in related industries. For example, large airlines have in some cases been accused of abusing their market power to the detriment of local suppliers. In addition, in parallel with recent trends in privatisation, deregulation and to some extent liberalisation, the airline industry has seen the emergence of strategic alliances and code sharing agreements among airlines of different countries. These initiatives can increase efficiency and reduce costs by rationalising the use of

> **Box 2.12. Destination management operators in St. Lucia**
>
> International tour operators establish vertical links with firms in destination countries to manage the tourist experience in a comprehensive manner. In general, tour operators tend to rely on larger companies as they are most likely to meet higher standards and understand their needs better (*e.g.* knowledge on of European and North American markets and technical requirements on safety and liability issues). In St. Lucia, so-called destination management operators have emerged as a response to the needs of international tour operators, acting as ground agents and providing a wide range of services, such as local transfers, tours and special events.
>
> St. Lucia Reps is the leading destination management company in the country, controlling 80% of the total packaged tours and 64% of total tourist arrivals. Complaints have been raised about abuse of its dominant position to the detriment of small local providers. In particular, St. Lucia Reps was allegedly able to reduce the prices of restaurants and providers in situ, refusing to bring business unless they were prepared to accept low rates. These concerns are aggravated because 60% of restaurants in the country are dependent on destination management companies.
>
> *Source:* Stewart, 2006.

resources (*e.g.* check-in facilities and ground personnel), and can also expand existing networks. On the other hand, they may restrict competition and thus minimise benefits, particularly if airlines collectively achieve a dominant position on given routes (Diaz, 2001).

Anticompetitive business practices may additionally take place in hotel and related services. For instance, merger control issues or oligopolies may arise in major tourism destinations which feature large hotels and resorts belonging to highly concentrated international chains. Anticompetitive behaviour may also occur in the building and construction sectors on which the hotel industry relies. A number of cases of cartels or abuses of dominant position in these sectors have already been found in several industrialised countries (Souty, 2002).

Policy implications

Reforms at the national level

The preceding analysis has highlighted a number of areas for policy makers to consider when developing their tourism sectors, given its critical economic importance in many countries. Strengthening backward linkages is essential in order to unleash the sector's full potential, and particularly important is building service capacity and infrastructure. In order to realise this potential, substantial capital and expertise are needed. If appropriately designed, private sector participation and trade and investment liberalisation in services can be a means to complement national efforts in this direction.

Building service capacity

International air transport is the key to delivering tourists to their destinations, accounting in developing countries for nearly 80% of international tourist arrivals (UNESCAP, 2005b). Ideally, air transport should provide adequate access to tourism destinations at reasonable prices. Trade in air transport, though, has been heavily restricted by governments around the world since the Chicago Conference of 1944. Market access is largely determined by a complex system of some 3 500 bilateral agreements which typically determine the airlines permitted to operate on bilateral routes, their traffic rights, tariffs, and the number and frequency of their flights.

Nevertheless, over the years the regulatory framework of air transport has become increasingly more liberal. Deregulation has allowed for the entry of new carriers, including more recently low-cost carriers, and opened domestic routes to competition. Liberalisation of international air services has taken place particularly through the emergence of "open skies" agreements, which have relaxed restrictions on capacity and fares, and grant traffic rights up to a certain level. These reforms are seen as a way of improving efficiency and reducing costs, while maintaining service quality and extending regional and international connections.

Physical infrastructure including accommodation, airports, harbours, electricity, and water and sewage must also meet the needs of increasing tourist arrivals (as well as those of local residents), or tourism assets and market position may be damaged. However, national investment in infrastructure in developing countries often lags behind tourism growth. Innovative partnerships between governments and developers are engaging the private sector in helping to finance the infrastructure and operate the services. Large hotels also typically provide their own infrastructure, such as stand-by generators, water and sewage treatment plants. These initiatives are often able to increase a destination's carrying capacity.

The telecommunications and IT infrastructure is a vital driver for tourism development. Telecommunications liberalisation – coupled with technological innovation, particularly the introduction of cellular phones – has considerably expanded services in many countries. Expansion of IT also had a major impact on the structure of the tourism industry, and has become increasingly linked to the development of a number of other services that support tourism, from advertising to reservations and financial services. IT allows tourism suppliers, in particular small businesses, to have direct access to customers and allows customers to reach suppliers.

An effective financial system is a key enabler of tourism growth. Public financial institutions have typically been the main investors in infrastructure and partners in tourism development, but it is domestic and foreign private banks and investors – such as developers, constructors and real estate firms – that are now becoming increasingly important. If appropriately managed, these private players can attract the capital required, reduce costs and provide more specific financial products to finance the industry's growth and quality upgrading. At the retail level, enhanced credit card options and ATM penetration, which are generally linked to financial sector liberalisation, are increasingly indispensable to the international traveller.

Marketing and promotion are essential in order to generate viable levels of demand for tourism products and to succeed in a very competitive world. Well-targeted promotion can also contribute to tourism diversification and sustainability. In many countries, the public and private sectors now join forces to undertake promotional programmes. The government normally leads by allocating funds for national promotion, creating an overall image of the country and its main tourism assets, and improving perceptions of its attractiveness (for investors as well as tourists). The private sector promotes specific tourist accommodation and services, creating opportunities for enhanced trade and investment.

Growth of the tourism sector has a direct impact on a country's employment and human resources development, creating demand for professionals, specific skills and related education and training facilities. The need to develop and appropriately train the staff required at all levels and in all segments of the tourism industry has been widely acknowledged. Private education in tourism is growing significantly due to the rising burden on public finances from tourism's expansion. Another development has been the increasing importance of specialised training needed to expand tourism markets, including management and leadership training, information technology and languages. Strong leadership in management is crucial to capture the potential of high yield niche markets and to optimise the participation of SMEs in global value chains and networks.

The investment environment

Attracting investors to a country or destination requires an economic, social and political environment conducive to private sector investment. At the same time, the growth of a successful tourism sector requires that investments in accommodation and services, basic infrastructure and human resource development are carefully planned and appropriately phased. Tourism can expand in a sustainable manner if the carrying capacity of the assets is not exceeded, thus minimising the potential negative impact on the host society and environment. Due consideration also needs to be given to the development of national capacity to minimise financial leakages. Another important dimension is to ensure that local populations, including those in remote areas, are able to participate effectively in tourism.

Competition and other regulation

To limit the risks of anticompetitive practices in tourism, the development and enforcement of competition rules needs to accompany liberalisation, particularly in developing countries where such rules are often inadequate or absent. There may also be a need to strengthen co-operation between competition policy institutions in OECD and non-OECD countries. In addition, most of the services needed to support tourism, including transport, education, energy and environmental services, are often provided by the public sector to achieve a range of public policy objectives. Private sector participation and liberalisation in these services is no easy task and requires sound regulation and effective institutions to address market failure and meet social goals.

Government policies and institutions

A successful tourism sector requires strong public sector management and support. Given the cross-sectoral nature of tourism, tourism policy needs to be coherent and integrated with the country's overall economic, environmental and social policies. Partial policy mechanisms will be inadequate to address the needs and impact of the industry. Instead, governments need to establish a comprehensive policy framework that improves the business environment and addresses the underlying economic relationships as well as social and physical constraints.

To perform these tasks appropriately, the right institutional framework needs to be in place. Whatever the institutional setting, governments require a team of people with the capacity and expertise to prepare and implement a comprehensive policy framework. Such a framework needs to include a coherent set of programmes, notably in the following areas: i) institutional framework and medium- and long-term strategic vision; ii) conservation, preservation and development of the natural and cultural heritage; iii) support for the elaboration, development and diversification of products and innovation; iv) marketing and promotion of regions; *v*) human resources development (development of careers and skills); *vi*) use of information and communication technology; *vii*) information, economic monitoring and research for industry; *viii*) networks, poles and strategic alliance programmes; ix) strengthening of enterprise capacities, especially the smallest; and x) role of local authorities (promoting regional tourism).

Strong tourism agencies are needed that are capable of co-ordinating with other arms of government and other stakeholders such as local authorities, the private sector and NGOs. The preferred policy and institutional arrangements for tourism will have to reflect local conditions in each country, the size and characteristics of the sector and its growth prospects. Regular evaluations of the performance of tourism-related policies will be instrumental in identifying gaps, duplications or contradictions between policies, in assessing the quality of the institutional framework and in adapting the programmes to change. Such evaluations will be important in fostering a balance between tourism development policies and the broader objectives of economic, environmental and social development.

Co-operation in bilateral and regional initiatives

Regional tourism liberalisation is another important dimension where an increasing number of initiatives are being established, including in developing countries. For example, in Africa several regional initiatives have incorporated tourism in their liberalisation and co-operation efforts. The Southern African Development Community (SADC), the Common Market of Eastern and Southern Africa (COMESA) and the East African Community (EAC) are all examples of such initiatives. They include or are in the process of establishing protocols on services trade liberalisation, including tourism, or specific protocols for the integration of tourism markets. These initiatives also often include protocols or discussions on air transport, at times with specific reference to the benefits these could bring to tourism.

In Asia, in recognition of the growing importance of tourism for economic and social development, the Asia Pacific Economic Co-operation (APEC) established a Tourism Working Group in 1991. The basis for APEC's tourism co-operation is the APEC Tourism Charter, endorsed by members in 2000, which established several policy goals. A key objective relates to the removal of impediments to tourism business and investment, including measures taken through regulatory reform and the liberalisation of services trade related to tourism under the GATS. Other goals relate to increasing the mobility of visitors and the region's tourism competitiveness, by measures such as facilitating travel, fostering marketing, and managing tourism sustainably. The Charter also provides for the development of individual and collective action plans for implementation, through regular peer review mechanisms and independent assessment to ensure outcome delivery.

The Economic Partnership Agreement (EPA) negotiations between the EU and the African, Caribbean and Pacific (ACP) countries represent another initiative incorporating tourism, as part of broader efforts dealing with trade in services. In these negotiations, the linkages between tourism and the development of other services figure prominently. For instance, discussions between the EU and the Pacific members of ACP countries have focused on ways to promote the development of tourism industries, through measures such as the promotion of synergies between air transport and tourism, ways to address infrastructure deficiencies and obstacles created by the institutional and legal environment, and co-operation on tourism training and marketing.

Regional tourism liberalisation and regulatory co-operation is likely to be more effective than unilateral endeavours. They can create more expansive tourism destinations, help to increase the number of long-term tourists and also provide an opportunity to join forces to expand service and achieve sustainable tourism objectives. However, with the possible exception of APEC, in most regional initiatives implementation challenges have been identified, and progress on EPA negotiations has been slow. Although these initiatives have brought to the forefront the importance of regional co-operation in fostering tourism development, to date there have been few sustained results. For the most part, initiatives are confined to the level of good intentions and discussions about policy strategy; more emphasis is needed on implementation and the creation of robust enforcement mechanisms.

The GATS complementing role

Enhanced GATS commitments could contribute to the advancement of national and regional policies aimed at strengthening the tourism sector. By creating a more transparent and predictable legal framework, the GATS can improve the investment climate and help attract foreign investment to enhance the quality of services and infrastructure. The high level of commitments in the tourism sector indicates that WTO members widely recognise the important complementing role that the GATS can play in tourism development.

Yet, the complete bound liberalisation of the industry is far from having been achieved. At the level of W/120, there remain modal and sub-sectoral imbalances in the commitments and, most importantly, the generally low level of commitments in related sectors adds to the complexity of tourism liberalisation. The cross-sectoral dimension of tourism has been acknowledged in services negotiations by a number of developed and developing country members. Indeed, while tourism did not receive much attention recently, the sector featured prominently in the early stages of the negotiations.

In 1999, the Dominican Republic, El Salvador and Honduras circulated a proposal to create a GATS Annex on Tourism (WTO, 1999). One of the main rationale for the Annex was that the current GATS structure does not address the needs of the sector with respect to sectoral coverage. The Annex thus proposed the possibility of treating tourism as a cluster, on the basis of the definitions provided in the TSA. The Annex was subsequently joined by a number of other developing countries,[4] and nine other negotiating proposals followed, which stressed the widespread connection that tourism has with most other services sectors.[5] A "checklist" approach was suggested as a possible way forward in the negotiations.[6]

Improved GATS commitments in telecommunications and financial services are among the more readily attainable goals and can significantly contribute to the development of the tourism sector. Enhanced liberalisation of transport services and infrastructure under the GATS would also lead to substantial gains for the tourism sector, though in this case regulatory capacity requirements are more substantial. Yet, significant reforms have taken place in recent years, particularly in maritime services, which have created scope to achieve more progress on these services at the multilateral level.

Even in the air transport sector, which as noted has been until recently highly restricted and is largely excluded from the GATS,[7] there are a number of desirable initiatives that could be taken by WTO members. Consideration could be given to expand commitments in the ancillary services already covered by the Agreement,[8] to negotiate an amendment to the Annex on Air Transport to include ground handling services, and even to the more ambitious possibility of commitments in charter services. While these initiatives could be potentially highly beneficial to tourism, it is crucial that they be pursued without neglecting air safety and security.

Multilateral progress in other infrastructure services, such as waste treatment or energy, and in education services, while also very important for tourism development, is more difficult to attain in light of the more challenging regulatory environment. However, with respect to tourism, there are areas where regulatory capacity requirements are moderate in these services as well. For example, as noted, it is common for large hotels to have their own waste water treatment plants. These can be contracted out to the private sector, including to foreign firms. This business to business activity entails much fewer regulatory risks and represents an increasingly larger share of environmental firms' operations.

Similarly, there seems to be significant scope for private education for tourism, since the sector covers various activities. People employed in many tourism-related sectors often do not need formal education, but only some skill development programmes or short-term training. In addition, as seen earlier, specialised training, in such areas as management and leadership, information technology and languages, is expanding rapidly and represents a growing international business supplementing the public education system. Availability of these services can help to develop a more efficient workforce, playing a key role in the sustainable development of tourism.

The other main rationale for the Annex on Tourism was the development of safeguards to address international anticompetitive practices in tourism and related industries (the Telecoms Reference Paper was the model for the Annex). However, the Annex proposal has subsequently largely been ignored because of the difficulties to apply disciplines to the wide range of services that are related to tourism. This includes air transport which as noted remains largely excluded from the Agreement. Perhaps a way forward in this case could be exploring the feasibility of developing disciplines on anti-competitive practices with a narrow sectoral focus covering tourism as defined in W/120. As seen in Section VI, anticompetitive behaviour is prevalent in some of these segments, such as tour operators.

Conclusion

The economic and social importance of tourism means that the industry is high on the list of development priorities of many developing countries and LDCs. This report suggests that in order to have a successful tourism export industry, effective linkages need to be established with many different sectors, most of which are services. If appropriately designed, trade and investment liberalisation at the national, regional and multilateral levels can be a means to complement national efforts to achieve these goals. At the multilateral level, in light of the importance of so many services sectors for the development of tourism, the element of the benefits to tourism in making GATS commitments could feature more prominently in the negotiations.

Notes

1. The adoption of policies to ensure that the benefits flowing from tourism are widely shared and spread to poor communities, and adverse environmental impacts are minimised.

2. The category is divided into four sub-sectors, the first three of which have associated listings under the United Nations Provisional Central Product Classification (CPC). These sub-sectors and their respective CPC numbers are as follows: A. Hotels and restaurants (including catering) (CPC 641-643); B. Travel agencies and tour operators services (CPC 7471); C. Tourist guides services (CPC 7472); and Other. No further sub-classifications are provided for under W/120.

3. CRSs were developed by large air carriers in the 1960s for flight reservations. They then expanded to offer further airline services, *e.g.* information storage, marketing and sale of tickets, and other services supplied to tourists, such as package tours, hotels and vehicles rentals. GDSs connect the various CRSs, providing single terminals with access to all services. There are four main GDSs operating: SABRE, Amadeus, Galileo and Worldspan.

4. Bolivia, Ecuador, Nicaragua, Panama, Peru and Venezuela.

5. The proposals were from Australia, Chile, the European Communities, New Zealand, Norway and Switzerland (WTO, 2005); Brazil, Colombia, the Dominican Republic, El Salvador, India, Indonesia, Nicaragua, the Philippines and Thailand (WTO, 2004a); Canada (WTO, 2001a), Colombia (WTO, 2001b); Costa Rica (WTO, 2001c); Cuba (WTO, 2002); the EC (WTO, 2000a, and WTO, 2000b), and MERCOSUR (WTO, 2001d).

6. Such checklist of "tourism-related" sectors would be used as an aide-memoire during the negotiations of these sectors. The results would be scheduled in the relevant GATS sectors other than tourism (see WTO, 2000a and WTO, 2000c).

7. Air traffic rights are expressly excluded from the GATS. The exclusion, though, must be reviewed at least every five years with a view to consider expansion of the application of the Agreement.

8. Repair and maintenance, selling and marketing and computer reservation systems.

Bibliography

Barbados Private Sector Team (2004), "Anticompetitive Practices in the Global Tourism Industry: Implications for Barbados", August, Barbados.

Barbados Private Sector Team (2006), "What Does an EPA Have to Do with Tourism?", April, Barbados.

Cai. J., P. Leung and J. Mak (2005), "Tourism's Forward and Backward Linkages", University of Hawaii at Manoa, Department of Economics, Working Paper No. 200516.

Christie, I. and D. Crompton (2001), "Tourism in Africa", *Africa Region Working Paper Series No. 12*, World Bank, Washington DC.

Christie, I. and D. Crompton (2003), "Madagascar Tourism Sector Study", *Africa Region Working Paper Series No. 46*, World Bank, Washington DC.

Christie, I. (2005), "The Tourism Sector in Madagascar", *Africa Region Findings No. 250*, World Bank, Washington DC.

Cockburn, M. and C. Low (2005), "Output-based Aid in Mozambique: Private Electricity Operator Connects Rural Households", *Global Partnership on Output Based Aid (GPOBA)*, World Bank, Washington DC.

ComMark Trust (2006), "Clear Skies Over Southern Africa: the Importance of Air Transport Liberalisation for Shared Economic Growth", Johannesburg.

Department of Environmental Affairs and Tourism (DEAT) (1996), "White Paper on the Development and Promotion of Tourism in South Africa", Government of the Republic of South Africa.

Diaz, D. (2001), "The Viability and Sustainability of International Tourism in Developing Countries", Symposium on Tourism Services, 22-23 February, WTO, Geneva.

Economist Intelligence Unit (2006), "Country Report Mozambique, February 2006".

Foreign Investment Advisory Services (FIAS) (2005), "Corporate Responsibility and the Tourism Sector in Cambodia", International Finance Corporation (IFC) and World Bank.

Gollub, J., A. Hosier and G. Woo (2002), "Using Cluster-Based Economic Strategy to Minimise Tourism Leakages", paper prepared for UNWTO.

Government of India (2005), "Mid -Term Appraisal of the Ninth Five Year Plan (2002-2007)", Available at: *http://planningcommission.nic.in.*

Jahangir A., S. Dunaway, and E. Prasad (2006), "China and India: Learning from Each Other: Reforms and Policies for Sustained Growth", International Monetary Fund.

Kruger-Cloete, E. (2006), "Foresight Tourism Report", the National Research and Technology Foresight Project, Department of Science and Technology, Government of the Republic of South Africa.

Leung, P., T. Lam and S. Wong (1998), "Tourism Development in Cambodia: An Analysis of Opportunities and Barriers", *Asia Pacific Journal of Tourism Research.*

Meyer, D. (2003), "The UK Outbound Tour Operating Industry and Implications for Pro-Poor Tourism", Overseas Development Institute, Working Paper No. 17, September 2003, London.

MINTEL (2006a), "Mozambique Travel and Tourism Intelligence".

MINTEL (2006b), "India Travel and Tourism Intelligence".

Nathan Inc. (2006), "Liberalisation of Mozambique Aviation Policy", prepared for review by USAID.

National Council of Applied Economic Research of India (NCAER) (2006), "Tourism Satellite Account for India 2002-03", commissioned by Indian Ministry of Tourism.

OECD/FIAS (2006), "The Tourism Sector in Mozambique: A Value Chain Analysis", Vol. I.

Sinha, A. (2001), "Tourism Development in India", Press Information Bureau, Government of India.

South African Tourism (2006), *2005 Annual Report*, South African Tourism Strategic Research Unit.

Souty, F. (2002), "Passport to Progress: Competition Challenges for World Tourism and Global Anti-Competitive Practices in the Tourism Industry", Paper prepared for UNWTO.

United Nations (UN) (1994), Recommendations on Tourism Statistics, United Nations (Series M, No. 83). New York, 1994.

United Nations Conference on Trade and Development (UNCTAD) (2002), "Trade in Services and Development Implications", Note by the UNCTAD Secretariat, Document TD/B/COM.1/55, 20 December 2002.

United Nations Economic and Social Commission for Asia and the Pacific (UNESCAP) (1999), "Human Resource Development Requirements of the Tourism Sector in India".

United Nations World Tourism Organisation (UNWTO) (2007), Statistical Yearbook, UNWTO, Madrid.

USAID (2004), "Removing Obstacles to Economic Growth in Mozambique: A Diagnostic Trade Integration Study".

United States Department of Transportation (2005), "United States, India Sign Open Skies Aviation Agreement", available at: *www.dot.gov/affairs/dot6005.htm.*

World Bank (2003), "Madagascar – Transport Infrastructure Investment Project", Report No. 27140-MG, World Bank, Washington DC.

World Bank (2005), "Mozambique Country Economic Memorandum: Sustaining Growth and Reducing Poverty", Report No. 32615-MZ, World Bank, Washington DC.

World Travel and Tourism Council (WTTC), Policy Research and Tourism Satellite Account Country reports, available at *www.wttc.org.*

ANNEX 2.A2

Tourism Constraints, Policy Responses and Results in the Five Case Study Countries

	Constraint	Policy response	Results
Cambodia	No tourism policy.	Tourism Law proposed to lead to national and regional tourism development plan.	In progress.
	Lack of infrastructure; high-priced and inadequate electricity supply.	Japanese-funded master plan for Siem Riep to tackle infrastructure, environmental and utility issues.	In progress.
	Limited financial system. Insufficient marketing. Limited education and training services. Over-concentration of tourists at Siem Reap. Few backward linkages.	In all these areas, Cambodia is developing policy responses and exploring the possibilities for wider private sector involvement. Developments are at an early stage, however, given wider economic development concerns.	
India	Restrictive air transport policies and limited air transport capacity.	Air transport liberalisation in progress.	New domestic carriers in operation, reducing fares and raising passenger numbers. Open skies agreements with USA and Australia.
	Poor infrastructure, notably airports.	Public/private partnerships introduced in airport management.	No information.
	Inadequate accommodation capacity.	Improvements in land availability in progress, and fiscal incentives introduced for hotel development.	No information.
	Limited access to capital.	Reserve Bank of India reforms to raise activity levels of foreign banks.	More competitive financial sector.
	Under-developed marketing and promotion.	Promotional expenditure increased.	Strong growth in demand.
	Deficient education and training.	Strengthened Advisory Board on tourism training – training and craft centres established.	
Madagascar	Limited competition in air transport services and airports.	Air liberalisation commenced in 1997; airport management reforms.	International and domestic air traffic increased; scope for further action.
	Inadequate hotel accommodation and standards.	Privatisation of government-owned hotels.	No information.
	Lack of effective marketing and promotion.	Comprehensive tourism policy framework under development.	Awaiting policy implementation.
	Inadequate and high-cost telecommunications.	Competition introduced in telecommunications.	Better telecommunications and wider spread of mobile telephones and Internet access.
	Inadequate training and education.	Comprehensive tourism policy framework under development.	Awaiting policy implementation.

2. GLOBALISATION, SMES AND TOURISM DEVELOPMENT

	Constraint	Policy response	Results
Mozambique	Poor air access and limited international services; no provision for charter flights.	Move to privatise national airline, and liberalise the industry.	Reforms not yet implemented.
	Inadequate domestic air transport network.	Domestic air liberalisation initiatives.	Some improvement in services.
	Unreliable and high-cost utilities.	Telecommunications reform; private sector able to produce and sell energy.	Improved connectivity and mobile telephone services; Improved supplies and lower costs.
	Inadequate tourism marketing. Poor network of local ground tour operators. Urgent need for tourism education and training.	Ministry of Tourism created in 2000; National Tourism Policy issued in 2003; Strategic Tourism Development Plan issued 2004.	These issues part of the on-going development process.
South Africa	Inadequate supply of trained staff.	Involvement of private sector in training programmes; public/private partnership increased funds for training.	No information.
	More scope for air transport liberalisation.	Policy environment encouraged new entrants and more open international skies.	Sharp increase in passenger volumes where new carriers/competition increased.
	Inadequate rural transportation services.	Service gaps persist in road transport.	Further investment required.
	Tourism marketing inadequately co-ordinated across all provinces.	Involvement of private sector and all nine provinces in improved marketing; public/private partnership increased funds to training.	Tourism numbers increasing rapidly, but further improvements required.
	Tourism security inadequate.	Steps taken to improve security.	Further reductions in tourist crimes and violence still required.

Chapter 3

Country Profiles: Tourism Policy Developments and Trends

Table of Contents

Synthesis 87

OECD MEMBER COUNTRIES

Australia 95
Austria 101
Belgium 107
Canada 112
Czech Republic 116
Denmark 120
Finland 125
France 129
Germany 133
Greece 137
Hungary 140
Iceland 145
Ireland 148
Italy 153
Japan 157
Korea 161
Luxembourg 166
Mexico 169
The Netherlands 173
New Zealand 176
Norway 181
Poland 185
Portugal 190
Slovak Republic 194
Spain 198
Sweden 202
Switzerland 205
Turkey 209
United Kindom 213
United States 218

OECD NON-MEMBER ECONOMIES

Romania 225
South Africa 230
Annex 3.A1. National tourism administration and related websites 234

Synthesis

The following chapter presents summary details of the tourism sector in 32 countries, 30 of which are OECD members, in addition to Romania and South Africa. Each country section is set out under five main headings:

- Tourism in the economy.
- Tourism organisation.
- Tourism budget.
- Tourism related policies and programmes.
- Statistical profile

For further information, a synopsis table in Annex 3.A1 indicates the main websites for national tourism administrations, national tourism organisations and other important Tourism related organisations.

This chapter focuses mainly on international tourism (inbound and outbound). It also includes some partial data on domestic tourism based on Tourism Satellite Account sources or on national surveys. The measurement of domestic tourism, in terms of the number of tourist trips taken each year, is not generally provided by most countries on a consistent basis and does not readily lend itself to aggregations and international comparisons.

International tourist arrivals, however, are recorded for almost all countries. Data for 2005, the latest year for which complete data are available, show that globally there were 802 million international tourist arrivals (World Tourism Organisation). In the OECD member countries, international tourist arrivals in that year totalled 481.5 million, and thus these countries account for 60.0% of all international tourism by this measure (Figure 3.1).

Eight out of the top ten international tourism destinations are included in this chapter, the exceptions being China and Russia. These eight – France, Spain, USA, Italy, UK, Germany, Mexico and Austria – together accounted for 308.9 million arrivals in 2005, 38.5% of the global total.

Tourism in the economy

The importance of the tourism sector in the economies of these 32 countries varies widely. To generalise however, tourism accounts for an important share of Gross Domestic Product (GDP) and of services exports in many countries (see Chapter 1, *New Paradigm for International Tourism Policy*), and also generates a substantial share of total employment. Although data coverage of these measures is variable (see individual sections for country details), an idea of tourism's economic importance is given in the Figure 3.2.

3. COUNTRY PROFILES: TOURISM POLICY DEVELOPMENTS AND TRENDS – SYNTHESIS

Figure 3.1. **International tourist arrivals, world, 2005**

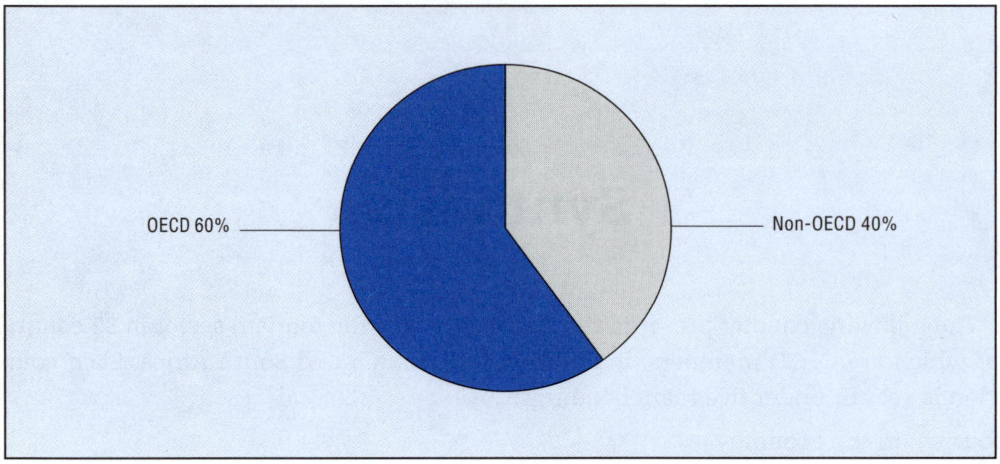

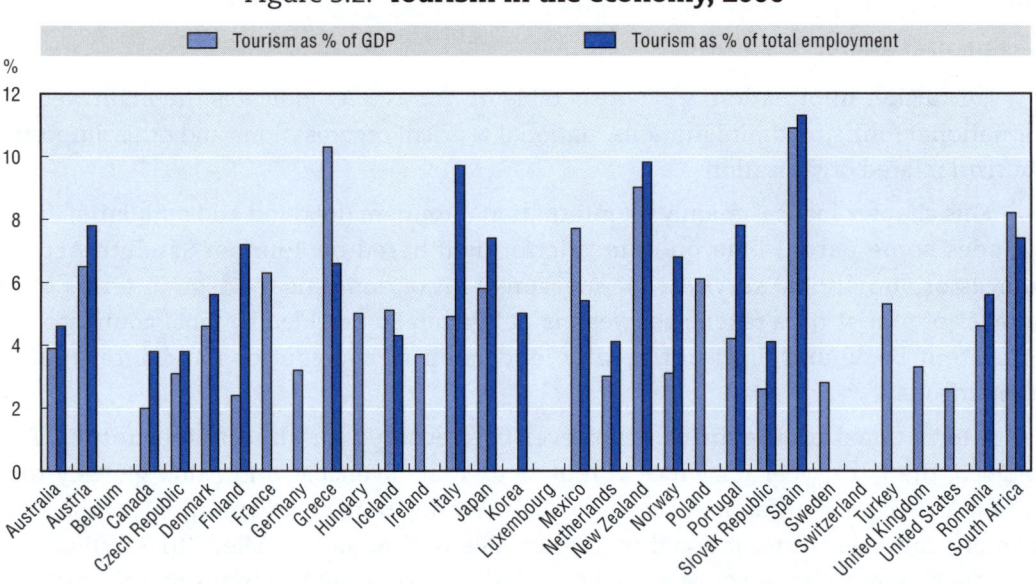

StatLink http://dx.doi.org/10.1787/153030008744

Figure 3.2. **Tourism in the economy, 2006**

StatLink http://dx.doi.org/10.1787/152847245261

Clearly tourism is an important economic force in many of the countries covered here. For some of the world's major tourism destinations, tourism plays a crucial role in sustaining employment and in earning foreign currency receipts.

Tourism organisation

The treatment of the tourism sector within the government structures of the countries covered in this chapter varies considerably. Moreover, due to variations in government structures it is difficult to be precise about which portfolio includes tourism. However, the growing economic and political importance of tourism is reflected by the fact that 15 OECD countries have a Ministry or a Secretariat of State with Tourism named in their title.

Several countries have their own dedicated tourism ministries (Greece, Mexico and New Zealand), however in most cases, the tourism portfolio is attached to Economy,

Industry, Trade or SME ministries (Australia, Austria, Canada, Denmark, Finland, France, Germany, Netherlands, Norway, Portugal, Romania, Slovak Republic, Spain, Sweden, Switzerland and United States). For a few others, the tourism portfolio is linked to Regional Development (Czech Republic and Hungary), Culture and Sports (Ireland, Korea, Poland, Turkey and United Kingdom), Environment (South Africa) or Transportation (Japan).

Tourism budgets

A comparison of tourism budgets is complicated by issues of exchange rates and, especially, of the different approaches to the public funding of tourism support adopted by governments. Readers are referred to the country sections for details.

As a generalisation, however, the largest item in public budgetary support for tourism tends to be the marketing budgets granted to national tourist offices or their equivalents for international marketing purposes. Again as a generalisation, it is typically the national tourist office that is responsible for marketing the country as a tourism destination to foreign visitors. Regions or specific destinations within countries are then responsible for their own promotion within the country concerned, but generally national governments discourage regions from direct (and usually costly) international marketing themselves. In some countries, such as the United States for example, where it is felt that the country's international profile is inherently high, international marketing budgets are limited.

For domestic tourism, countries are becoming increasingly aware of the economic benefits to be gained from encouraging nationals to take their holidays in their own countries, both in terms of balance of payments benefits (by avoiding expenditure on holidays abroad) and in terms of the economic stimulation that a vigorous domestic tourism sector can generate. As a result, national tourist offices or other public tourism organisations are taking on more responsibility for the active promotion of tourism opportunities within their own countries to their resident population.

Tourism related policies and programmes

Public investment in tourism is again highly varied across countries, and the reader is referred to the country sections for detailed information.

As an economic activity with the potential to create jobs, add value and earn foreign exchange, tourism is increasingly being seen as a sector in which public investment can be justified, in a number of areas. The most common are:

- Investment programmes in infrastructure which can contribute to facilitating access to the tourism industry for nationals and foreigners alike.
- Programmes supporting the small business sector which, in terms of the number of enterprises engaged, is dominated by SMEs; programmes to enhance quality in tourism most commonly through action of training.
- Programmes aimed at the quality of tourism facilities and services (these often involve the introduction and maintenance of national quality standards and quality accreditation schemes).
- Licensing schemes for personnel engaged in tourism (*e.g.* the licensing of tourism guides).
- The creation of a business and investment climate that is supportive of the tourism sector and which encourages the participation of the private sector as prime investors.

Governments are also increasingly conscious of their role in facilitating international access for visitors to their countries by means of the pursuit of increasingly liberal air transport policies. In the area of environmental policy and conservation, governments are also becoming more directly involved in the promotion of ecologically-friendly policies aimed at minimising the adverse impact of tourism on the physical environment and maximising the sustainability of their tourism sectors.

The concept of public-private partnerships in tourism is being pursued actively by a number of countries, both in the financing of national tourist offices and the development of tourism networks such as those providing information to tourists at a local level, as well as investment programmes geared to leveraging private investment in the tourism sector by means of public pump-priming money.

Policy advice and enabling measures are also increasing, led by national governments, to assist tourism industries and especially small businesses to meet the fast-growing competition in global tourism. A notable emphasis is now being seen on maximising the use of on-line technologies to enable tourism businesses to benefit from and cope with the rapid globalisation of tourism marketplaces and of tourism marketing. Information and reservation systems are at the heart of many of these initiatives, as the direct linkages via the Internet between the tourist and the tourism service supplier strengthen and disintermediation (the elimination of the need for the use of travel intermediaries such as travel agents) increases.

Finally, in addition to the pursuit of national policies and programmes and the promotion of tourism clusters and networks, governments are becoming increasingly aware of the potential benefits to be gained from international co-operation in tourism marketing and promotion and generally take the lead in developing tourism linkages with other, often contiguous, states.

Summary

To summarise, tourism is gaining in importance in the eyes of governments as an economic activity which justifies serious consideration at the level of national policy. Tourism in many countries has already surpassed in economic importance some of the more traditional sectors such as agriculture which historically have commanded greater political attention at national government level. Governments are becoming more aware of the benefits and of the potential pitfalls of the tourism sector in national economic development terms. Closer study of this chapter will illustrate the many initiatives taken by governments in the tourism field and will assist the reader in comparing their own national experience with international best practice.

Basic methodological references

The following definitions are based on UN and UNWTO (1994), International Recommendations on Tourism Statistics (IRTS), UN, Madrid and New York.

Inbound tourism

Arrivals associated to inbound tourism correspond to those arrivals by international (or non-resident) *visitors* within the economic territory of the country of reference.

Visitors include: a) *Tourists (overnight visitors)*: "a visitor who stays at least one night in a collective or private accommodation in the country visited"; b) *Same-day visitors*: "a visitor who does not spend the night in a collective or private accommodation in the country visited".

When a person visits the same country several times a year, an equal number of arrivals is recorded. Likewise, if a person visits several countries during the course of a single trip, his/her arrival in each country is recorded separately. Consequently, *arrivals* cannot be assumed to be equal to the number of persons travelling.

Tourism receipts data are obtained from the item "travel, credits" of the Balance of Payments of each country and corresponds to the "expenditure of non-resident visitors (tourists and same-day visitors)" within the economic territory of the country of reference.

Fare receipts data are obtained from the item "transportation, passenger services, credits" of the Balance of Payments of each country and corresponds to the "fare expenditure of non-resident visitors (tourists and same-day visitors)" within the economic territory of the country of reference.

Outbound tourism

Departures associated to outbound tourism correspond to the departures of resident visitors outside the economic territory of the country of reference.

Tourism expenditure data in other countries are obtained from the item "travel, debits" of the Balance of Payment of each country and corresponds to the "expenditure of resident visitors (tourists and same-day visitor)" outside the economic territory of the country of reference.

Fare expenditure data in other countries are obtained from the item "transportation, passenger services, debits" of the Balance of Payment of each country and corresponds to the "fare expenditure of resident visitors (tourists and same-day visitor)" outside the economic territory of the country of reference.

Symbols and abbreviations used

.. Not available

OECD Member Countries

Australia

Tourism in the economy

In 2005-06, tourism generated about AUD 37.7 billion (approximately 3.9% of Australia's total GDP), an increase of 5.5% on the previous year. However, since the Australian economy as a whole grew at a faster rate, this resulted in a decrease in tourism's share of GDP from 4.0% in 2004-05 to 3.9% in 2005-06. In 2005-06, the tourism industry employed around 464 500 people; approximately 4.6% of total employment.

Domestic tourism represents approximately three quarters of all tourism consumption. Overall domestic tourism expenditure grew by 5.7% in 2006. The number of domestic trips also increased by 4.0% and the number of domestic visitor nights by 3.6%. In 2006, there were 5.5 million foreign visitor arrivals, an increase of 0.6% on 2005 (Table 3.1). International visitors spent AUD 14.0 billion while in Australia, up 14.7% (or by AUD 1.8 billion). Key foreign markets for Australia in 2006 were New Zealand (1.1 million, down 2.1% on 2005), the UK (734 000 arrivals, up 3.6%), Japan (651 000 arrivals, down 5.0%), the US (456 000 arrivals, up 2.2%), and China (309 000 arrivals, up 8.3%).

Tourism organisation

The Australian Government Department of Industry, Tourism and Resources (DITR) (Figure 3.3) is the primary source of tourism policy advice to the Australian Government, covering a wide range of areas including bilateral tourism relations with other countries, visas and passenger processing, transport and security, taxation and assistance, education and training, industry standards and regulation, and regional and niche tourism development.

In 2004, the Australian Government brought together four separate tourism entities to form Tourism Australia (TA): the Australian Tourist Commission (international marketing); See Australia (domestic tourism marketing); Bureau of Tourism Research (research and statistics); and the Tourism Forecasting Council (market forecasting). TA is responsible for international tourism marketing and marketing development, domestic tourism development, events and business tourism development and key research and forecasting functions.

All state/territory governments in Australia incorporate tourism into relevant areas of portfolio responsibility. Several Australian states/territories with a greater economic reliance on tourism have developed their own statutory authority bodies to market and develop international and domestic visitation in their respective states/territories.

The main role of the Tourism Ministers' Council (TMC) is to facilitate consultation and policy co-ordination among tourism Ministers from the Australian Government, each State and Territory Government and the New Zealand Government. TMC operates in conjunction with the Australian Standing Committee on Tourism (ASCOT), whose main objective is to improve co-operation and co-ordination of Government policies and activities as they

Figure 3.3. **Organisational chart of tourism bodies in Australia**

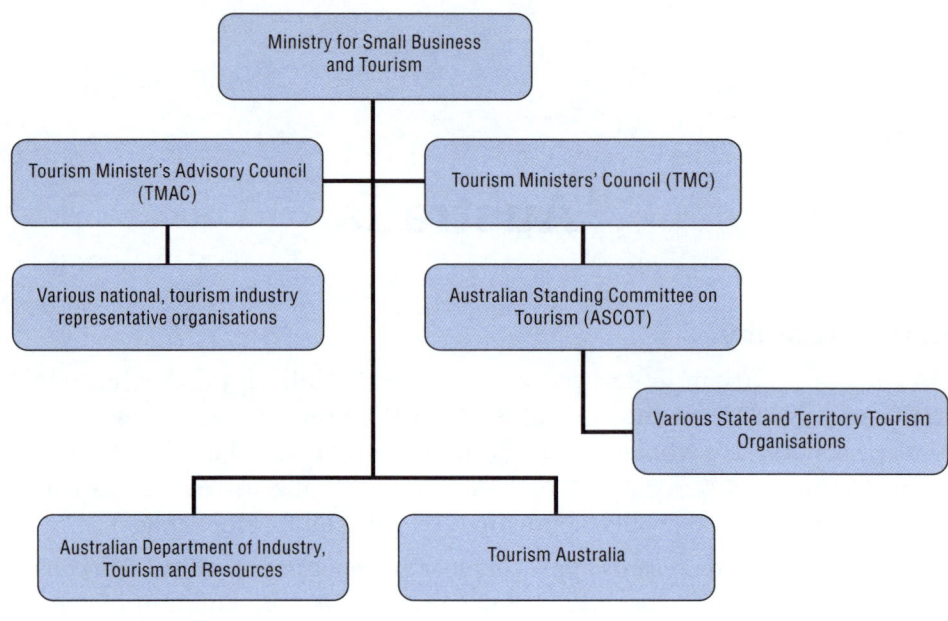

Source: OECD, adapted from Australian Government Department of Industry, Tourism and Resources, 2007.

affect tourism. ASCOT is the forum for senior officials to discuss issues at an operational level. Decisions taken by ASCOT are then passed to the TMC for consideration.

The Australian Tourism Development Program (ATDP) is a highly competitive merit-based grants program which assists in the development of tourism throughout Australia by providing funding to industry initiatives that increase Australia's competitiveness as a tourism destination and increase visitation and yield throughout Australia.

Tourism budget

Tourism Australia (TA) is the national tourism organisation assigned with responsibility to develop and market tourism internationally and domestically. In the 2005-06 Australian Federal Budget, TA was appropriated AUD 137.82 million.

From 2004-08, the Australian Government allocated AUD 3.5 million to the ATDP to increase the diversity of tourism products and services. To date, more than AUD 13.7 million has been provided to 88 projects across Australia.

The Australian Government's Tourism White Paper launched in December 2003 included additional funding of AUD 235 million, increasing the Australian Government's total direct expenditure on the tourism sector to AUD 600 million over four and a half years. The Paper identified the importance of sustainable development to the ongoing prosperity of the tourism industry. The White Paper recognised the need to develop partnerships that would deliver new nature-based tourism products, benefits for conservation, and economic opportunities in regional communities. Under the Tourism White Paper initiative, the Australian Government has allocated:

- AUD 31.5 million over four years to June 2008 for the Australian Tourism Development Program to encourage the development of tourism, particularly in rural and regional Australia. Box 3.1 illustrates an innovative project in the region of Victoria.

> **Box 3.1. A case of innovation at the Sovereign Hill museum**
>
> Sovereign Hill is a major interactive museum in regional Victoria, which recreates daily life in Australia during the gold rush period of the 1850s. A feature at Sovereign Hill is the open-air light and sound show, named Blood on the Southern Cross, which tells the story of the Eureka Stockade in 1854. While Sovereign Hill itself enjoys good international visitation, the museum's managers noticed that Blood on the Southern Cross did not so. Only 7% of visitors attending Blood on the Southern Cross were international, despite international visitors forming 28% of all visitors to the museum. With the assistance of a AUD 100 000 Australian Tourism Development Program grant (which the museum matched), Sovereign Hill was able to improve its foreign language narration service. Using radio frequencies and headsets, Sovereign Hill now broadcasts the narration in French, German, Japanese, Mandarin, Cantonese and English. One year since introducing the foreign language narration, Sovereign Hill has seen German visitors attending the show increase by 27%, Japanese visitors by 30%, and the Chinese market by 100%.

- AUD 3.8 million over four years to June 2008 for the Business Ready Program for Indigenous Tourism to help indigenous tourism businesses develop business and management skills and gain a better understanding of the tourism industry.
- AUD 3.7 million over three years to June 2007 for the Tourism and Conservation Partnerships Initiative to help facilitate the development of nature-based tourism attractions.

As part of the 2006-07 Federal Budget, the Australian Government provided AUD 3.9 million to strengthen Australia's administration of the China Approved Destination Status (ADS) scheme.

Tourism related policies and programmes

The DITR liaises with those Australian Government departments responsible for national and industry-wide labour resources policy (Box 3.2). DITR also plays a liaison role with the states and territories through the TMC and ASCOT forums in order to co-ordinate a tourism industry-wide approach to labour resources policy. DITR has convened an Industry-Government Working Group on the Tourism and Hospitality Industry Labour Market. The group is now working with the Australian Department of Employment and Workplace Relations to conduct a series of pilot surveys in specific tourism regions to ascertain the nature and extent of labour and skills shortages at a regional level.

Public/private partnerships

In terms of public/private partnerships, a number of groups support a co-ordinated approach to national tourism policy by strengthening relationships between governments, within government and with the tourism industry. Such groups include the Tourism Minister's Advisory Council (TMAC) and National Tourism and Aviation Advisory Committee (NTAAC).

TMAC is a forum which among other activities provides advice on strategic issues affecting the sustainable development and growth of the tourism industry. TMAC is chaired by the Federal Minister for Small Business and Tourism, and has a membership drawn from the tourism industry, TA, ASCOT and the DITR.

> **Box 3.2. Key tourism policy developments in 2006-07**
>
> - Further implementing the Tourism White Paper and subsequent Government Policy.
> - Further implementing the Korea Building Framework for Sustainable Inbound Tourism Action Plan.
> - Implementing The Action Plan for Japanese Tourism: Embracing Change.
> - Further developing other key markets around the world.
> - Shifting international consumers from a preference to visit Australia to an intention to visit Australia.
> - Continuing to engage in Air Services Agreement negotiations.
> - Building a more resilient tourism industry that is better prepared to respond to threats.
> - Implementing the recommendations of the National Tourism Investment Strategy.
> - Implementing the recommendations of the Emerging Markets Strategy.

Several measures are targeted at the development of small and medium-sized enterprises (SMEs). In 2006, the Australian inbound tourism industry, with funding from the Australian Government, launched the Australian Tourism Export Code of Conduct. This voluntary accreditation program, which can be accessed through *www.qualitytourism.com.au* incorporates standards of practice designed to ensure that the Australian tourism experience for international visitors is delivered ethically, professionally and with integrity. The Portal, developed in consultation with the tourism industry, also provides information and assistance on sectoral and generic tourism accreditation programs, enabling online accreditation applications, in addition to providing resources relating to business improvement. A voluntary Code of Conduct for inbound tour operators in the Korean market has been developed by the DITR and the Korean Inbound Tour Operators Council of Australia, in consultation with other key stakeholders.

NTAAC membership comprises officials from the tourism and transport portfolios of the Australian Government, officials representing the state and territory governments, and industry representatives from the tourism and aviation sectors. NTAAC supports a strong and viable tourism industry by establishing formal working relations between major stakeholders in tourism and aviation.

In February 2006, the Australian Government announced that it will continue its policy of seeking liberalisation of international air service agreements. International air transport is a key driver of the Australian economy and is crucial for serving and expanding the tourism industry. Accordingly, current Australian air services policy will:

- Recognise "open skies" as an aspirational goal to be sought on a case-by-case basis, where it is in the national interest.
- Recognise the contribution that an Australian-based airline makes to the economy.
- Negotiate capacity ahead of demand.
- Expand access to a range of aviation hubs.
- Encourage major foreign carriers to commit to a long-term presence in Australia.
- Attract services to regional parts of Australia.
- Seek liberalisation through multilateral forums.

Indigenous tourism

Tourism can provide much needed opportunities for employment, social stability and the preservation of culture within indigenous communities. Research also suggests that there is strong demand for indigenous tourism products from international and domestic tourists. The Business Ready Program for Indigenous Tourism (BRPIT) assists indigenous tourism operators to develop, establish and run successful tourism businesses by addressing the lack of management, business and strategic planning skills. The program has funding over four years starting 2004-05, which allows selected mentors to identify indigenous tourism businesses in their region and work to improve their business management and strategic planning skills, increase business potential for commercialising tourism products or services, and ensure that the businesses are capable of operating successfully within the Australian tourism industry.

TA supports the education industry to boost Australia's profile as an educational tourism destination through its corporate and consumer websites in informing international students about the range of educational experiences on offer in Australia, including a marketing brochure highlighting travel and study options.

In the light of Australia's projected increase of visitor arrivals from India and China in the next 10 years, the Australian Government undertook a National Tourism Investment Strategy consultancy study, which looked at issues associated with investment in the tourism industry.

The Sustainable Tourism co-operative Research Centre is currently developing tourism satellite accounts for Australia's States and Territories. Also, Tourism Research Australia has developed a new concept of yield, Total Inbound Economic Value (TIEV), to measure the financial contribution of inbound tourism to the economy. TIEV reflects the total trip spending by inbound visitors less key leakages of this spending to non-Australian entities (such as the share of payments to overseas based airlines, wholesalers and travel agents). Estimates of TIEV are now included in the International Visitor Survey.

Statistical profile

Table 3.1. Inbound tourism: International arrivals and receipts

	Units	2002	2003	2004	2005	2006
Visitors	Thousands	**4 841**	**4 746**	**5 215**	**5 499**	**5 532**
of which:						
New Zealand	Thousands	790	839	1 033	1 099	1 076
United Kingdom	Thousands	643	673	676	709	734
Japan	Thousands	715	628	710	685	651
United States	Thousands	435	422	433	446	456
China	Thousands	190	176	251	285	308
Tourism receipts	Millions AUD	18 342	19 041	20 656	22 086	..

StatLink http://dx.doi.org/10.1787/153411735353

Source: Australia Bureau of Statistics, 2007.

Table 3.2. Outbound tourism: International departures and expenditure

	Units	2002	2003	2004	2005	2006
Departures	Thousands	3 461	3 388	4 369	4 756	4 941
Tourism expenditure	Millions AUD	11 156	11 119	13 925	14 738	..

StatLink http://dx.doi.org/10.1787/153414175733

Source: Australia Bureau of Statistics, 2007.

Table 3.3. Tourism in the national economy

	Units	2001-02	2002-03	2003-04	2004-05	2005-06
Tourism as % of gross domestic product	Percentage	4.5	4.4	4.2	4	3.9
Tourism as % of gross value added	Percentage	4.1	4	3.8	3.6	3.5
Total tourism employed persons	Thousands	446.6	450.7	448.6	458.6	464.5
Tourism as % of total employment	Percentage	4.9	4.8	4.7	4.7	4.6

StatLink http://dx.doi.org/10.1787/153474621624

Source: Australia Bureau of Statistics, 2007.

Austria

Tourism in the economy

According to Tourism Satellite Accounting methods, the direct value-added effects of tourism in 2006 were of the order of EUR 16.5 billion, 6.4% of GDP. In 2006, 168 000 people (2005: 164 100) were employed in hotels, restaurants and similar establishments, 5.1% of total national employment. Of the total, around 60% were females.

In 2006, the number of international tourist arrivals was 20.3 million, a 1.5% rise on 2005, while domestic arrivals totalled 9.87 million, 5.2% up on 2005. Overnight stays amounted to 119.4 million, just 0.1% up on 2005. Tourism receipts from foreign visitors in 2006 were EUR 13.3 billion (excl. fare receipts), 2.7% up on the previous year. Tourism accounts for more than one third (Table 3.7) of Austria's total exports of services. (Despite an 3.0% rise in Austrians' tourism expenditure abroad in 2006, Austria maintains a strong positive balance on the tourism account of EUR 5.8 billion.) Although Austria's leading origin market, Germany, has been in decline recently, smaller markets, particularly those in Central and Eastern Europe, have grown.

The total number of accommodation establishments in Austria in the winter season 2005-06 was 60 900 and 68 200 in the 2006 summer season. The majority are small and medium-sized enterprises, although during the last ten years, the number of beds in small establishments (private rental accommodation) decreased by 17%, whereas the figure for larger hotels of the four and five-star categories expanded by 27%.

Tourism organisation

In Austria, tourism is part of overall economic policy and in particular of SME policy. Under Austria's constitution, legislative authority in tourism affairs is vested not in the federal government, but in the country's nine federal provinces. Nevertheless, as tourism is a typical cross-cutting sector, many federal laws impinge on it. Tourism is also affected by European Union legislation, *e.g.* in the realm of consumer protection.

At the national level, tourism policy lies within the purview of the Federal Minister of Economics and Labour. In December 2006, the Austrian parliament established a new parliamentary committee on tourism (Figure 3.4).

The Austrian National Tourist Office (ANTO or *Österreich Werbung*) is the country's national tourism marketing organisation. It receives basic funding from the Federal Ministry of Economics and Labour (75%) and the Austrian Federal Economic Chamber (25%), and also provides services on a fee basis for firms in the Austrian tourism industry. ANTO operates 33 offices worldwide, which carry out marketing activities in 61 countries, in some cases with the support of the representatives of Austrian Trade, Austria's foreign trade promotion organisation, which is part of the Austrian Federal Economic Chamber.

Figure 3.4. **Organisational chart of tourism bodies in Austria**

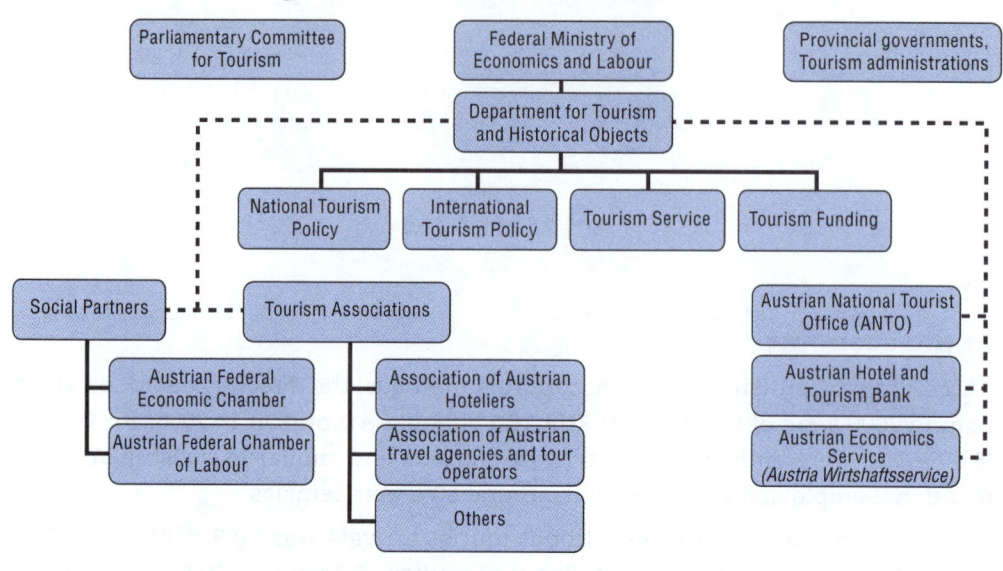

Source: OECD, adapted from Austrian Federal Ministry of Economics and Labour, 2007.

ANTO carries out strategic marketing activities based on product knowledge and market trend analysis. It has defined five main points for its activities in the years ahead: managing and developing the "Vacation in Austria" brand, supporting innovation in the design of new offers and products, promoting internationalisation (i.e. diversification) of Austria's guest structure, encouraging year-round tourism, and intensifying co-operation with partners.

Tourism budget

In 2006, the national tourism administration had a budget of around EUR 58 million, of which EUR 27 million was for the support and loans to SMEs and was administered by the Austrian Tourism Bank, EUR 24 million was contributed to ANTO, and a further EUR 7 million dispensed by the Federal Ministry of Economics and Labour in the form of individual subsidies, for research and other projects. In addition, a total of EUR 30 million in European Recovery Programme (ERP)-funds was available for loans to SMEs in the tourism industry. All nine federal provinces also have their own tourism budgets and tourism development programmes.

Tourism related policies and programmes

The objectives of the national tourism administration are to boost quality and competitiveness in the sector and support sustainable tourism development. A number of key projects are described below.

Improving the quality of data for decision making and developing an evaluation culture to enhance productivity

Tourism Satellite Account (TSA)

The need both to assess tourism's economic importance and establish a platform to monitor current developments, led to the implementation of a TSA in Austria which was first produced in 2001 with 1999 as the initial reporting year. This joint project carried out by Statistics Austria and the Austrian Institute of Economic Research has since been produced on a regular basis. For the 2004 reporting year, the economic analysis of the tourism sector provided by the TSA was supplemented by data on direct and indirect employment effects. This made possible for the first time a determination of the total contribution to employment made by the tourism and leisure industry. A regional breakdown of TSA core tables has been carried out for the federal provinces of Vienna, Upper Austria and Lower Austria; implementation for the other federal provinces is envisaged in the near future.

Tourism Monitor Austria (T-MONA)

T-MONA, an innovative guest monitoring system was launched in 2004 and was a joint project of ANTO, the Federal Ministry of Economics and Labour, the Austrian Federal Economic Chamber, all nine provincial tourism organisations, and many regions. T-MONA is a web-based management information system based on gathering travel behaviour and socio-demographic data, and provides an up-to-date picture of domestic and foreign tourists in Austria. Direct collation of data obtained in surveys makes it immediately available for analysis and also permits easy presentation of results in the form of statistical diagrams or tables.

> **Box 3.3. Major forms of tourism in Austria**
>
> The T-MONA (Tourism MONitor Austria) guest monitoring system has been developed to provide Austrian tourism regions with information on their strengths and weaknesses, guest structure, and guests' motivation for visiting specific regions.
>
> An analysis of all regions indicates that guests have the following main motivations for visiting Austria: 30% skiing and snowboarding, 27% mountains and hiking, 18% water sports and lakes, 16% cities and culture, and 15% spa treatments (multiple answers are included here). Austria also ranks among the top ten international destinations for meetings and conventions worldwide (ICCA, 2005). In 2005, the winter and summer seasons were of roughly equal importance, accounting for about 60 million overnight stays each.

Destination Management Monitor Austria (DMMA)

DMMA, which is intended to enhance the international competitiveness of Austria's destinations and holiday regions, grew out of a strategic programme of the Federal Ministry of Economics and Labour in 2002. The 19 participating destinations together account for more than 23% of the value-added generated by Austrian tourism. Members of DMMA collaborate on various projects, such as market research and the development of professional management and marketing instruments (*www.dmma.at*).

Benchmark system for the hotel industry

The new online benchmarking system "*Webmark Hotellerie*" was developed to give the Austrian hotel industry direct access to industry-specific data and key statistics to assist in their strategic decisions. It has five modules giving both quantitative and qualitative information which provide an anonymous comparison with peers in essential areas of a hotel's business. The benchmarking system was a joint initiative of the Federal Ministry of Economics and Labour, the nine federal provinces, the Division for Tourism and Leisure

Industry of the Austrian Federal Economic Chamber, Austrian Hotel Association, and Austrian Tourism Bank. The system can also be used by these institutions in their decision-making.

Helping tourism SMEs face global competition

Public sector support to stimulate the tourism industry is based on public-private partnerships. The Federal Ministry of Economics and Labour appointed the Austrian Tourism Bank, a wholly private institution, to handle its funding programmes for tourism SMEs. These programmes include in part EU co-financing measures. The Ministry's objectives for such funding programmes range from encouraging investment, improving the quality and size of tourism enterprises and upgrading the quality of software and training, to enhancing co-operation, optimising enterprises' financial structure, encouraging new business start-ups, and attracting new sources of finance for tourism enterprises (*www.oeht.at*).

Enhancing co-operation and networking

Best Health Austria

Best Health Austria was initiated by the Federal Ministry of Economics and Labour and is now a co-operation of key players in Austrian health tourism. The body oversees the "Best Health Austria" quality designation, which is based on the officially recognised Austrian Seal of Quality. By May 2007, around 50 Austrian companies had received the quality seal, and a further 30 were in the accreditation process (*www.besthealthaustria.com*).

Culture Tour Austria

Culture Tour Austria is a strategic programme for cultural tourism in Austria, which was recently launched by the Federal Ministries of Economics and Labour and of Education, the Arts and Culture. The programme is the first in a series that aims to promote the development and modernisation of cultural tourism. Development of a strategy for the future "*Kulturtourismus Austria 2010+*" is a core project for focusing Austrian cultural tourism in the years ahead. Apart from organisational and structural innovations, the key launch projects include preparation of a premium product catalogue for leading brands in the Austrian cultural tourism field, brand and quality management tailored to the needs of cultural tourism, and future-oriented cultural and quality marketing co-operation (*www.culturetour.at*).

Improving human resource development and planning

"*Tourism, Employment and Training*" is a project to develop a package of measures to improve labour potential through co-ordination with tourism sector players. The project consists of four components: future criteria for success in tourism, labour market conditions, training and continuing education in tourism, and taxation framework for tourism employees. In 2007, a guide entitled "*A Job in the Tourism and Leisure Industry – Attractive and Promising*" was published, providing valuable information on education and training opportunities in the field of tourism. The handbook is targeted at pupils, students, teachers, parents and those undertaking re-training.

Acting as a mediator within the tourism industry

Since 1997, the tourism service agency in the Federal Ministry of Economics and Labour has served as an information point for inbound and outbound travellers, companies, authorities, and institutions for inquiries, complaints, information and other Tourism related matters. The tourism service agency processes some 2 500 to 3 000 queries and complaints each year. As a special service, the agency offers free mediation in disputes between companies in the tourism industry, such as hotels, restaurants, tour operators, and travellers.

Enhancing international and cross-border co-operation

Bilateral and multilateral co-operation in tourism aims to position Austria as a constructive, competent and reliable partner in international tourism development. Austria contributes to international exchanges of best practice and organises many international events. The Federal Ministry of Economics and Labour is involved in a number of EU co-financed projects implemented in co-operation with neighbouring countries. Apart from networking and co-operation, these projects focus on sustainable development (such as bicycle routes, national parks and eco-friendly travelling/soft mobility), culture and tourism (for example, pilgrimage routes and castle routes), health tourism and marketing.

Statistical profile

Table 3.4. **Inbound tourism: International arrivals and receipts**

	Units	2002	2003	2004	2005	2006
Tourists (overnight visitors)[1]	Thousands	**18 611**	**19 078**	**19 374**	**19 952**	**20 269**
of which:						
Germany	Thousands	10 349	10 468	10 256	10 367	10 107
Netherlands	Thousands	1 350	1 418	1 426	1 484	1 516
Italy	Thousands	995	1 090	1 101	1 102	1 106
Switzerland	Thousands	817	888	896	895	926
United Kingdom	Thousands	685	663	722	757	802
Tourism receipts	Million EUR	11 578	11 917	12 203	12 904	13 255
Fare receipts	Million EUR	1 620	1 612	1 695	1 796	1 892

StatLink http://dx.doi.org/10.1787/153477657025

1. Including arrivals in private rental accommodation.
Sources: Statistics Austria and OeNB (Austrian Central Bank), 2007.

Table 3.5. **Outbound tourism: International departures and expenditure**

	Units	2002	2003	2004	2005	2006
Departures[1]	Thousands	8 265	8 384	8 371	8 206	10 042
Tourism expenditure	Million EUR	7 416	7 647	7 171	7 200	7 420
Fare expenditure	Million EUR	888	1 003	1 170	1 217	1 342

StatLink http://dx.doi.org/10.1787/153525645168

1. Including business trips and visits to friends and relatives; excluding same-day visits abroad.
Sources: Statistics Austria and OeNB (Austrian Central Bank), 2007.

Table 3.6. **Employment in tourism**

	Units	2002	2003	2004	2005	2006
Dependent employment in the tourism sector	Employees	**153 164**	**156 467**	**159 019**	**163 644**	**168 038**
of which:						
Hotels and similar accommodations	Employees	58 497	59 317	59 919	60 663	62 084
Restaurants	Employees	86 443	88 832	90 656	93 451	97 604
Male	Employees	59 484	61 043	62 411	64 451	66 470
Female	Employees	93 680	95 424	96 608	99 194	101 567

StatLink http://dx.doi.org/10.1787/153535753377

Source: BMWA BALI based on data of the Main Association of Austrian Social Security Institutions, 2007

Table 3.7. **Tourism in the national economy**

	Units	2002	2003	2004	2005	2006
Tourism Satellite Account aggregates						
Tourism as % of gross domestic product[1] (direct effects)	Percentage	6.5	6.8	6.3	6.5	6.4
Total tourism value added[1]	Million EUR	14 376	15 280	14 937	15 872	16 498
Total tourism consumption	Million EUR	26 097	27 419	27 939	29 229	30 381
of which: Foreign visitors	Million EUR	13 907	14 548	14 822	15 428	15 968
Domestic visitors[2]	Million EUR	12 190	12 871	13 117	13 801	14 413
Tourism as % of employment[3]	Percentage	..	7.7	7.7	7.8	..
Other aggregates						
Tourism as % of service exports	Percentage	42.4	41.6	40.2	38.1	35.9
Domestic tourism as % of final consumption[4]	Percentage	10.9	11.2	11.0	11.1	11.2
Return of investment (ROI) in the industry	Percentage	4.6	3.9	3.8	..	..

StatLink http://dx.doi.org/10.1787/153558778267

1. Including business trips.
2. Including expenditure staying in weekend and second homes.
3. Concept of full time equivalents.
4. Final consumption does not include imports, tourism consumption only for domestic trips.

Sources: Statistics Austria, BMWA BALI based on data of the Main Association of Austrian Social Security Institutions, Vienna University for Economics and Business Administration, KMU Forschung Austria, 2007.

Belgium

Tourism in the economy

Since 2004, tourism is under the responsibility of the different regions (Walloon region, Flemish region and Brussels-Capital Region). There is no tourism policy undertaken at federal level. This country profile presents the current policies developed in the Walloon and Flemish regions.

In 2006, the tourism sector accounted for EUR 8 billion in Belgium. During the same period, Belgium received about 7 million international arrivals, of which 52% in the Flanders Region, 32% in the Walloon Region and 16% in the Brussels Region (Table 3.8). In the Walloon Region, tourism represents approximately 4.8% of GDP (2003).

FLANDERS REGION

Tourism organisation

Since 2004, the National Tourist Office, *Toerisme Vlaanderen*, has become an "*Intern verzelfstandig agentschap*", which means it has no longer a Board of Directors. *Toerisme Vlaanderen* has responsibility both for the set-up of the tourism sector in the region (all activities regarding the inspection, care and improvement of the tourist offer) and for the marketing of the product.

A new tourism unit has been created in the Flemish Department of Foreign Affairs (Figure 3.5). This unit is entrusted with supporting the delineation of policy and with subsequently evaluating the measures taken. Furthermore, it directs and monitors the execution of policy, carried out by *Toerisme Vlaanderen*.

Tourism budget

The budget for *Toerisme Vlaanderen* in 2006 is EUR 59.8 million. This budget is used for all the tasks of *Toerisme Vlaanderen*: marketing of the destination, licences for hotels, campsites and travel agencies and the investments in the product itself.

Tourism related policies and programmes

In 2005, an Advisory Committee ("Raadgevend comité") was installed, comprising representatives of the regional and local governments and of the private sector. The Minister for tourism has four major policy lines for tourism:

- Maximising the tourism performance but in a sustainable manner.
- Co-operation with and for all tourism actors.
- Putting Flanders on the map as a quality-destination.

● Regulations with ample space for efficient tourism management.

In Flanders, there are three major forms of tourism:

● The cities, which attract tourists from all over the world.
● The Flemish coast, which mainly attracts tourists from Belgium and the neighbouring countries.
● The countryside, which mainly attracts tourists from Belgium, the Netherlands and Germany.

Figure 3.5. **Organisational chart of tourism bodies in Flanders Region, Belgium**

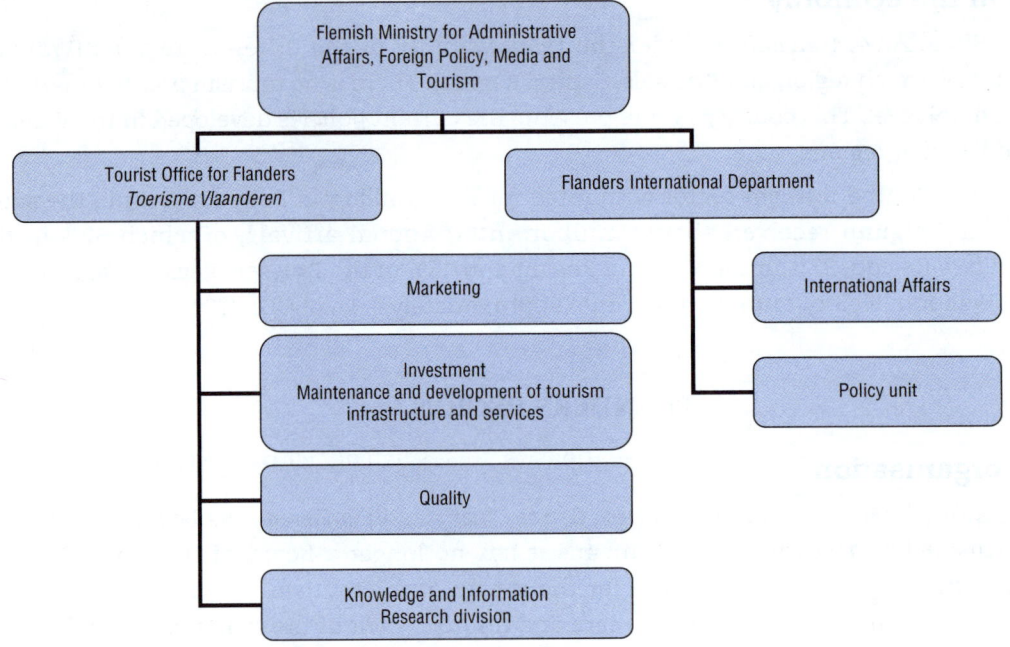

Source: OECD, adapted from Tourist Office for Flanders, 2007.

WALLOON REGION

Tourism organisation

In 2004, the Walloon Government adopted the draft *Decree on the Organisation of Tourism* and created a new public body, the General Commission for Tourism (*Commissariat Général au Tourisme*, CGT) (Figure 3.6). The CGT is responsible for implementing the general policy of the Walloon Government in the field of tourism and for managing the tourism infrastructure that belongs to the region.

There are various advisory bodies, such as the Higher Council for Tourism (*Conseil Supérieur du Tourisme*), which give opinions on tourism policy in general and on any draft decrees or orders in the field of tourism. There are also various technical committees that give opinions on specific issues of tourism policy, on licences, authorisations and exemptions and on subsidies to the private sector. These bodies make it possible to work with the accommodation sector (hotels, campsites, rural tourism accommodation and social tourism), the travel agency sector and the tourist office sector.

Figure 3.6. **Organisational chart of tourism bodies in Walloon Region, Belgium**

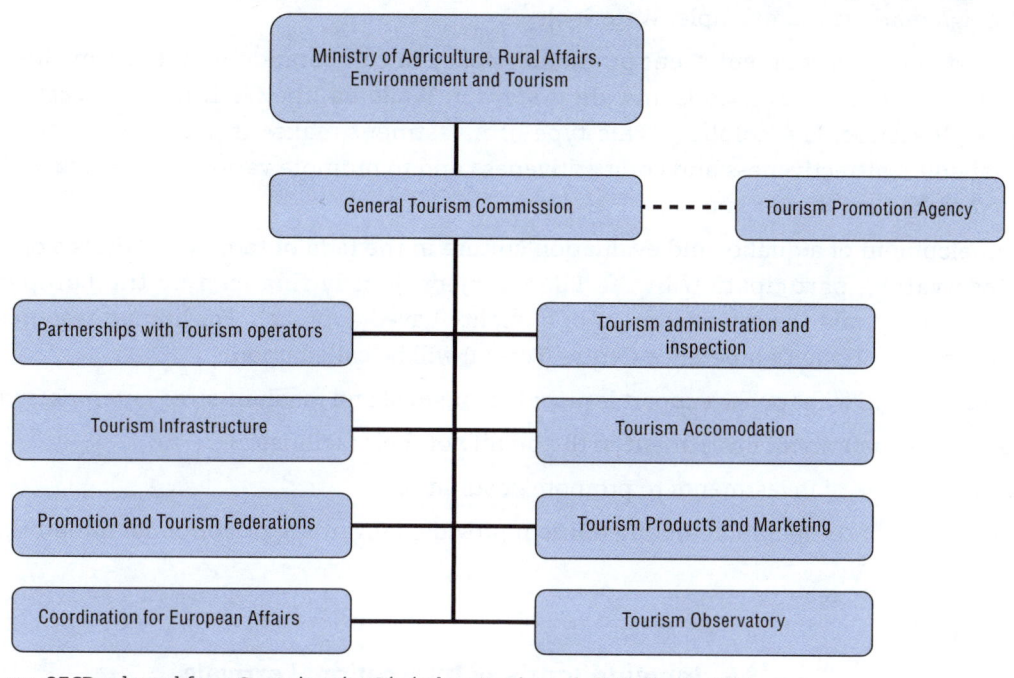

Source: OECD, adapted from Commissariat Général au Tourisme de la Wallonie, 2007.

The Walloon Tourism Observatory (*Observatoire wallon du tourisme*) is aimed at promoting co-operation among the various sectors of activity with a view to measuring the impact of tourism in Wallonia.

Tourism budget

For 2005, the budget for public tourism structures was approximately EUR 44.2 million (including Walloon co-financing of European projects) and the budget of the Wallonia-Brussels Tourism Promotion Office (*Office de Promotion du Tourisme Wallonie-Bruxelles*), a public interest foundation, was roughly EUR 13.6 million.

Tourism related policies and programmes

The Walloon Region has set six priorities for the development of tourism:
- To finalise the Walloon Tourism Code.
- To invest in human capital (creation of a Competence and Knowledge Centre aimed at making knowledge and know-how available to Walloon tourism).
- To develop synergies with other sectors (*e.g.* nature discovery tourism).
- To ensure that tourism products are promoted effectively.
- To develop the right to leisure and access to tourism for all.
- To improve the quality of tourism services for visitors.

In this context, Wallonia is giving priority to the following:
- Investment in the modernisation of accommodation in hotels and campsites and rural tourism in order to improve quality. New regulations governing tourism accommodations came into force in 2005.

- Improvement of facilities at major tourism sites to make them more competitive in foreign markets (for example, Waterloo).
- Investment in a coherent event promotion policy in co-operation with tourism sites in order to promote excursions and short stays in Wallonia (the festival "*L'eau d'heure en fête*", Waterloo, Francofolies). This type of investment makes it possible to improve Wallonia's attractiveness and competitiveness and to promote various tourism facilities and make them better known.
- Development of a quality and evaluation culture in the field of tourism: activities of the Observatory, participation in the Eden project, jointly financed by the European Community, and the establishment of a quality-based approach. For human resources, the Tourism Trade Competence Centre (Forem) will be called upon.

Lastly, significant public support is provided for small and medium-sized enterprises via:

- Subsidies to promote investment in the quality of their facilities.
- A programme of investments to promote destinations.
- Promotion of co-operation among tourism providers regarding promotional initiatives.

Statistical profile

Table 3.8. **Inbound tourism: International arrivals**

	Units	2002	2003	2004	2005	2006
Belgium	Thousands	6 825	6 807	6 710	6 747	6 995
Flemish Region	Thousands	3 477	3 391	3 394	3 455	3 608
Brussels Region	Thousands	2 262	2 335	2 251	2 199	2 247
Walloon Region	Thousands	1 086	1 081	1 065	1 093	1 140

StatLink http://dx.doi.org/10.1787/153740876728

Source: FPS Economy – Directorate-general Statistics and economic information, 2007.

Table 3.9. **Inbound tourism: International overnight stays**

	Units	2002	2003	2004	2005	2006
Belgium	Thousands	16 194	16 206	15 545	15 553	16 040
Flemish Region	Thousands	8 882	8 724	8 437	8 478	8 775
Brussels Region	Thousands	4 350	4 436	4 198	4 118	4 206
Walloon Region	Thousands	2 962	3 046	2 910	2 957	3 059

StatLink http://dx.doi.org/10.1787/153763124348

Source: FPS Economy – Directorate-general Statistics and economic information, 2007.

Table 3.10. **International tourism receipts and expenditure**

	Units	2002	2003	2004	2005	2006
Tourism receipts	Million EUR	7 317	7 243	7 423	7 934	8 164
Fare receipts	Million EUR	703	577	708	836	1 045
Tourism expenditure	Million EUR	10 736	10 807	11 274	12 047	12 172
Fare expenditure	Million EUR	1 149	1 053	1 209	1 469	1 842

StatLink http://dx.doi.org/10.1787/153615188608

Source: National Bank of Belgium, 2007.

Table 3.11. **Outbound tourism: International departures**

	Units	2002	2003	2004	2005	2006
Belgium	Thousands	**7 912**	**8 646**	**10 190**	**10 881**	**8 844**
Brussels Region	Thousands	1 019	1 157	1 375	1 490	1 335
Flemish Region	Thousands	4 556	5 161	5 884	6 435	5 002
Walloon Region	Thousands	2 338	2 328	2 931	2 956	2 507

StatLink http://dx.doi.org/10.1787/153658751380

Source: FPS Economy – Directorate-general Statistics and economic information, 2007.

Table 3.12. **Number of collective establishments**

	2002	2003	2004	2005	2006
Brussels Region	183	181	167	168	170
of which: Hotels	175	173	159	160	162
Camp sites	0	0	0	0	0
Flemish Region	1 961	1 915	1 959	1 901	1 968
of which: Hotels	1 114	1 081	1 080	1 055	1 129
Camp sites	220	213	266	252	250
Walloon Region	1 504	1 463	1 412	1 380	1 347
of which: Hotels	721	704	683	684	664
Camp sites	320	314	314	302	299
Belgium	**3 648**	**3 559**	**3 538**	**3 449**	**3 485**
of which: Hotels	2 010	1 958	1 922	1 899	1 955
Camp sites	540	527	580	554	549

StatLink http://dx.doi.org/10.1787/153662858372

Source: FPS Economy – Directorate-general Statistics and economic information, 2007.

Canada

Tourism in the economy

Tourism (domestic and international) contributes just over 2% to Canada's GDP and accounts for 3.8% of national employment (Table 3.16). The sector's contribution to both these measures has remained broadly stable over the past five years.

In 2006, Canada's most important international market, the United States, which accounts for 86% of all inbound visitors, is in decline. Overall arrivals from the United States declined by 8.8% in 2006, falling below 30 million for the first time since record keeping started in 1972. The first half of 2007 has also shown decreases in arrivals.

A high proportion of international visitors (50%) come to Canada for leisure purposes (including outdoor activities and sports), followed by visiting friends and relatives (18%), with business (including convention and employment) in third place (10%).

Tourism organisation

In Canada, the federal government, the ten provinces and three territories, as well as municipalities, all have a role in supporting tourism.

Within the federal government, the Minister of Industry has the lead responsibility for tourism policy, and through the Canadian Tourism Commission (a Crown corporation), for tourism marketing and research (Figure 3.7). Several other federal government departments and agencies, such as Canadian Heritage, Parks Canada, Infrastructure Canada and regional development agencies also provide significant support for tourism.

In most provinces and territories, the responsibility for tourism resides in Economic Development departments or in Recreation, Culture or Heritage departments. The federal government, as well as several provincial, territorial and municipal governments, have established agencies with a focus on marketing and partnerships.

Tourism budget

The Canadian government invests in excess of CAD 400 million annually in supporting the tourism sector. It provides funding for tourism marketing and research, provides tourism development support through regional development agencies, and invests in National Parks and historic sites, as well as events and Tourism related infrastructure.

Tourism related policies and programmes

On 4 December 2006, the federal Minister responsible for Tourism met with provincial and territorial counterparts and agreed on a National Tourism Strategy framework which identified six key priorities for immediate action and collaboration. The priorities reflect the input obtained from the tourism industry through consultation and were selected

Figure 3.7. **Organisational chart of tourism bodies in Canada.**

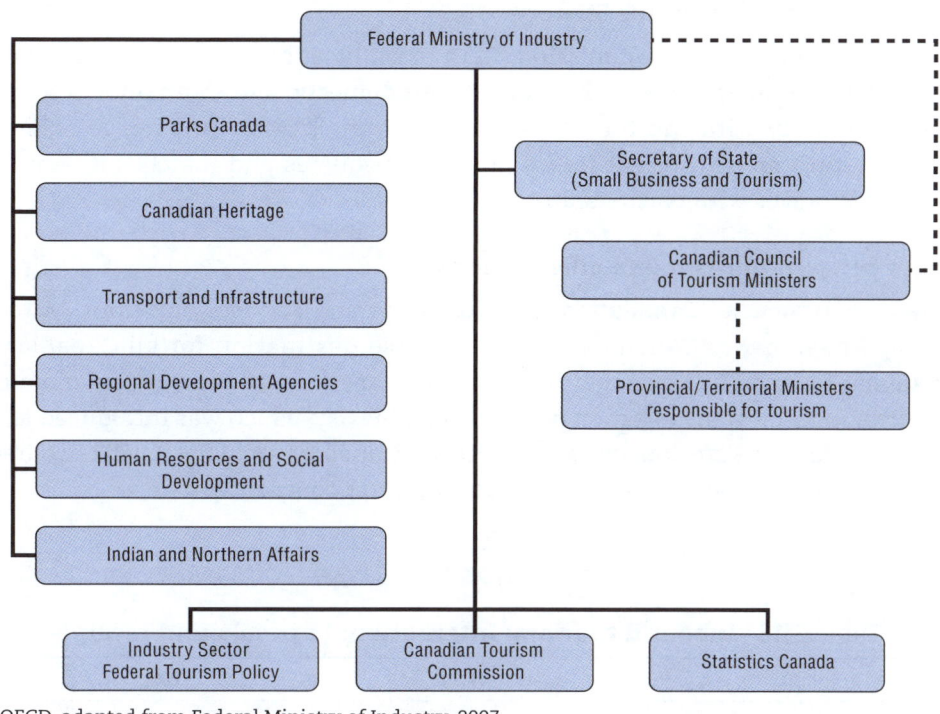

Source: OECD, adapted from Federal Ministry of Industry, 2007.

because of their national significance or importance to the industry at large. These priorities require the collaboration of governments to effect change and are as follows:

- *Accessible Destination – Border Crossing*: The goal is to ensure the efficient flow of tourists to and from Canada.

- *Accessible Destination – Transportation*: The goals are to i) emphasise the need to implement transport policies and programmes that take into consideration national, provincial/territorial, and regional tourism economic benefits; and ii) emphasise the importance of ensuring that transport policies enhance the ability of tourists to travel to and within Canada.

- *Exceptional Experiences – Product Development*: The goal is to ensure that existing products are enhanced and new products developed to take advantage of new and emerging opportunities.

- *Exceptional Hosts – Human Resources*: The goal is to ensure that the supply of tourism and hospitality sector labour is consistent with demand.

- *Exceptional Reputation – Tourism Information and Statistics*: The goals are to i) improve access by governments, business, and stakeholders to relevant information and analysis for decision- making; and ii) improve the measurement of tourism's performance and of its impact on the economy.

- *Exceptional Reputation – Tourism Marketing*: The goals are to i) harmonise and co-ordinate marketing activities more effectively between the Canadian Tourism Commission and provinces/territories in order to improve the positioning of Canadian destinations; and ii) optimise existing resources through increased government collaboration.

Tourism Ministers also agreed to establish a committee of senior officials to develop an action plan to implement the Strategy.

The Canadian Tourism Commission (CTC) recently launched a new Canada brand as part of a global strategy aimed at increasing both domestic and international travel. The CTC works closely with the tourism sector, both public and private, to achieve the maximum return on investment for its financial resources and matches its funding for marketing initiatives with partnership contributions.

Linkages between tourism and other policies

The Government of Canada reduced the Goods and Services Tax from 7% to 6% in July 2006, which makes Canada a more affordable destination for all Canadians and international tourists. In November of the same year the government also announced a new international air transportation policy called Blue Sky, which was introduced to create opportunities for travellers, businesses and the air transport industry. It will encourage the development of new markets, new services and greater competition.

Statistical profile

Table 3.13. **Inbound tourism: International arrivals and receipts**

	Units	2002	2003	2004	2005	2006
Tourists (overnight visitors)	Thousands	**20 057**	**17 534**	**19 145**	**18 771**	**18 265**
of which:						
United States	Thousands	16 167	14 232	15 088	14 391	13 855
United Kingdom	Thousands	721	691	801	888	842
Japan	Thousands	423	250	391	398	364
France	Thousands	312	275	337	351	361
Germany	Thousands	292	253	296	311	298
Tourism receipts	Million CAD	16 741	14 776	16 745	16 674	16 598
Fare receipts	Million CAD	3 278	2 275	2 750	2 756	2 640

StatLink http://dx.doi.org/10.1787/153822745512

Source: Statistics Canada, 2007.

Table 3.14. **Outbound tourism: International departures and expenditure**

	Units	2002	2003	2004	2005	2006[1]
Departures	Thousands	17 705	17 739	19 595	21 099	22 732
Tourism expenditure	Million CAD	18 401	18 727	20 747	22 059	23 311
Fare expenditure	Million CAD	4 192	4 157	4 875	5 973	6 471

StatLink http://dx.doi.org/10.1787/154004112870

1. Preliminary data.
Source: Statistics Canada, 2007.

Table 3.15. Employment in tourism

	Units	2002	2003	2004	2005	2006
Transportation	Thousands	77.9	78.5	78.4	78.6	79.4
Accommodation	Thousands	160.5	158.8	161.5	162	163.9
Food and beverage services	Thousands	144.8	146.2	145	146.1	151.1
Other tourism industries[1]	Thousands	107.4	108.0	109.9	113.0	114.7
Total tourism industries	Thousands	**490.5**	**491.5**	**494.9**	**499.7**	**509.1**
Other industries[2]	Thousands	120.7	120.7	121.1	121.9	124.6
Total Tourism Activities	Thousands	**611.2**	**612.2**	**616.0**	**621.6**	**633.7**

StatLink http://dx.doi.org/10.1787/154020546060
1. Includes recreation and entertainment services and travel agency industries.
2. Includes non-tourism industries that benefit from tourism (eg. Retail trade).
Sources: Statistics Canada, National Tourism Indicators, 2007.

Table 3.16. Tourism in the national economy

	Units	2002	2003	2004	2005	2006
Tourism as % of gross domestic product (Basic prices)	Percentage	2.18	1.98	2.00	2.01	2.03
Tourism as % of total employment	Percentage	3.9	3.8	3.8	3.8	3.8
Total tourism demand	Million CAD	**56.6**	**54.8**	**58.7**	**62.7**	**66.7**
Tourism domestic demand	Million CAD	38.4	39.2	41.2	45.7	50.3
Tourism demand by non-residents	Million CAD	18.1	15.6	17.5	17.0	16.5

StatLink http://dx.doi.org/10.1787/154026501111
Source: Statistics Canada, 2007.

Czech Republic

Tourism in the economy

According to tourism satellite account (TSA) methodology, the contribution of the tourism industry to the Czech Republic's GDP in 2005 was 3.1% (Table 3.20), with hotels and restaurants accounting for about 1.8% of GDP. Employment in the tourism sector (hotels and restaurants) reached 3.8% of total employment in the same year. Foreign currency revenues amounted to EUR 3 760 million in 2005 and their contribution to GDP was 3.8% and to exports 5.9%. Because of the rapid rate of growth in the national economy, however, and the stagnation of the tourism sector, tourism's share of foreign currency revenues is declining.

The level of nominal wages in this sector is well below the average of the Czech Republic. The total number of enterprises registered in this sector was 50 233 in 2005.

The number of arrivals of foreign visitors reached 23.4 million in 2005. Foreign tourists represented about 39% of all foreign visitors. Consumption of inbound tourism reached EUR 4 089 million in 2005.

Tourism organisation

At central government level, the Tourism Department of the Ministry for Regional Development manages the development of tourism (Figure 3.8). The Ministry contributes to

Figure 3.8. **Organisational chart of tourism bodies in the Czech Republic**

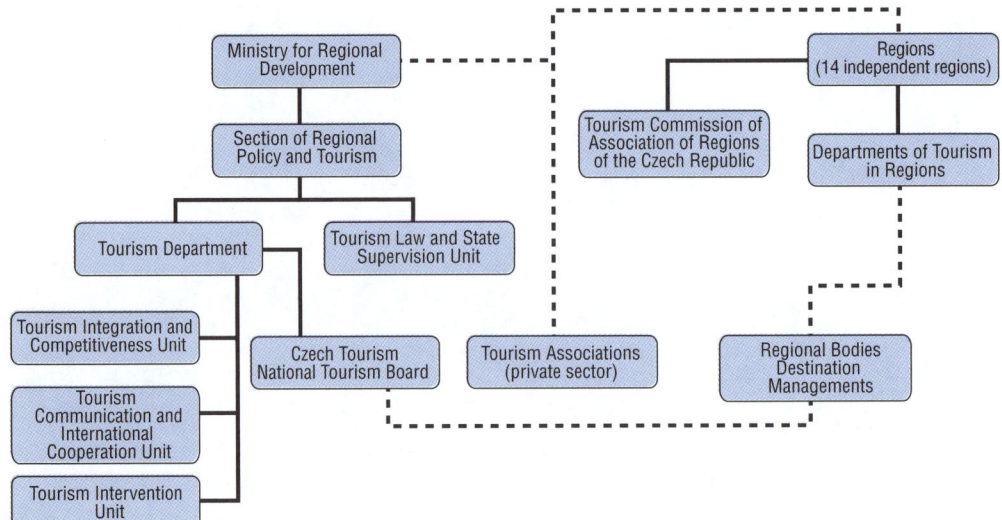

Source: OECD, adapted from Ministry for Regional Development, 2007.

i) the preparation of relevant legislation; *ii)* the dissemination and analysis of statistical information; *ii)* the development of tourism at regional and local levels; *iv)* the development of activities that foster quality in tourism services; and *v)* the implementation of measures that enhance co-operation in the field of tourism.

The Czech National Tourism Board (CzechTourism) is a subsidised organisation of the Ministry for Regional Development. Its principal mission is to create and maintain awareness of the Czech Republic as a country with a wide tourism potential. To this end, CzechTourism takes part in tourism activities and exhibitions abroad, operates 28 foreign agencies across 27 countries, and manages advertising.

The Czech Republic's administrative system of 14 self-governing regions came into effect in 2000. This long-awaited regional set-up significantly changed the organisation of tourism in the country so that, regions are now individually represented by regional administrations, while individual communities and municipalities represent local interests.

The budget of the Ministry for Regional Development, the Czech National Tourism Board, the regions and the provision for co-financing European structural funds in tourism from the national budget totalled EUR 49.5 million in 2006, up 46% on 2005 which in turn was 22% up on the 2004 figure of EUR 27.9 million. The Czech National Tourist Board's budget for 2006 was EUR 9.69 million, up by 7.2% on 2005 which in turn was 9.4% up on 2004's budget of EUR 8.27 million.

Tourism is supported through the budget of the Tourism Department of the Ministry for Regional Development under the following programmes:

- **National Programme of Support for Tourism:** Support is provided in the form of a systemic investment subsidy from the state budget. Subsidies may not exceed 50% of the eligible expenditure of a given project, with the balance financed from the applicant's own resources.

- **Joint Regional Operational Programme:** Support is provided by EU funds through the contribution from the European Regional Development Fund (ERDF). ERDF funds can contribute up to 75% of the government's expenditure on a project, with the balance financed by the state and the applicant's own resources (shares vary according to the type of project).

Tourism related policies and programmes

The main strategic document is the State Tourism Policy, endorsed by the government in 2002. This document outlines a comprehensive approach to tourism development. The Czech Republic's entry into the EU in 2004 required a further updating of the policy in early 2005. The principal policy measures are summarised in Box 3.4.

Recently, a new State Tourism Policy has been prepared for the period 2007-13, in line with the programming period of the European Union. The Czech Republic is aiming to implement all the recommendations of the European Commission in the field of the Tourism.

The Ministry for Regional Development promotes close co-operation among the stakeholders involved in tourism and a better coherence of tourism policies. Major stakeholders include the regional and local authorities, industry, associations (such as the National Hotels and Restaurants Federation, Associations of the Tour Operators and Travel Agencies, Association of Tourism Guides) and tourist destinations.

> **Box 3.4. Major measures of the state tourism policy**
>
> - To set up and implement the Tourism Satellite Account (TSA).
> - To create and implement a system for receiving European Union financial assistance in the area of tourism and determining its focus after 2006.
> - To set up an integrated information system for tourism.
> - To support the development of the tourism product, focusing primarily on sectors such as Spa Tourism, Congress and Incentive Tourism, Rural Tourism, Ecological Tourism and Cycle Tourism.
> - To increase the efficiency of foreign promotion of the Czech Republic on the world tourism market.
> - To secure more effective marketing of tourism in the Czech Republic.

As an important European cultural, historical and natural tourism destination, the country is focusing on the following markets:

- Urban and cultural tourism, nature tourism, sports tourism and spa tourism.
- Meeting, incentive travel, conventions and exhibitions (MICE).

In November 2006, the Czech Statistical Office (CZSO) published the first results of the Tourism Satellite Account of the Czech Republic for 2003-05. The CZSO is currently considering undertaking a regional TSA. There is also an inter-ministerial commission for the co-ordination of tourism development, which links tourism with other policies and examines ways in which national tourism development policies can be made more effective.

Statistical profile

Table 3.17. **Inbound tourism: International arrivals and tourism consumption**

	Units	2001	2002	2003	2004	2005
Visitors[1]	Thousands	..	..	19 004	22 517	23 387
Tourists (overnight visitors)	Thousands	5 405	4 743	5 076	6 061	6 336
of which:						
Germany	Thousands	1 652	1 451	1 439	1 569	1 607
United Kingdom	Thousands	303	306	412	651	657
Italy	Thousands	317	250	281	391	405
United States	Thousands	238	190	221	293	304
Netherlands	Thousands	242	190	239	274	296
Tourism consumption[2]	Billion USD	..	..	3.56	4.58	5.08

StatLink http://dx.doi.org/10.1787/154041521023

1. Visitors include transit passengers.
2. Tourism Satellite Account (TSA) methodology.
Sources: Czech Statistical Office, Tourism Satellite Account, 2007.

Table 3.18. **Outbound tourism: International departures and tourism expenditure**

	Units	2003	2004	2005
Departures[1]	Thousands	36 074	36 650	36 190
Tourism expenditure[2]	Billion USD	2.21	2.44	2.71

StatLink http://dx.doi.org/10.1787/154042832352

1. Data according to the border statistics.
2. Tourism Satellite Account methodology.
Sources: Czech Statistical Office, Tourism Satellite Account, 2007.

Table 3.19. **Employment in tourism**

	Units	2001	2002	2003	2004	2005
Employment in hotels and restaurants	Thousands	**159.4**	**171.7**	**170.7**	**174.8**	**181.7**
Men	Thousands	70.0	76.9	80.0[1]	81.9	84.2
Women	Thousands	89.5	94.8	90.7[1]	92.9	97.4

StatLink http://dx.doi.org/10.1787/154057681317

1. Estimated data.
Sources: Czech Statistical Office, 2007.

Table 3.20. **Tourism in the national economy**

	Units	2001	2002	2003	2004	2005
Tourism as % of gross domestic product	Percentage	..	..	3.4	3.4	3.1
Tourism as % of employment	Percentage	3.4	3.6	3.6	3.7	3.8
Tourism as % of gross value added	Percentage	..	..	3.4	3.1	2.8

StatLink http://dx.doi.org/10.1787/154060800356

Sources: Czech Statistical Office, Tourism Satellite Account, 2007.

Denmark

Tourism in the economy

Tourism accounts for 2.8% of Danish GDP and 3.6% of total employment. The total tourism consumption in Denmark was DKK 64 billion in 2005.

In 2004, there were 9 936 Danish enterprises/firms in the tourism sector, employing almost 29 000 full time employees. More than 50% of these enterprises/firms had no employees (Table 3.23).

In 2006, there were 22.14 million domestic bed nights and 22.25 million foreign bed nights registered in Denmark, almost exactly a 50/50 split. Recent trends are summarised in Table 3.21. The recent fall in bed nights is largely due to a reduction in the key German market.

Tourism organisation

Territorial organisation: Denmark's national tourism organisation, VisitDenmark, is responsible for strategic development and promoting the country as a travel destination in foreign markets (Figure 3.9). At regional level, five regional tourism development organisations receive funding from five newly established regional administrative entities to develop and promote tourism in each region. At local level, the vast majority of Denmark's 98 municipalities operate local tourist information centres, which are funded predominantly by each municipality.

Organisation and links between the national tourism authority and the provinces/regions: Since the beginning of 2007, representatives from the five regions have had a seat on VisitDenmark's governing board. Also, representatives of VisitDenmark have a seat on the governing boards of all five regional tourism development organisations together with tourism enterprises. VisitDenmark and the five regional tourism development companies co-operate extensively on issues relating to developing tourism destinations, new products and regionally-based marketing campaigns serving to promote Denmark in foreign markets.

At national level, tourism policy comes under Denmark's Ministry for Economic and Business Affairs. In February 2006, the Danish Parliament adopted a renewed governmental tourism strategy.

"VisitDenmark" is Denmark's national tourism organisation responsible primarily for developing and promoting Denmark as a travel destination in foreign markets. VisitDenmark operates 8 overseas offices (in Germany, Sweden, Norway, The Netherlands, Italy, Great Britain, Japan and the United States). In addition, VisitDenmark is active on an *ad hoc* basis in selected markets in South East Asia, Spain, France, Russia and Poland.

VisitDenmark, whose legal status is as a business foundation under the Ministry of Economic and Business Affairs, receives its core funding from the state budget. It also generates additional funding from the tourism industry in conjunction with specific

Figure 3.9. **Organisational chart of tourism bodies in Denmark**

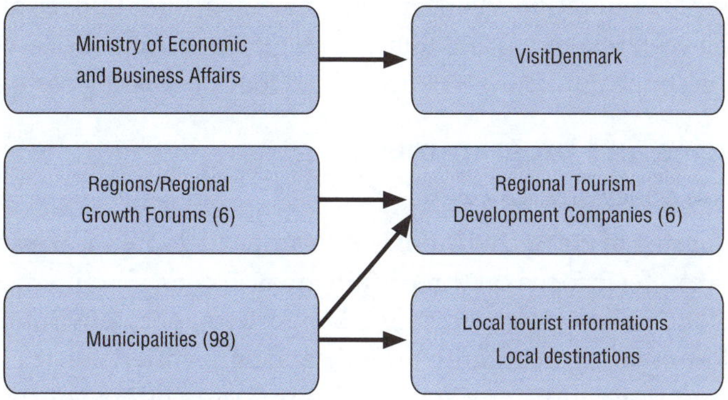

```
Ministry of Economic           →    VisitDenmark
and Business Affairs

Regions/Regional               →    Regional Tourism
Growth Forums (6)                   Development Companies (6)

Municipalities (98)            →    Local tourist informations
                                    Local destinations
```

Note: Bracketed number indicates number of bodies.
Source: OECD, adapted from VisitDenmark, 2007.

activities. As an integral part of the ministry, VisitDenmark has been delegated a range of policy tasks relating to the OECD, EU, the Nordic Council of Ministers and national political administration and development.

Denmark has six regional tourism development companies covering the whole country. Most have been re-structured during 2005-06 as a result of an administrative reform, which reduced the number of Denmark's regional administrative entities from fourteen to five (see below). The sixth regional tourism development company covers the Baltic island of Bornholm.

The main tasks of the six are to develop tourism within Denmark's five administrative regions, to promote regional tourism to the domestic market and to contribute actively in international marketing activities conducted by VisitDenmark. The companies also aim to bring together regional interests in order to develop an agreed tourism policy for their region. These regional companies receive their core funding from the regional administrations.

At local level there are a large number of tourist offices responsible for implementing and co-ordinating tourist services and information as well as product development and marketing at the local level. These are mainly financed by local authorities.

Tourism budget

The main source of funding public tourism promotion and development in Denmark is the national budget. Unlike some other European countries, Denmark has no tradition of using specific tourism taxes to fund public tourism policy activities. In 2006, the national tourism administration (*i.e.* the Ministry of Economic and Business Affairs) had a total budget of around DKK 156 million.

The vast majority of the national tourism budget is allocated to VisitDenmark. The remainder is allocated for funding innovation activities relating to the three primary business areas in Danish tourism; *i)* coastal tourism, *ii)* citybreak tourism and *iii)* MICE tourism. Large parts of this funding are predominantly allocated to VisitDenmark on an *ad hoc* basis because VisitDenmark is a formal part of the ministry and is tasked with implementing national tourism policy initiatives.

For 2006, VisitDenmark received from the Ministry of Economic and Business Affairs DKK 112 million in core funding and DKK 17 million in activity-based funding, raising the total to DKK 129 million from the national budget. Further funding is generated through activities and comes mainly from the private sector. In 2006, the combination of state- and co-funding with private interests resulted in VisitDenmark having a total budget of DKK 224 million for 2006. During the year, marketing and tourism development activities accounted for 62% of total expenditure, with the remaining 38% accounted for by operating costs.

Tourism related policies and programmes

i) National tourism policy strategy 2006-09

In the first quarter of 2006, the Danish Parliament adopted a new national tourism policy which put a strategic focus on three main areas: i) coastal tourism, ii) citybreaks and iii) MICE tourism. The policy aims to create a supportive policy environment by pursuing measures aimed at creating economic growth and innovation for the industry and, in particular, creating the conditions for developing innovative tourism products and destinations through public-private partnerships at national, regional and local level.

The policy also seeks to establish closer institutional ties, co-ordination and co-operation between the national tourism organisation, VisitDenmark, and the six regional tourism development companies, to improve tourism research and education, and to influence policy on transport, infrastructure and accessibility to and within Denmark. In total, DKK 60 million has been earmarked for co-funding in the three main areas of coastal, city breaks and MICE tourism.

ii) "Action Plan for the Global Marketing of Denmark"

The *Action Plan for the Global Marketing of Denmark* was launched by the government in April 2007, partly reflecting a perception that Denmark – as a nation in which to do business, invest, study and visit – is not well known abroad and suffers from a weak and relatively blurred image affecting Denmark's global competitiveness. The action plan sets out to generate a clear and positive image of Denmark abroad and ensure a strong position in the global competition for creative and competent workers, tourists, students, investment and global market share. The objective is for Denmark to be ranked among the top ten OECD and new growth countries in 2015 in terms of awareness of the country's strength and competencies. In the 3rd quarter of 2006, Denmark ranked fourteenth.

The action plan contains a number of cross-cutting initiatives aiming to ensure a more effective and co-ordinated marketing. They include a general initiative called "the Branding Denmark Initiative" (*DanmarksInitiativet*) seeking to boost awareness of Denmark and improving coherence in marketing messages. The main cross-cutting initiative is the creation of the Marketing Denmark Fund (*Fonden til Markedsføring af Danmark*) with the purpose of boosting awareness of Denmark's strengths and competencies abroad, especially by supporting and promoting larger-scale activities with promising potential such as events, campaigns, conferences, and promotional activities that generate publicity about Denmark.

The promotional action programme is based on four main themes: i) "responsible and balanced" ii) "high quality", iii) "experimental and courageous", iv) "environmental awareness, simplicity and efficiency". Total budget allocations for this programme are DKK 412 million, with DKK 60 million earmarked for co-financing the development, launch and implementation of initiatives relating to coastal tourism and city-break tourism. VisitDenmark will serve as an implementing body for the tourism initiatives in the action plan.

iii) Structural reform

In June 2004, Denmark revised its local government structure, reducing the number of local municipalities in Denmark from 274 to 99. This came into force in April 2007. Five new administrative regions were created: *i)* Northeast Zealand and metropolitan Copenhagen (including the island of Bornholm), *ii)* North Jutland, *iii)* Central Jutland, *iv)* South Denmark and *v)* Zealand.

The main area of responsibility for the five new regions will be healthcare and hospital services, but the regions will also carry out tasks relating to regional business policy, including tourism. Regional Growth Forums have been established as legal entities, with each forum responsible for administration and investment of comprehensive public funding (from *e.g.* state, regional and EU-sources) aimed at regional business development. Each forum has the option of allocating investment funds to selected sectors, including tourism, with the forums being governed by nominated members covering politicians, employer and employee representatives.

Co-operation with the tourism industry and civil society

Co-operation within the Danish tourism sector takes place on many different levels involving both private partners and public organisations. At national level, public-private co-operation is organised and implemented by VisitDenmark, whose high level of co-funding illustrates its success in this area. Such co-operation has been widely institutionalised through the establishment of consultative boards relating to coastal tourism, city-break and activity-intensive tourism.

The six regional tourism development companies are also funded by a combination of public grants and private sector co-operation, although important administrative restrictions have been imposed on most regional tourism development companies when it comes to investing public resource in specific marketing campaigns and activities abroad. Such activities must predominantly be co-ordinated with VisitDenmark. The traditional challenge of co-ordinating publicly-funded activities in tourism at the national and regional level has been tackled by giving each regional company a seat on the VisitDenmark board with VisitDenmark having reciprocal arrangements.

At the local level, most of Denmark's 98 municipalities tend to finance and run local tourist offices and tourism information centres, the main tasks of which are to provide relevant information to visitors and guests once they reach their chosen holiday region.

International and cross-border activities

Denmark plays an active role when it comes to co-operation at European level on tourism and participates in co-operation among the national tourist boards of the Nordic countries, the work carried out by the OECD Tourism Committee and the European Travel Commission's working groups concerning research, new media and marketing respectively.

Statistical profile

Table 3.21. **Inbound tourism: International arrivals and tourism consumption**

	Units	2001	2002	2003	2004	2005
Arrivals in hotels and similar establishments	Thousands	4 088	3 628	3 779	3 663	4 562
Bed nights in hotels and similar establishments	Thousands	23 117	23 311	23 777	22 496	21 620
of which:						
Germany	Thousands	15 003	15 113	15 345	13 941	13 246
Norway	Thousands	2 057	2 301	2 396	2 300	2 206
Sweden	Thousands	2 314	2 247	2 237	2 167	2 031
Netherlands	Thousands	976	960	1 106	1 155	1 115
Tourism receipts	Million DKK	33 404	37 500	34 639	33 975	30 087

StatLink http://dx.doi.org/10.1787/154220788185

Sources: Statistics Denmark and VisitDenmark, 2007.

Table 3.22. **Outbound tourism: International departures and expenditure**[1]

	Units	2002	2003	2004	2005	2006
Departures	Thousands	..	..	..	3 532	4 054
Tourism Expenditure	Million DKK	46 104	43 861	43 546	39 082	41 494

StatLink http://dx.doi.org/10.1787/154236207601

..: Data not available.
1. Long-term leisure travel involving journeys with a minimum of four bed nights spent on location.
Sources: Statistics Denmark and VisitDenmark, 2007.

Table 3.23. **Number of firms and full time employees in tourism by size class (2004)**

Size (Number of employees)	Number of firms	Full time employees
0	5 041	..
1-9	4 268	11 028
10-19	375	4 911
20-49	191	5 672
50-99	39	2 699
100+	22	4 589
Total	**9 936**	**28 899**

StatLink http://dx.doi.org/10.1787/154261255272

Source: Statistics Denmark, 2005.

Table 3.24. **Tourism in the national economy**

	Units	2001	2002	2003	2004	2005
Tourism as % of gross value added	Percent	4.1	4.2	4.1	4.2	4.6
Total tourism employed persons	Thousands	144.0	143.6	144.3	146.7	156.5
Tourism as % of total employment	Percent	5.2	5.2	5.3	5.3	5.6

StatLink http://dx.doi.org/10.1787/154304356182

Sources: Statistics Denmark and VisitDenmark, 2007.

Finland

Tourism in the economy

Domestic tourists account for nearly 73% of all overnights in Finland, although the share of international travellers is increasing. In 2006, the number of foreign visitors to Finland increased by over 6% to reach 5.3 million. The consumption of international visitors has increased by 12.5% between 2004 and 2006, and represents 26% of total tourism consumption (which was EUR 9.6 billion in 2005).

Finland provides Tourism Satellite Account data on an annual basis and has also developed a Regional Tourism Satellite Account system. Tourism accounted for 2.4% of GDP in 2005 (Table 3.28). At the end of that year, there were 22 400 tourism characteristic enterprises, employing some 130 000 persons full- or part-time. In 2005, tourism employment represented 7.2% of total employment. Tourism receipts were EUR 1 891 million, according to preliminary information for 2006.

Tourism organisation

The Finnish Ministry of Trade and Industry (MTI) is responsible for tourism policy, the overall development of inbound and domestic tourism and the co-ordination of supportive measures, drafting and co-ordination of tourism legislation and international tourism relations (bilateral and multilateral) (Figure 3.10).

Figure 3.10. **Organisational chart of tourism bodies in Finland**

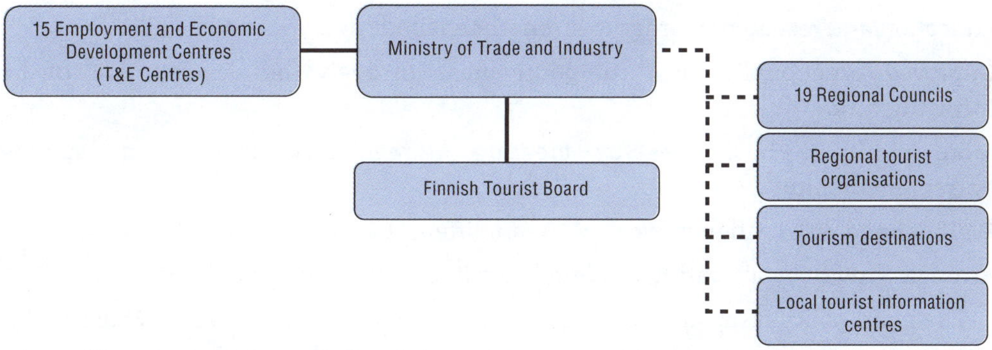

Note: There will be substantial changes in the administrative structure of Finnish ministries at the beginning of 2008. It is expected that the Ministry of Trade and Industry, the Ministry for Labour and certain divisions of the Ministry of the Interior will be merged to one new ministry.
Source: OECD, adapted from Finnish Tourist Board, 2007.

At the regional level, the partners are 19 regional councils and 15 Employment and Economic Development Centres (T&E Centres). Regional Councils are non-governmental, statutory joint municipal authorities, which are responsible for the development of their territories. T&E Centres are regional governmental agencies providing a comprehensive range of advisory and development services for businesses, entrepreneurs, and private individuals. Each has a business department (under the MTI), a rural department (under the Ministry of Agriculture and Forestry) and a labour market department (under the Ministry of Labour). The T&E Centres are significant specialists and contributors of EU funding.

Tourism budget

Budget of the National Tourism Administration

The National Tourism Administration is part of the Ministry of Industry and has no separate budget. One person is in charge of tourism related affairs. Tourism development is funded mainly by the general budget.

Budget of the National Tourism Organisation

In 2005, the total budget of the National Tourism Organisation (the Finnish Tourist Board) was EUR 21 million, of which 86% was allocated by the Ministry of Trade and Industry.

During the period 2000-03, a total of 3 555 partly or wholly publicly funded projects for the promotion of tourism were implemented. They amounted to EUR 383.2 million, of which 68% was funded from public resources.

Tourism related policies and programmes

The new national tourism strategy "*Finland's Tourism Strategy to 2020 and Action Plan for 2007-13*" was published at the beginning of June 2006. This has been developed through close co-operation with over 2 000 stakeholders. The government approved a new Tourism Policy in 2006. Following the adoption of these two documents, the government has worked to implement them, focusing on the following items:

- A stronger country image in tourism internationally.
- An unbroken service chain in order to raise customer satisfaction.
- Easy accessibility (country and destinations) crucial to the development of tourism industry.
- Education and research in order to strengthen labour and vocational skills.
- Improved functionality and competitiveness through the development of better infrastructure.
- More profitable businesses by creating a regulatory environment supporting entrepreneurship.
- Well-defined distribution of work between different tourism stakeholders.
- Stronger growth by allocating funding according to strategic guidelines.

The main policy issue at present is the reform of the Finnish Tourist Board (FTB), the government agency that works under the aegis of the Ministry of Trade and Industry. In future, the FTB's main functions will be focused on the promotion of Finland's image abroad, following up new market information and delivering better market intelligence to the tourism industry, and co-ordinating large tourism product development projects.

> Box 3.5. **Major forms of inbound tourism**
>
> The major forms of inbound tourism to Finland can be defined and measured on a general level in two ways – by trip purpose and by seasonality. In these groups there are numerous sub-groups whose importance is difficult to measure, such as Christmas tourism.
>
> In 2005, the most significant travellers (as measured by their economic importance) were business travellers (spending approx. EUR 553 million), closely followed by leisure travellers (EUR 522 million) and, of lesser economic importance, those visiting friends and relatives (VFR) travellers (EUR 114 million). Multi-purpose and other travellers spent approx. EUR 178 million. The summer tourism season (June-Sept.) is worth EUR 614 million and winter tourism (November-April) EUR 518 million. During the summer, leisure travellers are clearly the most significant group, but the importance of leisure travel during the winter is also increasing as more and more travellers are coming to Finland for winter holidays. In social terms, leisure travel with nature related activities and countryside accommodation is the most important form of tourism as it brings income and employment to otherwise declining regions in Finland.

Linkages between tourism and other policies

The MTI will soon produce a study of the impact of taxes and other regulatory payments on the tourism industry, together with a comparative study of the situation in other countries. The study will serve as a basis for possible governmental regulatory reform proposals.

The relationship between culture and tourism has benefited from enhanced co-operation over recent years, in particular at governmental level. The challenge for the future is to translate this to the entrepreneurial level.

A large study was completed in 2006, assessing the future needs, quantity and quality of education in tourism. The results will be used to formulate educational policy concerning tourism, such as in the Tourism Sector Education Committee. Also, a study of foreign direct investment in tourism in Finland has recently been completed.

Statistical profile

Table 3.25. **Inbound tourism: International arrivals and receipts**

	Units	2002	2003	2004	2005	2006
Visitors (including same day visitors)	Thousands	4 697	4 572	4 854	5 038	5 345
of which:						
Russia	Thousands	1 537	1 589	1 647	1 684	1 737
Sweden	Thousands	766	780	794	783	779
Estonia	Thousands	303	230	383	457	503
Germany	Thousands	394	347	363	342	369
United Kingdom	Thousands	276	264	251	233	317
Tourism receipts	Million EUR	1 664	1 656	1 669	1 757	1 891

StatLink http://dx.doi.org/10.1787/154323471050

Sources: Statistics Finland and Finnish Tourist Board, 2007.

Table 3.26. **Outbound tourism: International departures and expenditure**

	Units	2001	2002	2003	2004	2005	2006
Foreign trips from Finland	Thousands	5 825	5 857	5 586	5 798	5 902	5 756
Tourism expenditure	Million EUR	2 070	2 119	2 150	2 273	2 461	2 723

StatLink http://dx.doi.org/10.1787/154342388363

Sources: Statistics Finland and Finnish Tourist Board, 2007.

Table 3.27. **Employment in tourism**

	Units	2000	2001	2002	2003	2004
Employment in tourism sector	Employees	**170 680**	**168 830**	**168 221**	**169 090**	**170 499**
of which: Hotels and similar	Employees	13 052	12 747	12 401	12 077	11 871
Restaurants and similar	Employees	39 892	40 650	41 528	41 581	42 366
Passenger transportation	Employees	84 217	81 670	79 579	79 317	78 040
Travel agencies and similar	Employees	5 211	5 206	4 952	4 895	4 662

StatLink http://dx.doi.org/10.1787/154351325633

Sources: Statistics Finland and Finnish Tourist Board, 2007.

Table 3.28. **Tourism industry in the national economy**

	Units	2001	2002	2003	2004	2005
Tourism as % of gross domestic product[1]	Percentage	2.3	2.3	2.3	2.4	2.4
Tourism as % of employment[2]	Percentage	7.1	7.1	7.1	7.2	7.2
Domestic tourism as % of final consumption[3]	Percentage	6.0	6.1	6.2	6.3	6.5
Tourism share of service export						
Travel services	Percentage	15.9	15.4	16.7	14.0	14.5
Travel and international passenger transport services	Percentage	22.8	21.8	23.9	20.2	20.4
Tourism Satellite Account main aggregates						
Total tourism demand in Finland	Million EUR	7.97	8.29	8.61	9.01	9.60
Domestic leisure tourism demand	Million EUR	3.96	4.21	4.43	4.68	5.02
Inbound tourism demand total[4]	Million EUR	2.31	2.37	2.37	2.40	2.47
Value added generated by tourism demand[5]	Million EUR	2.85	2.93	2.97	3.11	3.26

StatLink http://dx.doi.org/10.1787/154424005751

1. Tourism value added as percentage of GDP at basic prices.
2. Total personnel in tourism characteristic activities.
3. Business trips paid by employers not included.
4. International passenger transport fares included.
5. Employers expenses included.

Sources: Statistics Finland and Finnish Tourist Board, 2007.

France

Tourism in the economy

Tourism is an important sector of the French economy. It accounts for 6.3% of GDP and generates some two million direct and indirect jobs in 200 000 companies, most of which are small or medium-sized. In recent years France, which is the world leader in the number of foreign tourist arrivals, has experienced exceptional growth, in particular up until 2001, making tourism activity the front ranking sector of the national economy in terms of the foreign currency inflow generated.

Tourism organisation

In a new context of globalisation that has many and at times unpredictable environmental, economic, cultural and social consequences, the central government is seen as being the guarantor of controlled, coherent and sustainable tourism development (Figure 3.11).

Figure 3.11. **Organisational chart of tourism bodies in France**

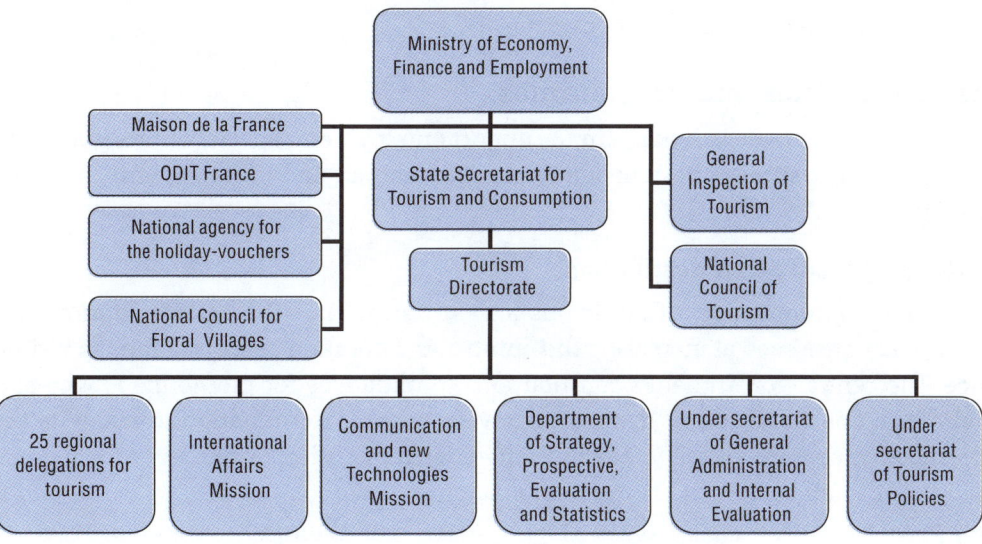

Source: OECD, adapted from Ministry of Economy, Finance and Employment, 2007.

This being the case, central government must anticipate developments that might have an influence on tourism activity, taking steps to develop the country's assets even further, ensuring that its structures are adapted to the national and international context and the sector's new requirements, strengthening the partnership between the National

Tourism Administration and public and private stakeholders and associations in the field of tourism, promoting the development of employment and social cohesion and, lastly, integrating into all its initiatives the key European and international dimension that makes France the world's top-ranking tourism destination.

The Interministerial Committees on Tourism (*Comités Interministériels sur le Tourisme*, CIT) convened by the Prime Minister successively in 2003 and 2004, constituted an important stage in the implementation of France's tourism strategy for the coming decade.

The Tourism Programme also includes the necessary modernisation of government. The organisation and functioning of the administration of tourism have been rationalised in recent years in order to meet tourism stakeholders' needs better by: i) encouraging the initiatives of the Public Interest Grouping *Odit France*, ii) renewing the National Tourism Council (*Conseil national du Tourisme*), a genuine partner of the tourism sector whose membership was reduced from 400 to 200 members to make it more effective and responsive, iii) consolidating most departments and bodies within the *Maison du Tourisme* in order to develop synergies and promote exchanges and, lastly, iv) increasing the resources devoted to the Regional Delegations for Tourism.

Tourism budget

The budget allocated to the Ministry responsible for tourism (*ministère délégué du Tourisme*) to implement its policies in 2007 will be EUR 86.2 million in commitment authorisations and EUR 83.7 million in appropriations, increases of 8% and 7% respectively on the initial 2006 budget.

The basic missions of the Tourism Programme for 2007 are to support the tourism economy by promoting France as a destination abroad and implementing the Tourism Quality Plan, and to widen access to holidays for all by reorganising the social component and continuing the policy of local contracts.

Tourism related policies and programmes

In order to create new dynamism to support employment, special efforts will be made to promote France's image both inside France and abroad and to implement the Tourism Quality Plan.

Promotion of France as a destination

The strong promotion of France as a destination and the efforts to enhance its attractiveness are aimed at increasing the number and duration of stays of foreign visitors in France. The central government's contributions to initiatives for promoting France abroad but also at home clearly show the central government's determination to make its action more effective abroad. This is a key challenge, for it is an important lever for increasing employment in all sectors of the tourism economy. The potential already exists and now needs to be supported (*Maison de la France*; the information, promotion and reservation platform *www.franceguide.com*; the reinforcement of promotional campaigns such as "bienvenue en France", "la France des trois océans", "la campagne vous invite à la campagne").

The quality of supply

Stimulating tourism consumption in France also requires improving the quality of supply. This will be promoted by implementing the Tourism Quality Plan and awarding the "Tourism Quality" label. The objective is to introduce greater clarity into French tourism supply and ensure better marketing. This "trademark" will receive specific financing for the third consecutive year.

In addition, there must be better knowledge of tourism demand both nationally and locally so that supply can be continuously adapted to consumer demand. It is for these reasons that the appropriations requested for 2007 for tourism have been increased.

Access to holidays for all

In order to enable everyone to gain access to holidays, the Tourism Programme is continuing its initiatives in support of social tourism. The objective is to give greater coherence to social initiatives and to work to enable specific sections of the public to go on holiday (seniors, the disabled, poor families for example). Continuing previous initiatives, and within the framework of the ministerial reform strategy, the Tourism Programme is continuing to modernise. The creation of a social component has been effective since November 2006 with the merger of the grant and voucher programmes *GIP Bourse Solidarité Vacances* and the *Agence Nationale pour les Chèques Vacances*.

In addition, specific local contracts are being signed in order to help professionals to bring their facilities into compliance with the Law of 11 February 2006 for the equal opportunity, participation and citizenship of disabled persons.

State-Region project contracts

The national public policies defined by the Minister responsible for tourism will be implemented at the local level by means of joint projects between central government and the regions through specific local contracts. This is enabling tourism to play an important role in centres of rural excellence and it is important to provide support both to local and regional units and to tourism destinations concerned with ensuring sustainable development.

Statistical profile

Table 3.29. **Inbound tourism: International arrivals and receipts**

	Unit	2002	2003	2004	2005	2006
Visitors[1]	Thousands	**77 012**	**75 048**	**75 121**	**75 908**	**79 100**
of which:						
United Kingdom	Thousands	14 958	14 845	14 648	13 436	13 642
Germany	Thousands	14 346	14 047	13 728	13 689	13 079
Belgium and Luxembourg	Thousands	8 472	8 614	8 771	10 216	9 806
Netherlands	Thousands	12 631	12 486	12 387	6 816	7 730
Italy	Thousands	7 874	7 511	7 400	6 961	7 624
Tourism receipts	Million EUR	34 190	32 347	36 409	35 381	36 906

StatLink http://dx.doi.org/10.1787/154455736688

1. Before 2005: Estimate Direction du Tourisme; since 2005: Survey of foreign visitors (DT/Banque de France/TNS Sofres).
Sources: Direction du Tourisme and Banque de France, 2007.

Table 3.30. **Outbound tourism: International trips and expenditure**

	Unit	2002	2003	2004	2005	2006
Number of trips	Thousands	18 316	18 575	22 500	22 300	22 400
Tourism expenditure	Million EUR	20 580	20 713	23 171	24 546	24 841

StatLink http://dx.doi.org/10.1787/154456751360

Sources: Direction du Tourisme and Banque de France, 2007.

Table 3.31. **Employment in tourism**[1]

	2001	2002	2003	2004	2005[2]
Total	**714 650**	**736 476**	**744 357**	**772 392**	**785 983**
of which:					
Hotels with restaurant	145 602	145 980	143 501	145 913	144 479
Hotels without restaurant	26 057	27 242	28 178	33 615	34 127
Camping sites	7 030	7 283	7 393	7 619	7 736
Traditional restaurant	283 249	294 083	302 790	319 555	325 418
Fast-food restaurant	98 954	105 236	109 093	109 637	116 189
Funicular, mechanic lifts	12 128	12 831	13 615	14 594	14 797
Travel agencies and tourism offices	46 796	47 421	47 954	47 808	48 560
Thermal activities and thalassotherapy	6 168	6 096	5 751	5 512	5 672

StatLink http://dx.doi.org/10.1787/154506072747

1. Employees to 31 December of the year.
2. Preliminary data
Source: UNEDIC, 2007.

Table 3.32. **Tourism in the national economy**

	Unit	2002	2003	2004	2005	2006
Tourism as % of gross domestic product[1]	Percentage	6.6	6.4	6.4	6.3	6.3
Travel as % of services exports[2]	Percentage	37.6	37.0	36.7	37.0	39.2
Internal tourism consumption as % of total consumption of households	Percentage	11.3	11.3	11.3	11.3	11.3
Public income generated by tourism[2]	Million EUR				8 333	8 596
Number of establishments[3]		127 397	129 178	133 074	134 197	..
of which: Hotels		21 683	21 417	21 485	20 906	..
Restaurants		70 178	72 445	76 345	77 760	..
Travel agencies		7 425	7 384	7 470	7 395	..

StatLink http://dx.doi.org/10.1787/154527732234

1. Ratio between internal tourism consumption and GDP.
2. Including the VAT of residents and of non-residents and other taxes. Excludes certain taxes related to tourism that are not immediately received.
3. Number of establishments linked to the UNEDIC on 31 December 2005 in Metropolitan France. Provisional figures.
Sources: INSEE, Direction du Tourisme and UNEDIC, 2007.

Germany

Tourism in the economy

According to TSA calculations, the direct added value effects of tourism in 2000 were about EUR 57.5 billion, 3.2% of GDP. Up to 2.8 million jobs in Germany depend directly or indirectly on tourism. There are some 52 900 accommodation facilities with more than 2.5 million beds.

Tourism in Germany employs some 776 000 people, of which 64% are female. The sector (hotels and restaurants only) employs some 2.12% of the national labour force (Table 3.35).

In 2006, 23.5 million international tourists arrived in Germany (up by 9.6% on 2005 which in turn was 6.8% up on 2004's figure of 20.1 million), generating 48.3 million overnight stays* (up by 9.8%) and spending EUR 26.2 billion (12.0% up on 2005). The main origin markets for incoming tourism in Germany in 2006 were the Netherlands, the United States of America, the United Kingdom, Switzerland and Italy (Table 3.33).

Germany is the favourite travel destination of the Germans themselves. The number of domestic arrivals in 2006 was 101.7 million (2.6% up on 2005 which in turn was 2.9% ahead of 2004's figure of 96.3 million). In 2006, Germans generated 295.7 million overnight stays in the country (0.8% up on the previous year), the equivalent of nearly 85% of all overnight stays in Germany.

City tourism is the motor of tourism in Germany generating a quarter of all overnight stays. Other important segments are cultural tourism, the MICE sector, spa and health tourism, and hiking and cycling.

In terms of the tourism industry's structure, various global players are based in Germany, such as TUI AG, Thomas Cook and Rewe Touristik, with aggregated turnover of over EUR 10 billion, in addition to major airlines and Deutsche Bahn AG. Nonetheless, 90% of the tourism industry consists of SMEs, with some 57 000 companies in the accommodation sector, 195 000 in catering, 17 000 travel agents, 2 000 tour operators, 3 000 camping ground operators, 5 800 bus companies, 296 airlines and 36 cruise lines.

Germany is the leading location for trade fairs worldwide and ranks second for conferences and congresses (2004) behind the USA. Among the world's most popular travel destinations (by revenue) Germany ranked seventh in 2005 behind the USA, Spain, France, Italy, United Kingdom and China.

Tourism organisation

Tourism policy is an integral part of the German government's economic policy. Tourism policy, which aims at strengthening business self-reliance, improving the policy

---

* Overnight stays in accommodation facilities including camping sites with nine and more beds.

Figure 3.12. **Organisational chart of tourism bodies in Germany.**

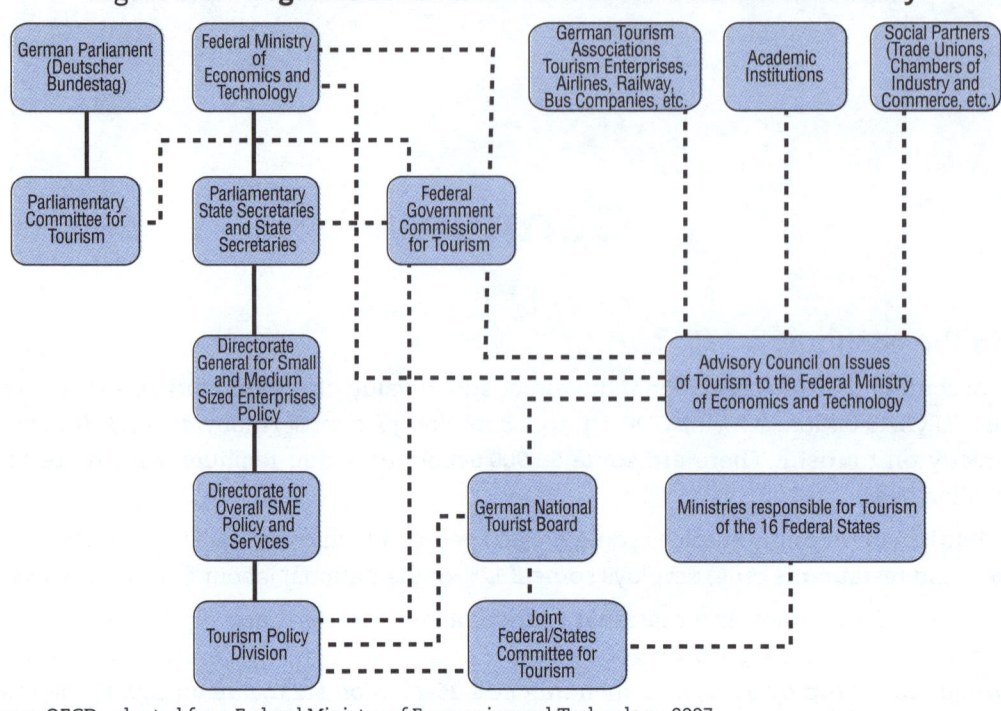

Source: OECD, adapted from Federal Ministry of Economics and Technology, 2007.

framework for the tourism industry and boosting its competitiveness, is the responsibility of the Federal Minister of Economics and Technology (Figure 3.12).

The planning, development and direct support of tourism is the responsibility of the 16 federal states (*Länder*). Each federal state has a ministry responsible for tourism and a separate tourism marketing organisation. The daily direct tourism business (information for German and foreign tourists, service and guidance, quality initiatives, co-operation with tour operators, etc.) is organised by local authorities and municipalities.

The German National Tourist Board (Deutsche Zentrale für Tourismus – DZT) is responsible for tourism marketing abroad. Its yearly budget is mainly funded by the Federal Government; this was EUR 25 million in 2007, compared to EUR 24.5 million in 2005. The Federal Government also supports various projects directly or indirectly linked to tourism, *e.g.* support of ecological tourism, accessible tourism for all, youth and children's tourism.

At the end of 2005, the office of a Federal Government Commissioner for Tourism was established in the Economics Ministry. The Tourism Commissioner acts as an intermediary between the tourism sector and government, with the various players at federal, state and local levels, with the aim of encouraging growth and employment in the sector.

A Parliamentary Committee for Tourism exists in the German Parliament (Deutscher Bundestag). The Federal Government reports regularly to the Tourism Committee. A Joint Federal-Länder Committee for Tourism has also been established to co-ordinate tourism policy. This consists of the Federal Ministry of Economics and Technology and the state tourism ministries. The Committee exchanges information, co-ordinates activities in the field of tourism policy, and co-ordinates joint measures by the Federal and the Länder governments. There is no written legal basis for the existence, responsibilities or tasks of this body, which is based on voluntary co-operation.

In order to bring together the interests of government, the tourism industry, the academic world, the municipal bodies and the trade associations, an "Advisory Council on Issues of Tourism to the Federal Minister of Economics and Technology" was set up in 1977. The Advisory Council is tasked with advising the Federal Minister on questions of tourism policy and supporting him with expertise.

Tourism budget

The 2007 budget of the National Tourism Administration (Federal Ministry of Economics and Technology) was EUR 25 million for the German National Tourist Board (DZT) and EUR 1.4 million for supporting projects to increase the performance of SME's in the tourism industry. The total 2007 budget for the DZT is EUR 34.3 million (including the EUR 25.0 million provided by the Federal Ministry of Economics and Technology).

Tourism related policies and programmes

German national tourism policy is focused on the following main points:

- Increasing economic growth and employment.
- Strengthening Germany as a tourism destination by developing higher quality tourism products and human resources, promoting the sustainable development of tourism, the use of new technologies and improving tourism and traffic infrastructure).
- Further high level support of the German national tourist board.
- Meeting the demographic challenges and promoting accessible tourism for all.

The development of tourism is strongly influenced by other policy areas, *e.g.* tax and fiscal policy, transport policy, health policy, labour, social and education policies, foreign policy, etc. Each of these policy fields has its own legislation which affects tourism to a greater or lesser extent. Further to this, some aspects of tourism are regulated by specific laws, *e.g.* on travel contracts, or the act on accommodation statistics. The Federal Ministry of Economics and Technology and the Parliamentary Committee for Tourism observe the draft decisions of new laws and take care that they will take into account the interests and needs of the tourism industry in an appropriate manner.

The Federal Government works closely together with the associations and enterprises within the German tourism industry with the aim of providing an appropriate policy framework for tourism companies and enabling them to meet global competition successfully.

Like all other small and medium-sized enterprises (SMEs), companies in the tourism sector can take advantage of the instruments of support for SMEs offered by the Federal and Länder governments, *i.e.* they can receive support when starting up, when investing, when accessing foreign markets, and in many other areas.

Co-operation with the tourism industry is mainly focused on the following issues:

- Advisory Council on Issues of Tourism to the Federal Minister of Economics and Technology.
- Annual meetings of the leading tourism associations.
- Advisory Councils and Boards of Directors of different institutions (*e.g.* German National Tourist Board (DZT), German Tourism Association (DTV), research facilities).
- Tourism Committee of the German Parliament (Bundestag).
- International Tourism Exchange Berlin (ITB), Germany Travel Mart and other events.

Statistical profile

Table 3.33. Inbound tourism: International arrivals and receipts

	Units	2002	2003	2004	2005	2006
Tourists (overnight visitors)[1]	Millions	**18.0**	**18.4**	**20.1**	**21.5**	**23.5**
of which:						
Netherlands	Millions	5.6	5.8	8.0	8.4	8.8
United States	Millions	4.0	3.7	4.3	4.4	4.7
United Kingdom	Millions	3.4	3.3	3.8	4.0	4.5
Switzerland	Millions	2.3	2.5	2.9	3.2	3.5
Italy	Millions	2.1	2.2	2.5	2.7	2.9
Tourism receipts	Billion EUR	20.3	20.4	22.2	23.4	26.2

StatLink http://dx.doi.org/10.1787/154532812128

1. Including camp sites.
Sources: Statistisches Bundesamt, Deutsche Bundesbank, 2007.

Table 3.34. Outbound tourism: International departures and expenditure

	Units	2002	2003	2004	2005	2006
Departures[1]	Millions	80.4	85.3	84.9	86.6	..
Tourism expenditures	Billion EUR	55.5	57.2	57.0	58.4	60.6

StatLink http://dx.doi.org/10.1787/154552586427

1. At least one overnight stay, including business travel.
Sources: Statistisches Bundesamt, Deutsche Bundesbank, 2007.

Table 3.35. Employment in tourism

	Units	2003	2004	2005
Employment of hotels and restaurants/total employment	Percentage	1.90	1.89	2.12
Hotels and restaurants (male employees)	Thousands	252	250	282
of which: Hotel and restaurant owners/executives	Thousands	118	117	123
Restaurant specialists, stewards	Thousands	89	87	89
Hotels and restaurants (female employees)	Thousands	437	427	494
of which: Hotel and restaurant owners/executives	Thousands	84	81	83
Restaurant specialists, stewardesses	Thousands	231	230	251

StatLink http://dx.doi.org/10.1787/154563212862

Source: Statistisches Bundesamt, 2007.

Table 3.36. Tourism in the national economy

	Units	2001	2002	2003	2004	2005	2006
Added value of tourism sector	Billion EUR	57.5[1]	..	..	..	..	..
Tourism as % of gross domestic product	Percentage	3.2[1]	..	..	..	..	..
Tourism[2] as % of total services	Percentage	4.10	4.06	4.03	4.14	4.26	..
Domestic Tourism as % of final consumption	Percentage	..	3.74	3.65	3.65	3.62	3.64

StatLink http://dx.doi.org/10.1787/154632346824

1. Data refer to the year 2000.
2. Aggregated sectors: Hotels and restaurants, transport sector including flight services, shipping services.
Sources: Statistisches Bundesamt, Deutsche Bundesbank, 2007.

Greece

Tourism in the economy

According to recent assessments the contribution of tourism (direct and indirect impact) to the Greek economy represents 18.2% of GDP. The "hotels and restaurants" sector represents half of tourism activities and directly contributes 10.4% to GDP. In 2005, the average tourist expenditure per capita was USD 1.073, placing Greece in 10th position worldwide. Taking into account international tourist receipts, which in 2005 totalled EUR 11 billion, this is the equivalent of EUR 1 200 for each resident, placing Greece in fifth position in world tourism by this measure.

It is estimated that 840 000 people are employed directly and indirectly in the tourism sector, 19% of the workforce. In 2006, 32 000 new jobs were created in the tourism industry, confirming that, for every 30 arrivals, a new job is created. This corresponds to 6.8% of the unemployed total in 2005. International tourist arrivals rose by 5.6% in 2005 and 7.5% in 2006, leading to total arrivals of some 16 million. Tourism receipts rose by 4.7% in 2005 and 5% in 2006.

Tourism organisation

The Ministry of Tourism, established in 2004, is the competent authority for policy making and programming in tourism (Figure 3.13). The Ministry of Tourism supervises the National Tourism Organisation, the Organisation for Education and Training, the Hotel Chamber of Greece and the Tourism Development Company. The National Tourism Organisation is responsible for implementing marketing programs and for licensing hotels and tourism enterprises under the guidance of the Ministry of Tourism. It is also responsible for the promotion of Greece, advertising and communications policy and for arranging the country's participation in international exhibitions, conferences and events in Greece and abroad.

The regional tourism authorities come under the supervision of the National Tourism Organisation and are responsible for the implementation of tourism policy at the regional level.

Tourism budget

In 2006, the budget of the Ministry of Tourism is about EUR 71 million, including a budget of EUR 34 million for the National Tourism Organisation. The National Tourism Organisation also receives funding from other sources.

Figure 3.13. **Organisational chart of tourism bodies in Greece**

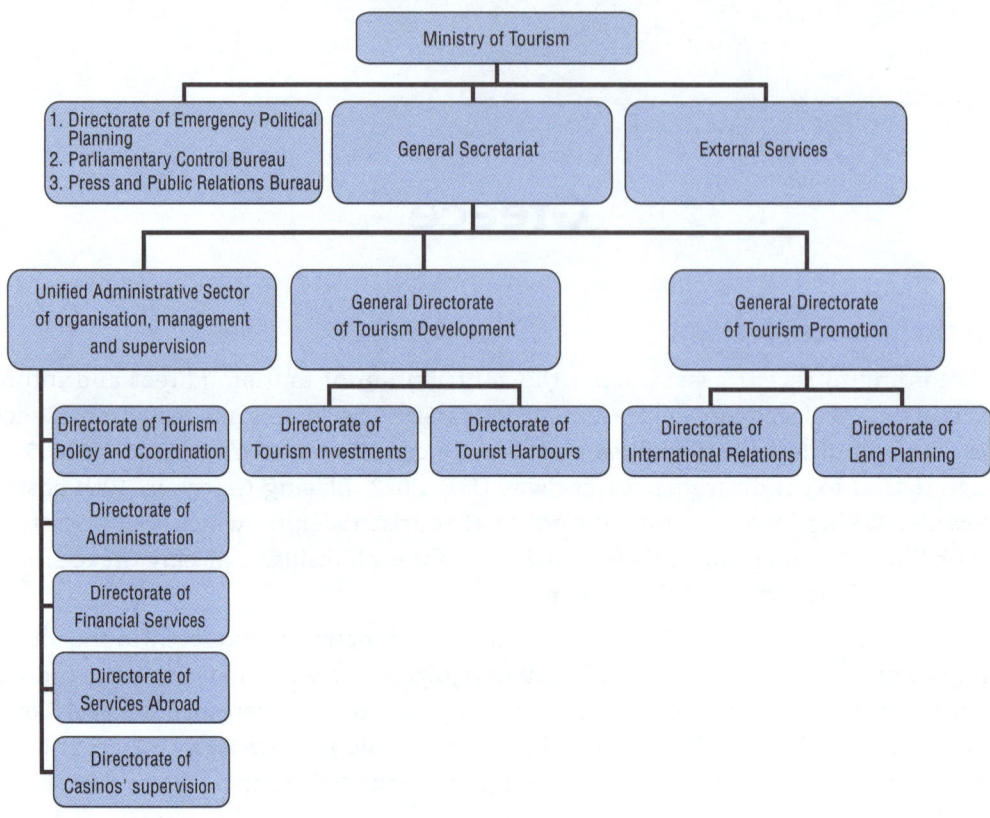

Source: OECD, adapted from Ministry of Tourism, 2007.

Tourism related policies and programmes

Tourism is an important sector of the Greek economy and a priority sector in the national agenda. Greece has a rich cultural and natural heritage which are important assets for the development of tourism. The challenge of current tourism planning in Greece is to develop a strategy which offers opportunities for investment and employment but also respects and enhances the country's rich endowment in the long term and contributes to the broader development strategy of the country.

Greece is developing a 10-year strategy of which the main objectives are upgrading, diversifying and enriching the quality of the tourist product. Tourism is developed in coherence with the national strategy for sustainable development. The strategy will contribute to:

- A new handling of Greece and a stronger positioning of the destination internationally.
- Co-operating regionally by, for example, creating alliances in marketing by developing common itineraries along historical routes with other countries in the region.
- Capitalising on the opportunities that exist in order to diversify the product, through the development of special types of tourism such as spa and thalassotherapy, beauty and wellness; gastronomy, cultural and urban tourism; conventions, exhibitions and business tourism (MICE); eco-tourism, adventures in nature; and agro-tourism such as sea tourism, diving and yachting.

- Promoting Greece as a place for investment, capitalising on the wider modernisation that has taken place as a result of the Olympic Games.

The private sector is actively involved in policy development in the sense that there is a lot of communication and discussion about the problems and concerns of the Greek tourism community and how these can be solved. The Ministry of Tourism is currently promoting incentives for public–private partnerships, such as partnerships to further develop large scale events.

The Ministry of Tourism has been instrumental in promoting greater co-operation, which has lead to the creation of co-operative platforms among public agencies and international stakeholders responsible for the analysis of tourism.

The World Travel and Tourism Council Tourism Satellite Account (WTTC TSA) is currently being integrated, has been delivered to the Ministry and is about to be put in practice.

Statistical profile

Table 3.37. **Inbound tourism: International arrivals and receipts**

	Unit	2001	2002	2003	2004	2005	2006
Tourists	Thousands	**14 679**	**14 918**	**14 785**	**14 267**	**15 938**	**17 284**
of which:							
United Kingdom	Thousands	2 932	2 858	3 008	2 870	2 719	2 616
Germany	Thousands	2 345	2 511	2 267	2 189	2 242	2 268
Italy	Thousands	890	805	866	898	1 129	1 188
France	Thousands	727	736	715	621	677	712
Netherlands	Thousands	716	721	636	612	666	782
Tourism receipts	Million EUR	10 580	10 285	9 495	10 348	11 037	..

StatLink http://dx.doi.org/10.1787/154711857537

Sources: Ministry of Tourism and National Statistical Service of Greece, Tourism Statistics Section, 2007.

Table 3.38. **Outbound tourism: International departures and expenditure**

	Unit	2000	2001	2002	2003	2004[2]	2005	2006
Departures[1]	Thousands	461	470	456	478	894	1 096	1 037
Tourism expenditure	Million EUR	..	4 651	2 549	2 136	2 310	2 785	..

StatLink http://dx.doi.org/10.1787/154754431214

1. Data estimated by a survey on the demand side tourism statistics.
2. The methodology of the survey has been changed from 2004.

Sources: National Statistical Service of Greece, Tourism Statistics Section and Bank of Greece, 2007.

Table 3.39. **Tourism in the national economy**

	Units	2001	2002	2003	2004	2005	2006
Tourism as % of gross national product	Percentage	9.9	10.0	9.6	10.0	10.3	10.4
Tourism as % of employment	Percentage	6.4	6.5	6.5	6.1	6.6	6.4
Tourism as % of services exports	Percentage	25.2	25.5	21.8	21.4	21.2	20.4
Tourism as % of national consumption	Percentage	9.9	9.8	10.0	10.5	10.7	10.5
Number of enterprises in tourism	Establishments	**8 684**	**8 666**	**9 041**	**9 230**	**9 377**	..
of which: Hotels and similar establishments	Establishments	8 342	8 329	8 689	8 899	9 036	..
Tourist camp sites	Establishments	342	337	352	331	341	..

StatLink http://dx.doi.org/10.1787/154844678657

Source: National Statistical Service of Greece, 2007.

Hungary

Tourism in the economy

The direct contribution of tourism to GDP is 5%, but rises to 8.5% when the indirect effects are taken into account. Some 75 400 enterprises were registered at the end of 2005 in tourism sector (Table 3.43), of which 72% were sole entrepreneurs and the remaining 28% were incorporated.

The number of employees in the field of tourism is 398 000, 8.9% of the total number of employees in the country. However, estimation shows that indirectly – taking into consideration the Tourism related industry – some 490 000 are employed in tourism, 12.5% of total employment.

According to the latest figures, 3.3 million foreign guests spent a total of 10 million guest nights in commercial accommodation in 2006. The proportion of foreign guests to the total number of guests was almost 46.0%. Foreigners spent eight out of ten guest nights in a hotel.

Tourism organisation

Government responsibility for tourism rests with the Ministry of Local Government and Regional Development (Figure 3.14). The Ministry oversees the activities of municipalities, regional development, housing issues, sports and tourism. The Minister performs Tourism related tasks through the State Secretary for Tourism and supervises the activities of the Hungarian National Tourist Office (HNTO), which is responsible for tourism promotion.

Figure 3.14. **Organisational chart of tourism bodies in Hungary**

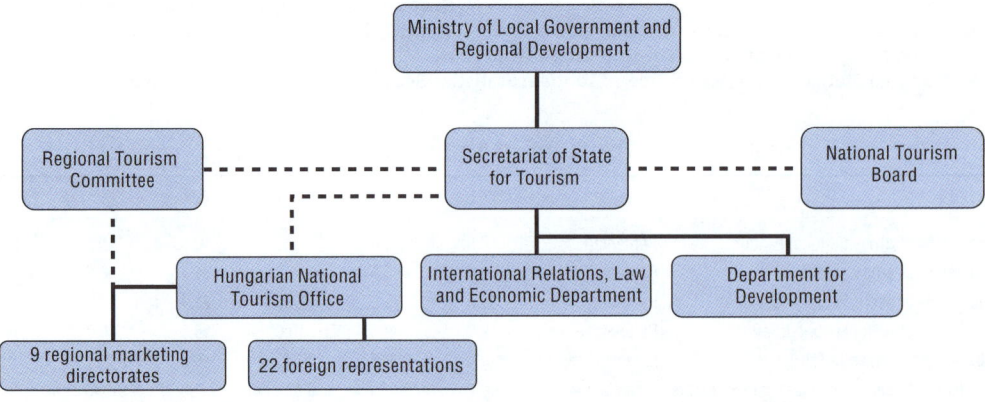

Source: OECD, adapted from Ministry of Local Government and Regional Development, 2007.

The country is divided into nine tourist regions. In each there is a Regional Tourism Committee which includes local government representatives and tourism professionals. The Regional Tourism Committees were established in February 1998 and are supported by Regional Marketing Directorates responsible for regional tourism promotion.

The HNTO was established in 1994 with the core objective of promoting Hungary's tourism attractions and services and thereby contributing to the development of domestic and international tourism. The HNTO carries out its international marketing operations mainly through its global network, which consists of over 20 representations abroad.

The National Tourism Committee (NTC) was established by the Minister for Economy in 1996 as an advisory body. The committee includes representatives from the main business organisations and from the Regional Tourism Committees.

Tourism budget

The state budget includes a yearly allocated Tourism Fund, which is dedicated to support specific tourism development schemes and to finance tourism promotion. In 2006, the Fund amounted to EUR 47.6 million. For 2007, it is EUR 35.6 million. The European Union, on the basis of the National Development Plan of Hungary, ensured an amount of approximately EUR 118 million (with national co-financing) for tourism development, mainly for attractions and accommodation between 2004-06. Between 2007-13, EUR 1.197 billion is expected to be allocated to the regions for tourism development.

Tourism related policies and programmes

A National Tourism Development Strategy (NTDS) for the period to 2013 was approved by the government in 2005 (Box 3.6). The Implementation Plan was adopted by the government at the end of 2005 and the major goals of the plan were incorporated into the country's National Development Plan. The NTDS was compiled with the involvement of all stakeholders who made significant contributions to the document.

> ### Box 3.6. **Key areas of National Tourism Development Strategy (NTDS)**
>
> - **Sustainability and competitiveness:** Tourism shall offer various benefits for its stakeholders: a good quality of life for the inhabitants, fair income for the entrepreneurs and an enjoyable stay for tourists.
> - **Accessibility:** The transport infrastructure shall be developed, both in terms of the quantity and quality of services, which shall be improved in a way that is helpful to tourism.
> - **Human resource development:** The lack of balance between the high-skilled and the low-skilled persons available on the job market should be improved as the education system focuses mainly on white-collar training.
> - **Tourism product development:** Hungary's leading products of spa, wellness and health tourism should receive priority, together with cultural attractions and conventions.
> - **Organisational structure of tourism:** Subsidiarity should be reflected in the structure, and thus regional capacities shall be strengthened with the enhancement of co-financing and co-decision making of tourism stakeholders.

The HNTO created an on-line tourist information system including key attractions and facilities, and also launched a new promotional campaign with the slogan "Talent for entertaining".

A promising initiative to decrease seasonality in Budapest, the most popular destination of Hungary, was launched at the end of 2006. Co-operation was established between the Hungarian Hotel Association, Budapest Airport, the Hungarian Airlines Malév, the Budapest Tourist Office and the Hungarian National Tourist Office to launch a campaign called "Budapest Winter Invasion" offering foreign visitors four guest nights for the price of three and including a free Budapest card, which permitted free use of transport facilities and free entrance to museums.

The financial support of the EU Phare-CBC (cross-border co-operation) and INTERREG programmes were widely used for tourism development with neighbouring countries.

> Box 3.7. **Special tourism marketing actions in Hungary in 2006**
>
> A major thematic campaign for gastronomy and wines called "The grand tour of flavours".
>
> The holiday cheque system was further developed, with a 36% increase in the issuance of cheques, totalling HUF 10 bn in 2005 and HUF 25 bn in 2006. The number of people supported by this programme has reached 600 000, of which 280 000 belong to socially disadvantaged groups. From 1 January 2007, the holiday cheque system has been extended to health prevention and leisure activities.
>
> The Hungarian Tourism Quality Award is a voluntary system aiming at increasing the quality of services and the competitiveness of the industry. The quality award system was established to recognise hotels and restaurants, and will be further developed to include tour operators, guides, thermal baths and spas, and camping operators.
>
> In order to decrease the number of complaints against the ticket control system in Budapest, the HNTO has launched a communication training campaign for ticket inspectors, a three language information package for tourists and a new tourist ticketing system. Rather than paying a fine, all tourists travelling without valid tickets now have the choice of buying for the same cost a tourist ticket offering three days of travel on all public transport facilities in Budapest.
>
> Since 2006, three international regional airports (Budapest, Debrecen and Sármellék) have been operating in Hungary with 24 hours border service.

To develop co-operation and social dialogue further between the government and the tourism industry, the National Tourism Employers' Association, and the Trade Union of the Hungarian Tourism and Catering Employees have established the Tourism and HORECA (Hotels, Restaurants and Catering) Branch Dialogue Committee. This Committee represents the interests of these branches in the negotiations with government in its efforts to find new ways for the further development of the tourism industry and to solve the different problems facing these branches. The committee constitutes part of the national social dialogue process and regular meetings are organised.

International and cross-border activities

In 2004, Hungary signed a three year co-operation programme with the Socialist Republic of Vietnam on the execution of the Memorandum of Understanding. In 2005, Hungary concluded a Memorandum of Understanding with the Republic of Korea. Hungary is member of the World Tourism Organisation and its Executive Council for 2005-09, and of the OECD Tourism Committee.

Hungary co-operates closely with the Visegrad Countries (Czech Republic, Hungary, Slovakia and Poland) in joint tourism promotion in overseas markets, especially in China, Japan and the USA. This co-operation was intensified in 2006 and as a result, the four countries undertake joint marketing activities (www.european-quartet.com). The joint tourism marketing activity is promoted under the slogan "European Quartet, one melody".

Hungary is also an active member of the Central European Initiative Working Group on Tourism, where the country's special interest is to develop co-operation in the field of eco-tourism. Hungary participates in a Joint Tourism Committees with the neighbouring countries, meeting generally on a yearly basis and discussing the possibilities of bilateral co-operation.

Statistical profile

Table 3.40. **Inbound tourism: International arrivals and receipts**

	Units	2001	2002	2003	2004	2005
Visitors	Thousands	**30 679**	**31 740**	**31 411**	**33 934**	**36 172**
of which:						
Austria	Thousands	4 790	4 735	4 870	5 237	5 600
Germany	Thousands	2 726	2 739	2 875	3 136	3 199
Romania	Thousands	4 861	5 660	5 976	7 435	7 445
Slovakia	Thousands	3 889	4 051	4 425	5 548	7 322
Ukraine	Thousands	2 691	2 642	2 450	2 564	2 387
International tourism receipts	Million EUR	4 654	3 925	3 577	3 265	3 433

StatLink http://dx.doi.org/10.1787/154845632044

Source: Ministry of Local Government and Regional Development, 2007.

Table 3.41. **Outbound tourism: International departure and expenditure**

	Unit	2001	2002	2003	2004	2005
Departures	Thousands	11 167	12 966	14 283	17 558	18 622
International tourism expenditure	Million EUR	2 022	2 252	2 288	2 302	2 347

StatLink http://dx.doi.org/10.1787/155026877576

Source: Ministry of Local Government and Regional Development, 2007.

Table 3.42. Employment in tourism[1]

	2001		2002		2003		2004		2005	
	Male	Female	Male	Female	Male	Female	Male	Female	Male	Female
Total	**24 016**	**29 524**	**25 839**	**29 491**	**25 611**	**30 081**	**26 250**	**29 426**	**26 429**	**27 359**
Hotels and similar accommodation	8 001	9 045	8 914	9 506	8 571	9 541	8 914	9 473	8 544	8 556
Youth hostels, tourist hostels	2 130	4 842	2 170	4 573	119	96	152	115	194	191
Camp sites	276	243	326	289	299	293	253	206	225	180
Other provision of lodgings	264	441	189	255	2 143	4 630	2 145	4 497	1 614	3 411
Restaurants	10 955	11 444	11 668	11 366	12 238	11 515	12 739	11 188	13 139	11 433
Bars	1 255	1 313	1 222	1 456	1 151	1 679	999	2 060	1 496	1 429
Travel agencies	1 135	2 196	1 350	2 046	1 090	2 327	1 048	1 887	1 217	2 159

StatLink http://dx.doi.org/10.1787/155051256075

1. Full-time equivalent.
Source: Ministry of Local Government and Regional Development, 2007.

Table 3.43. Tourism in the national economy

	Units	2001	2002	2003	2004	2005
Tourism as % of GDP	Percentage	5.1	5.0	5.3	5.0	..
Tourism as % of services exports	Percentage	32.6	31.1	28.3	27.6	..
Number of enterprises in tourism	**Establishments**	**79 924**	**79 928**	**79 746**	**78 679**	**75 436**
of which: Hotels and similar accommodation	Establishments	2 362	2 421	2 498	2 497	2 455
Other provision of lodgings	Establishments	38 288	37 946	36 974	35 846	32 872
Restaurants	Establishments	25 319	25 301	24 781	24 465	24 115
Travel agencies	Establishments	2 407	2 410	2 491	2 543	2 597

StatLink http://dx.doi.org/10.1787/155065116644

Source: Ministry of Local Government and Regional Development, 2007.

Iceland

Tourism in the economy

International tourism in Iceland is one of the major contributors to the economy, accounting for 3.9% of GDP in 2001, 4.7% in 2002 and 5.1% in 2003, and reaching 6.3% in 2006. The sector also accounted for 12.6% of export earnings in 2006, up from 12.3% in 2005 (Table 3.46). International tourist receipts were EUR 500 million in 2006. Growth has been erratic since 2001, with arrivals increasing by 21% in the five years to 2005 and international tourism receipts by 43%.

In terms of employment, tourism accounted for around 4% of total employment in each of the four years between 2001 and 2004. Data show that total tourism sector employment reached 6 800 in 2004, the latest year for which figures are available. This represented an increase of 5.5% on 2001. There were some 930 tourism enterprises recorded in 2004

The number of visitors from overseas has been growing considerably over recent years, by 39.4% in the period 2000-06. The 422 280 foreign tourists recorded in 2006 spent 900 000 guest nights, 78.7% of the total guest nights that year. The major overseas markets are the Nordic countries, the UK, the USA and Germany. These markets account for 65% of all overseas visitors.

Tourism organisation

Government responsibility for tourism rests with the Ministry of Communication (Figure 3.15). The Icelandic Tourist Board (ITB) handles the implementation of tourism affairs for the ministry and has the following main responsibilities:

- Issuing licences, registration and monitoring in order to ensure that requirements for operations are met.
- Development, quality control, and organisational issues related to tourism, i.e. the implementation of a defined tourism strategy, the co-ordination of environmental and educational affairs, the dissemination of information, regional and local development, and international collaboration.
- Marketing and promotion of tourism services under the Minister's direction.

The Minister may, at his/her discretion, amend or extend the role and functions of the ITB including those related to individual projects under the Board's auspices. The ITB is authorised, upon obtaining the approval of the Minister, to assign to others the task of handling specific projects and acting as parties to collaborative projects, including acquiring ownership shares in companies operating in specific sectors.

The Minister of Communication appoints the Icelandic Tourism Council. The job of the Council is to make recommendations to the Minister, at least once a year, on the marketing and promotion of services to tourists and to act as the Minister's advisor on matters

Figure 3.15. **Organisational chart of tourism bodies in Iceland**

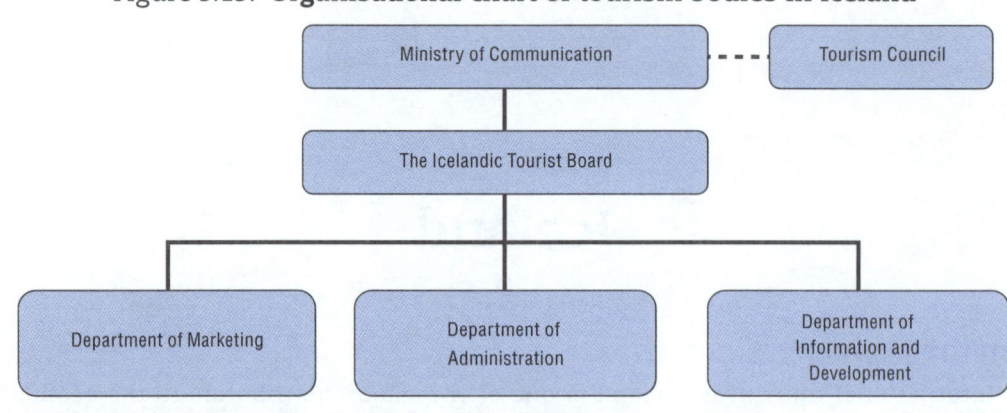

Source: OECD, adapted from Ministry of Communications, 2007.

concerning tourism planning. The Council also comments on amendments to Tourism related legislation and regulations and on other matters assigned to it by the Minister, and on any other matters that it deems appropriate in the interests of the tourism industry.

The Council comprises ten representatives. The chairman and vice-chairman are appointed by the Minister without nomination, and the remainder are appointed by the Minister upon receipt of nominations from the following: The Icelandic Travel Industry Association (three representatives); the Association of Local Authorities in Iceland (two representatives); the Iceland Tourism Association (two representatives), and the Trade Council of Iceland (one representative). The term of appointment are for four years, although the chairman and vice-chairman are limited to the appointing Minister's tenure in office. The Director of the Icelandic Tourist Board and a representative of the Ministry attend Tourism Council meetings and have the right both to address the meetings and to present proposals.

Tourism budget

The budget of the National Tourism Administration is ISK 72 million (plus ISK 206 million for administration, marketing and environmental issues, making a total of ISK 278 million), which is mainly funded through the general budget from state and local government as well as the private sector.

Tourism related policies and programmes

The primary policy objectives in support of the tourism industry during the period 2006-15 are as follows:

- To ensure that Iceland's nature and wilderness, culture, and a spirit of professionalism prevails in the development of Icelandic tourism.
- To ensure the maintenance of the competitive position of the tourism industry while maximising its performance.
- To distribute tourism as widely as possible throughout the country to the benefit of residents and without exceeding carrying capacities.
- To fortify and safeguard Iceland's image as a tourism destination.

Also, efforts are to be made to realise the following goals:

- The operating conditions created for the tourism industry shall be comparable to international best practice in Iceland's main competitor countries.

- Iceland shall be in the forefront of environment-friendly tourism.
- The build-up of national parks shall be followed up with the promotion of tourism that integrates outdoor activities and nature conservation.
- The responsibility of travellers and tourism companies with regard to environmental affairs shall be increased.

Statistical profile

Table 3.44. **Inbound tourism: International arrivals and receipts**

	Unit	2001	2002	2003	2004	2005
Tourists[1]	Thousands	**296**	**277**	**320**	**360**	**374**
of which:						
The Nordic countries[2]	Thousands	..	72	81	94	93
United Kingdom	Thousands	..	42	53	60	58
United States	Thousands	..	48	48	52	58
Germany	Thousands	..	31	37	39	37
France	Thousands	..	18	20	21	20
Tourism receipts[3]	Million EUR	262	266	284	300	331

StatLink http://dx.doi.org/10.1787/155110328463

1. Excluding arrivals from cruise ships.
2. Denmark, Norway, Sweden and Finland.
3. Excluding passengers fare.

Sources: Icelandic Tourist Board and Central bank of Iceland, 2007.

Table 3.45. **Outbound tourism: International departures and expenditure**

	Unit	2001	2002	2003	2004	2005
Departures	Thousands	..	..	292	345	391
Tourism expenditure[1]	Million EUR	417	388	460	561	790

StatLink http://dx.doi.org/10.1787/155147443731

1. Including passengers fare.

Source: Icelandic Tourist Board, 2007.

Table 3.46. **Tourism in the national economy**

	Units	2001	2002	2003	2004	2005
Tourism as % of gross national product	Percentage	3.9	4.7	5.1	..	..
Tourism as % of service export	Percentage	12.4	12.0	12.9	12.4	12.3
Employment of tourism sector	Employees	**6 456**	**6 104**	**6 156**	**6 814**	..
Tourism as % of employment	Percentage	4.13	3.91	3.95	4.33	..
Number of enterprises in tourism						
Travel agencies		65	78	83	96	102
Recreation		206	210	209	211	214
Hotels and guest houses		409	393	377	376	404
Car rentals		59	56	52	50	56
Tourist information centre		37	40	42	44	46
Museums and galleries		134	136	137	153	166

StatLink http://dx.doi.org/10.1787/155232108455

Sources: Icelandic Tourist Board, Central Bank of Iceland, 2007.

Ireland

Tourism in the economy

In 2006, total foreign and domestic tourism revenue of EUR 6.09 billion generated an overall GNP impact of EUR 5.63 billion after applying multiplier effects (direct, indirect, induced and "Government interacting"). As a result total tourism revenue accounted for 3.7% of GNP.

The estimated total number of people employed in the Irish tourism and hospitality industry in 2006 was 249 338 – an increase of 1.4% on the numbers employed in 2005. Of this number, almost 203 000 are year-round employees. Numbers employed in tourism related services in each year from 2004-06 are outlined in Table 3.49.

Government earned revenue estimated at EUR 2.75 billion through the taxation of tourism expenditure, of which EUR 2.27 billion came from foreign tourism. In 2006, the value of exported goods and services in Ireland is estimated at EUR 140.15 billion, of which EUR 4.69 billion can be directly attributed to tourism, accounting for 3.3% of exports.

2006 was a record year for Irish tourism with an all-time high of 7.7 million overseas visitors. This represents an increase of 10.5% on 2005 and of 9.9% in terms of associated revenues. Domestic holiday trips grew by 14% in the year.

Out-of-state tourist expenditure, including spending by visitors from Northern Ireland, amounted to EUR 4 billion in 2006 (EUR 3.7 billion in 2005). With a further EUR 0.66 billion spent by overseas visitors on fares to Irish carriers (EUR 0.60 billion in 2005), total foreign exchange earnings were EUR 4.69 billion (EUR 4.3 billion in 2005). Domestic tourism expenditure amounted to EUR 1.4 billion (EUR 1.16 billion in 2005) making tourism in total a EUR 6 billion industry in 2006 (EUR 5.4 billion in 2005).

Tourism organisation

There has been major reform of Irish tourism structures in recent years with the setting up of Fáilte Ireland (the national tourism development authority with responsibility for tourism development and domestic marketing) and Tourism Ireland (Figure 3.16). Tourism Ireland was established in December 2001 under the framework of the Northern Ireland Peace Agreement (Good Friday Agreement) with the responsibility of marketing the island of Ireland overseas as a tourism destination. More recently, the former Regional Tourism Authorities were dissolved and subsumed into Fáilte Ireland to ensure greater coherence in the development of regional tourism.

Tourism budget

Administration of the tourism sector at national level is carried out by the Tourism Division of the Department of Arts, Sport and Tourism. The overall budget for tourism in 2006 was over EUR 140 million. This amount is allocated to the tourism agencies – Fáilte Ireland and Tourism Ireland. For 2007, a record EUR 154 million has been provided for the

Figure 3.16. **Organisational chart of tourism bodies in Ireland**

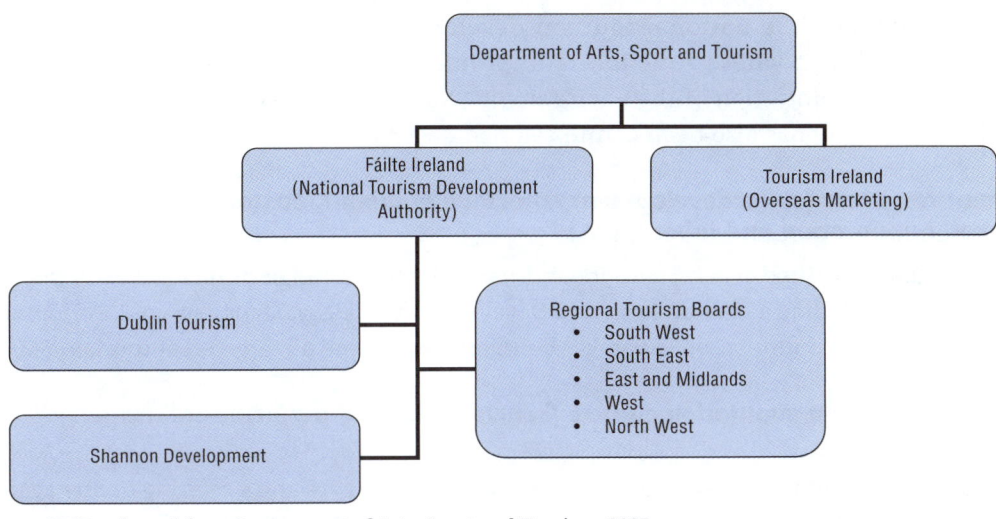

Source: OECD, adapted from Department of Arts, Sport and Tourism, 2007.

tourism services budget. These funds include specific provision for Product Development, Marketing and Promotion.

Apart from the private sector, the main source of funding is the general national tourism budget as detailed above. Certain tax incentives for tourism related developments have also been provided in recent years and some EU funding (Peace and INTERREG) has also gone towards tourism related activities.

Tourism related policies and programmes

Examples of recent tourism policy developments in Ireland include the following.

Legislative and regulatory environment

The Tourism Acts 1939-2003 provide for the establishment and corporate governance of the National Tourism Development Authority (Fáilte Ireland) as well as setting out the statutory framework for the promotion of tourism and the development of tourism facilities and services. 2006 saw the abolition of the Regional Tourism Authorities, which were quasi-independent companies, and their replacement with new Regional Tourism Development boards under the aegis of Fáilte Ireland.

Domestic/Inbound/Outbound tourism

In its report published in 2003, the Tourism Policy Review Group set targets of doubling the then level of overseas visitor expenditure by 2012 (which would have implied a total of EUR 8 billion) with an associated increase in visitor numbers from 6.4 million to 10 million. In fact, visitor numbers from all of Ireland's key markets in 2006 exceeded all targets set by Tourism Ireland for the year and it appears that the country is ahead of the 2003 plans, with 7.7 million visitors and receipts of EUR 4.7 billion having been reached in 2006.

Competitiveness (productivity, innovation, quality, etc.)

The Irish Tourist Industry Confederation has produced a report on competitiveness, which emphasises, *inter alia*, the importance of non-price elements in competitiveness.

Sustainable tourism (environmental, economic, social)

Fáilte Ireland (the national tourism development authority) has established an Environmental Unit whose function is to promote good practice within the tourism industry and the protection of the environment. A review of good environmental practice within the industry has also been commissioned.

Human resources (skills development, shortage of labour, obstacles in the labour market, immigration and labour, etc.)

Over the past three years, Fáilte Ireland has launched a range of new industry support programmes, including a Human Resource Development Strategy, Management Development Programme and a county-based capability building programme all targeted at tourism SMEs.

Development of an evaluation culture (benchmarking of performance, targets and indicators)

Tourism Ireland undertook a pilot project benchmarking Ireland's offering online against the country's key competitors in the top 4 markets in relation to cost, availability and choice of flights, hotels and car hire. Results show that Ireland is very competitive in these sectors.

> **Box 3.8. Examples of recent tourism initiatives in Ireland**
>
> - The Tourism Action Plan Implementation Group presented its final progress report in March 2006. It identified a number of key areas for action.
> - To date, over EUR 46.2 million has been allocated to 75 projects nationwide under the ERDF-supported Tourism Product Development Scheme.
> - The National Development Plan 2007-13, published in January 2007, provides for a record level of investment (EUR 800 million) in tourism product development and marketing up to 2013.
> - The national budget for 2007 introduced relief in relation to the reclaimability of VAT on certain conference related business.
> - A new pilot scheme to incentivise the sustainable development of tourism along the River Shannon was announced in January 2007.

International and intra-regional activities

There is strong co-operation between the relevant tourism authorities in the Republic of Ireland and Northern Ireland. Tourism Ireland Ltd. was established in December 2000 in the context of the Good Friday Agreement to market the whole island of Ireland as a tourism destination. A joint approach between the agencies North and South on the drawdown of future EU funding for tourism projects in the period 2007-13 has been agreed.

Major forms of tourism

Following extensive research, Tourism Ireland has established that in recent years, visiting places of cultural and historical interest was the most widespread pastime among overseas visitors. This segment, known as sightseers and culture seekers made up 39% of all holidaymakers to the Republic of Ireland. It is this segment which represents the best prospects for Ireland as a holiday destination. Tourism Ireland plans to highlight activities in a range of areas to attract this type of visitor in the years ahead.

Linkages between tourism and other policies

Taxation

In Budget 2007, several changes to the VAT system were signalled which will have a positive impact on tourism. These include allowing deduction of VAT on business accommodation costs in connection with attendance at conferences and the raising of the VAT registration threshold for services for small tourism businesses such as Bed and Breakfast accommodation.

Transport

The Department of Arts, Sport and Tourism and the tourism agencies work closely with the Department of Transport and the National Roads Authority. "Transport 21", Ireland's transport strategy encompasses many roads and rail elements that will be of significant benefit to tourism development when completed.

The Dublin Airport Authority has published a plan which includes the development of a new terminal by 2009 and other new facilities including an additional pier due for completion in 2007.

Culture

The development of Dublin's Abbey Theatre is currently the priority cultural infrastructure project of the Minister for Arts, Sport and Tourism. A suitable site has been identified and the necessary site investigation works completed. Planning has also commenced for a major redevelopment of the National Concert Hall. An inter-agency Steering Group and a Project Team have been put in place to oversee the redevelopment.

Education

Institutes of Technology across the country provide Tourism related education courses. 2 500 students took part in these programmes in 2006. Fáilte Ireland provides a range of training and education programmes for people employed in the tourism sector. It also has a dedicated resource facility for tourism careers information. It is expected that approximately 10 000 people will be trained by Fáilte Ireland in 2007, with an increased emphasis on helping to improve skill levels and industry capability. In 2006, Fáilte Ireland introduced a County Based Learning Network programme designed to provide action-learning support and development to owner/managers in tourism SMEs. 460 people participated in this programme in 2006.

Trade

Tourism Ireland participates in Irish trade missions abroad. Most recently (January 2007), it has been involved in a trade mission to the Middle East.

Foreign Direct Investment

In recent years, several international hotel chains have invested in hotels in Ireland. Most recently, the Ritz-Carlton group has decided to establish a presence in Ireland. The Ritz-Carlton Powerscourt Hotel in County Wicklow, which is scheduled to open later this year, is expected to generate up to EUR 60 million annually for the Irish tourism industry.

Public/private partnership

In May 2006, the Minister for Arts, Sport and Tourism established the Tourism Strategy Implementation Group, whose function is to address the outstanding recommendations of the

Report of the Tourism Policy Review Group, published in 2003. This Group works with the tourism industry and Government departments and agencies to address a number of key areas. The Irish Tourist Industry Confederation is closely involved with the work of the Group.

In 2006, Fáilte Ireland launched a county-based capability building programme specifically targeted at tourism SMEs and micro-enterprises

A new Tourism Best Practice Initiative, *Optimus*, was developed by Fáilte Ireland with Excellence Ireland and launched in May 2004. It is a total business excellence model and is linked to the European Foundation for Quality Management (EFQM) family of awards. The new strategies for special interest products incorporate recommendations with regard to quality assurance and maintenance of high standards

Statistical profile

Table 3.47. Inbound tourism: International arrivals and receipts

	Units	2001	2002	2003	2004	2005
Visitors	Thousands	5 990	6 065	6 369	6 575	6 978
of which:						
United Kingdom	Thousands	3 462	3 579	3 719	3 681	3 825
Other Europe	Thousands	1 357	1 392	1 497	1 600	1 912
United States and Canada	Thousands	912	849	904	977	951
Tourism receipts	Million EUR	3 935	3 989	4 057	4 065	4 272

StatLink http://dx.doi.org/10.1787/155404768056

Source: Department of Arts, Sport and Tourism, 2007.

Table 3.48. Outbound tourism: International departures and expenditure

	Units	2001	2002	2003	2004	2005
Departures	Thousands	4 216	4 634	4 929	5 409	6 113
Tourism expenditure	Million EUR	3 600	4 310	4 586	4 661	5 270

StatLink http://dx.doi.org/10.1787/155413460751

Source: Department of Arts, Sport and Tourism, 2007.

Table 3.49. Employment in tourism

	2004	2005	2006
Employment in tourism sector	244 089	245 959	249 338
of which: Hotels	53 637	54 095	55 768
Restaurants	41 367	43 309	45 200
Licensed premises	92 000	88 986	87 998
Tourism services and attractions	35 016	36 421	37 102

StatLink http://dx.doi.org/10.1787/155441646123

Source: Fáilte Ireland (Ireland's National Tourism Development Authority), 2007.

Table 3.50. Number of enterprises in tourism

	2001	2002	2003	2004
Number of enterprises in tourism	9 895	11 828	12 363	11 348
of which: Hotels	..	776	787	777
Restaurants	3 484	3 945	4 279	3 865
Bars	6 142	6 778	6 896	6 311
Travel agencies	269	329	401	394

StatLink http://dx.doi.org/10.1787/155472061304

Source: Central Statistics Office, Annual Services Inquiry, 2007.

Italy

Tourism in the economy

The vital role that tourism plays in the Italian economy is demonstrated by the foreign exchange registered by the Italian Foreign Exchange Office (UIC) and the Italian National Bank. This is expected to reach an all-time record of EUR 30 billion in 2006. The growth in foreign earnings announced by UIC is even greater than that for the international market and considerably larger than that for Western Europe.

Tourism organisation

The Italian Government's authority responsible for tourism is the Department for the Development and Competitiveness of Tourism (*Dipartimento per lo Sviluppo e la Competitività del Turismo*) (Figure 3.17). In 2006, tourism was placed under the Presidency of the Council of Ministers. The Tourism Policy Committee is under the presidency of the Vice-President of the Council of Ministers.

Regions play an essential role in Italian tourism. The Framework Law on Tourism defines the respective competences for the central government and the regions. It has been agreed with the regions that the Department for Tourism carries out the task of elaborating and defining general policy guidelines, principles and objectives for improving and developing the general tourism sector, preparation and monitoring of the relative guidelines, and the management of international and EU relations.

The regions participate in the executive board of the National Tourism Agency (ENIT), and are: Piemonte, Valle d'Aosta, Lombardia, Trentino-Alto Adige (which is composed of two autonomous Provinces: Trento and Bolzano), Veneto, Friuli-Venezia Giulia, Liguria, Emilia Romagna, Toscana, Umbria, Marche, Lazio, Abruzzo, Molise, Campania, Puglia, Basilicata, Calabria, Sicilia, Sardegna.

Tourism budget

In 2006, the budget for the National Tourism Administration was EUR 39 million, of which EUR 21 million was designated for the National Tourism Organisation. Other funds for tourism were managed directly by the regions.

Tourism related policies and programmes

The Department for Tourism has three main priorities:

1. *Harmonisation of the tourism sector, these measures involve:*
- Collaboration with the regions and other bodies for the constant improvement of the quality of the national tourism offer, by encouraging the responsible development of

Figure 3.17. **Organisational chart of tourism bodies in Italy**

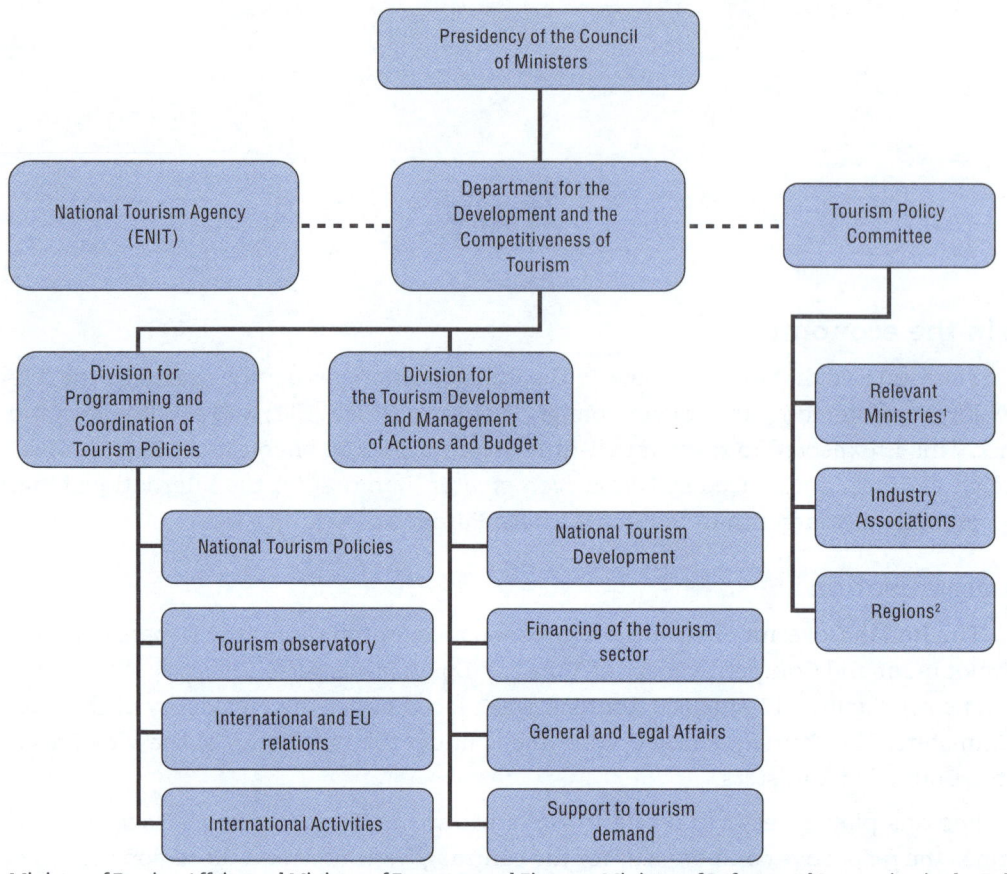

1. Ministry of Foreign Affairs and Ministry of Economy and Finance, Ministry of Reform and Innovation in the Public Administration (*Ministro per le riforme e le innovazioni nella pubblica amministrazione*); Ministry for the Environment and Territory (IMET), Ministry of Transport, Ministry of Regional Affairs Local Authorities.
2. Six regions which alternate and represent all regions during their tenure.

Source: OECD, adapted from Department for Development and Competitiveness of Tourism, 2007.

different Italian tourist resorts and through the careful acknowledgement of the needs of local and foreign tourists.

- Support to juridical and legal activities.
- Monitoring regional legislation and the legislation of other European countries.
- An example of innovation in tourism development is given in Box 3.9.

2. Improvement of the tourism sector, which involves:

- The Co-financing Fund for the Tourism Offer, and financing inter-regional tourism systems and other available means.
- Development of international and European Union relationships.
- Relations with regional and local administrations and operators.
- The realisation of studies, research and project implementation.

3. Assistance and support for the tourism demand, including:

- Support to the quality of the structures for tourists with special needs.

> **Box 3.9. A case of entrepreneurial innovation: Project of an "extended hotel" in Santo Stefano di Sessanio**
>
> This project was carried out by the "Sextanto" company in a semi-abandoned medieval borough located in the National Park of Abruzzo. The aim has been to create an "extended hotel" inside the borough. Besides offering accommodation and catering, there will be workshops for traditional craftsmanship, a wine cellar of the territory's wines and culinary products, an inn specialising in local cuisine, a conference hall, a wellness centre, and a centre for excursions. Fundamental to the demands of re-conversion, the project aims to fully conserve the historical and architectural heritage of Santo Stefano di Sessanio, one of the most interesting boroughs of the whole Apennine mountain range of the Abruzzo Region.

- Assistance to Italian tourists abroad who are in difficulty (Warranty Fund) and monitoring and information about journeys to countries at risk.
- A warranty system for foreign tourists in Italy (the Charter of Tourists' Rights).
- Support to social tourism (Rotation Fund – Systems of holiday vouchers).

> **Box 3.10. Major forms of tourism**
>
> In the tourism sector, Italy is one of the world's most competitive countries a consequence of the country's rich and varied natural, cultural and historical heritage. A survey carried out in 2006 interviewed 2 000 tourists about their holidays in Italy. The preferred choice for various destinations were (multiple answers were given): art cities (63.6%), the sea (24.8%), mountains (10.2%), lakes (8.3%), other (8.2%).

Co-operation with the tourism industry, consumers and other stakeholders

In pursuing the objective of raising the quality and harmonising the development of the national tourism system, the central administration co-operates with the regions, local entities, businesses, trade unions and other associations active in the tourism sector.

The most important forum for consultation and discussion with the relevant stakeholders is the National Conference on Tourism, which is organised by the Department for Tourism in collaboration with the regions. This takes place every two years in a different region and provides a general orientation for the drafting, updating and development of monitoring guidelines within tourism policy.

The Department for Tourism also monitors three national tourism entities: ENIT (the State Tourism Agency), which deals with the promotion and commercialisation of Italian tourism products; ACI (*Automobile Club d'Italia*), which represents and protects the general interests of the Italian motoring sector; and CAI (*Club Alpino Italiano*), which promotes awareness tourism, natural environment protection and the pursuit of consensus about sustainable mountain development.

Statistical profile

Table 3.51. **Inbound tourism: International arrivals and receipts**

	Units	2002	2003	2004	2005
Visitors	Thousands	**65 472**	**64 861**	**59 483**	**60 220**
of which:					
Germany	Thousands	..	14 057	11 997	11 059
Switzerland	Thousands	..	10 773	9 490	8 703
France	Thousands	..	8 942	8 262	8 434
Austria	Thousands	..	8 090	5 576	5 939
United Kingdom	Thousands	..	3 028	3 822	4 226
Tourism receipts	Million EUR	28 207	27 622	28 665	28 453

StatLink http://dx.doi.org/10.1787/155480005051

Source: Italian Foreign Exchange Office (UIC), 2007.

Table 3.52. **Outbound tourism: International departure and expenditure**

	Units	2002	2003	2004	2005
Departures	Thousands	49 601	51 056	43 335	46 030
Tourism expenditure	Million EUR	17 811	18 236	16 515	18 001

StatLink http://dx.doi.org/10.1787/155481284370

Source: Italian Foreign Exchange Office (UIC), 2007.

Table 3.53. **Tourism in the national economy**

	Units	2002	2003	2004	2005
Tourism as % of gross domestic product	Percentage	5.4	5.4	5.1	4.9
Tourism as % of employment	Percentage	9.4	9.8	9.4	9.7
Employment in tourism (hotels and restaurants)	Thousands	933	1 001	1 032	..
Domestic tourism as % of final consumption	Percentage	7.3	7.2	7.0	7.0

StatLink http://dx.doi.org/10.1787/155506710186

Source: ISTAT, Centro Internazionale di Studi Sull'Economia Turistica (CISET), 2007.

Japan

Tourism in the economy

Tourism in Japan is one of the biggest sectors of the economy. During fiscal 2005, it is estimated that JPY 24.4 trillion was spent on travel in Japan (including JPY 1.6 trillion spent by visitors to Japan from overseas). It is estimated that the Japanese spent a total of JPY 27.8 trillion (excluding the JPY 1.6 trillion spent by visitors to Japan from overseas) on travel during the year.

The "direct and indirect effects" of spending on travel in fiscal 2005 were worth JPY 55.3 trillion, some 5.8% of domestic output of JPY 949.1 trillion (Table 3.56), based on the 2000 input-output table. The value-added effects, estimated at JPY 29.7 trillion, represented 5.9% of the nominal GDP for fiscal 2005.

Travel spending also created 4.69 million jobs, 7.4% of the 63.7 million people employed in fiscal 2004. Tax revenues are estimated to be worth JPY 5 trillion, which represents 5.8% of the expected JPY 85.6 trillion of national and local tax revenue for fiscal 2005.

Partly as a result of the Visit Japan Campaign, the number of inbound tourists increased from 5.24 million in 2002 to 7.33 million in 2006, an increase of almost 40%. The main markets, as shown in Table 3.54, are South Korea, Taiwan, the USA, China and Hong Kong.

Tourism organisation

Japan's tourism policy falls under the jurisdiction of the Ministry of Land, Infrastructure and Transport, whose minister also acts as the Minister of State for Tourism Promotion (Figure 3.18). The number of Tourism related divisions in the ministry was increased from four to six in July 2006 to strengthen the organisational/personnel structure.

Tourism budget

The Government budgets related to tourism (the budgets of the Ministry of Land, Infrastructure and Transport, excluding those for the promotion of communities and for infrastructure construction) include a general budget of approximately JPY 6.5 billion. This budget covers the Visit Japan Campaign (JPY 3.6 billion) and subsidies for the Japan National Tourism Organisation (JNTO) of JPY 2.3 billion.

The total budget of the JNTO is approximately JPY 4 billion, of which JPY 2.3 billion comes in the form of government subsidies, JPY 360 million from contributions and convention income, JPY 330 million represents project income, and JPY 1 billion is from donations made by corporations and individuals.

Figure 3.18. **Organisational chart of tourism bodies in Japan.**

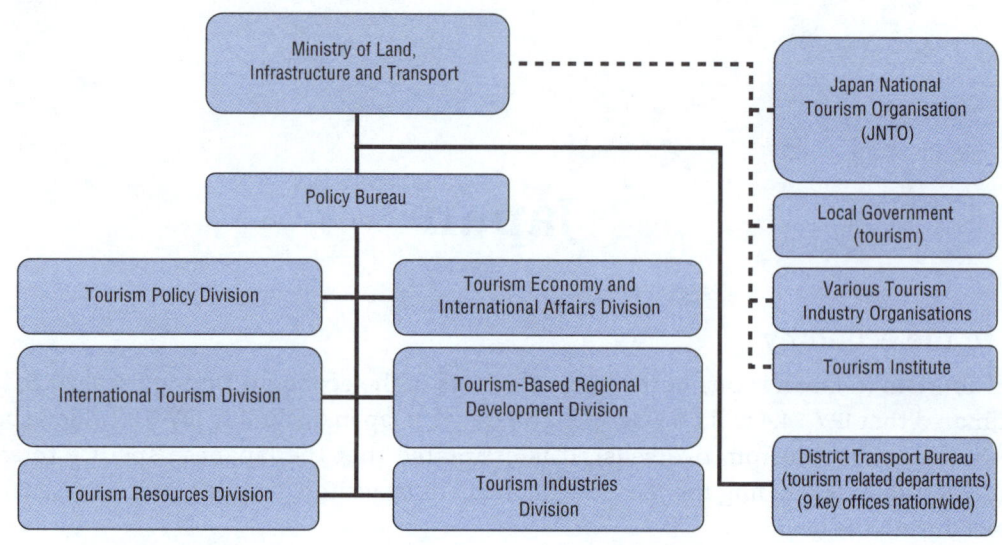

Source: OECD, adapted from Ministry of Land, Infrastructure and Transport, 2007.

Tourism related policies and programmes

Key tourism policy developments

The National Tourism Promotion Act, which positions tourism as a major pillar in Japan's 21st century economy, came into force on 1 January 2007. Based on this law, the government issued the National Tourism Promotion Plan in June 2007, which includes the basic policies for making Japan a tourism nation and sets out the goals to be attained.

Japan is undertaking the "Visit Japan Campaign" involving both the public and private sectors. The aim of the campaign is to increase the number of inbound tourists to 10 million per year by 2010 (the 2006 total was 7.33 million – up 9.0% on the previous year). The Prime Minister's policy statement indicates that "*the number of major international conferences hosted in Japan should be increased by 50% in the next five years to make Japan the largest conference-hosting nation in Asia*". Based on this objective, the "Visit Japan Campaign" now has a new item on its agenda to attract more international conferences. Box 3.11 illustrates a new approach to tourism development.

The first Japan-China-Republic of Korea tourism ministers' meeting was held in July 2006 in Hokkaido, at which the "Hokkaido Declaration on the Strengthening of Tourism Exchange and co-operation by Japan, China and the Republic of Korea" was agreed and announced. The Declaration set goals including those of increasing the number of tourists moving between the three nations to 17 million by 2010 (an increase of more than 5 million), by implementing tri-lateral measures to expand tourism.

Main areas of intervention and key changes

Human resources

In the field of human resources, the entry capacity of the nation's Tourism related schools or faculties/departments has increased by 1 095 places in the past five years. These are spread over 11 departments within various tertiary educational institutions. In fiscal 2006, the nation's educational institutions offered 3 000 places to future tourism students, in five schools (faculties) and 28 departments.

> **Box 3.11. New types of tourism under development in Japan**
>
> In recent years, many tourists' travelling styles have changed from the traditional, excursion-type group tours to more individual, exchange-oriented tours. These individual tours immerse tourists in the nature, lifestyle, culture, and people of the destinations they visit. "New tourism," including long-stay tourism, cultural tourism, industrial tourism, and other travelling styles, using the attractions of local areas for a wider variety of travelling experiences. Smaller group tours are aimed more specifically at the attractions of one tourism destination, enabling participants to discover or utilise new features of the destination. One example is "health tourism" where tourists enhance their health through activities during their tours. In order to spread this concept, symposiums on health tourism and trial health tours are being held in many other regions.
>
> This type of tourism for smaller and more diverse groups, and for higher added-value tourists, may contribute substantially to the revitalisation of local communities, the creation of new lifestyles, and the opportunity for the visitor to appreciate the nation's cultural and natural wealth more fully. For these reasons, the government wants actively to encourage the development and distribution of "new tourism" products. The creation of a "new tourism" market should be supported through building a new database, the implementation of verification projects, and general promotion and distribution of new tourism products.

Domestic tourism

From the viewpoint of promoting competitive tourist destinations, the government in 2005 created a subsidy system for supporting the private sector's activities aimed at revitalising tourism destinations.

Consumer issues (protection measures, information, ethics)

A registration system has been put in place for persons engaged in the travel business to maintain fair transactions, ensure the safety of travel, and promote the convenience of tourists. Persons engaged in travel businesses are classified into four categories according to the scope of their business and required to deposit an amount of security money which is determined by their classification, and also to meet certain other obligations.

Statistical profile

Table 3.54. **Inbound tourism: International arrivals and receipts**

	Units	2002	2003	2004	2005	2006
Tourists (overnight visitors)	Thousands	5 239	5 212	6 138	6 728	7 334
of which:						
Korea	Thousands	1 272	1 459	1 588	1 747	2 117
Taiwan	Thousands	878	785	1 081	1 275	1 309
United States	Thousands	732	656	760	822	817
China	Thousands	452	449	616	653	812
Hong Kong	Thousands	291	260	300	299	352
Tourism receipts	Billion JPY	759	1 326	1 552	1 715	1 336

StatLink http://dx.doi.org/10.1787/155530156556

Sources: Japan National Tourist Organisation and Bank of Japan, 2007.

Table 3.55. **Outbound tourism: International departures and expenditure**

	Units	2002	2003	2004	2005	2006
Departures	Thousands	16 523	13 296	16 831	17 404	17 535
Tourism expenditure	Billion JPY	4 360	4 212	5 211	5 298	4 379

StatLink http://dx.doi.org/10.1787/155553571525

Sources: Ministry of Justice, Japan National Tourist Organisation and Bank of Japan, 2007.

Table 3.56. **Tourism in the national economy**

		Units	2001	2002	2003	2004	2005
Tourism as % of gross domestic product	Direct effects	Percentage	2.1	2.1	2.4	2.4	2.4
	Direct and indirect effects	Percentage	4.6	4.7	5.3	5.6	5.8
Tourism as % of employment	Direct effects	Percentage	2.8	2.8	3.6	3.6	3.6
	Direct and indirect effects	Percentage	5.9	6.0	7.2	7.3	7.4
Tourism as % of service export		Percentage	8.9	9.2	14.7	14.7	14.1
Domestic tourism consumption as part of final consumption		Billion JPY	20 953	21 256	24 049	24 463	24 425
Government's revenues from	Direct effects	Billion JPY	1 694	1 757	1 940	1 913	1 983
	Direct and indirect effects	Billion JPY	4 421	4 460	4 787	4 806	5 003

StatLink http://dx.doi.org/10.1787/155605275547

Sources: National Statistical Office of Japan and Ministry of Land, Infrastructure and Transport, 2007.

Table 3.57. **Number of enterprises in tourism**

	2001	2002	2003	2004	2005
Number of enterprises in tourism (total)	82 877	81 250	79 506	77 682	75 259
of which: Western-style hotels	8 363	8 518	8 686	8 811	8 990
Japanese-style hotels (Ryokan)	63 388	61 583	59 754	58 003	55 567
Travel agencies	11 126	11 149	11 066	10 868	10 702

StatLink http://dx.doi.org/10.1787/155617304161

Sources: Ministry of Health, Labour and Welfare, Ministry of Land, Infrastructure and Transport, 2007.

Korea

Tourism in the economy

Total tourism revenues in 2006 reached USD 5.3 billion, a decrease of 8.6% over the previous year. According to the Tourism Satellite Account, in 2004 the total value added by tourism was KRW 17 606 billion, representing 2.26% of GDP in Korea. The total number of tourism employees is 852 471, or 5.04% of the total number of employees in Korea (Table 3.60).

In 2006, the number of foreign tourist arrivals increased by 2.2% on 2005, to reach 6.155 million, mostly from other Asian countries. Japan is Korea's dominant market, accounting for 38% of all international arrivals in 2006. The 2006 increase is smaller than in 2004, when arrivals grew by 22.4%, and in 2005 when the increase was 3.5%, but indicates nonetheless a continuation of an upward trend. Since 2003, the Korean Wave phenomenon (Box 3.13) had a strong effect on Korea's tourism industry. In 2005, this phenomenon produced good results for various marketing and public relation activities and contributed to the achievement of a record 6 million arrivals.

Tourism organisation

The Ministry of Culture and Tourism is one of Korea's most important central government agencies (Figure 3.19). The ministry is responsible for culture, arts, religion, tourism, and sports and has one industry office and four divisions related to tourism. The

Figure 3.19. **Organisational chart of tourism bodies in Korea**

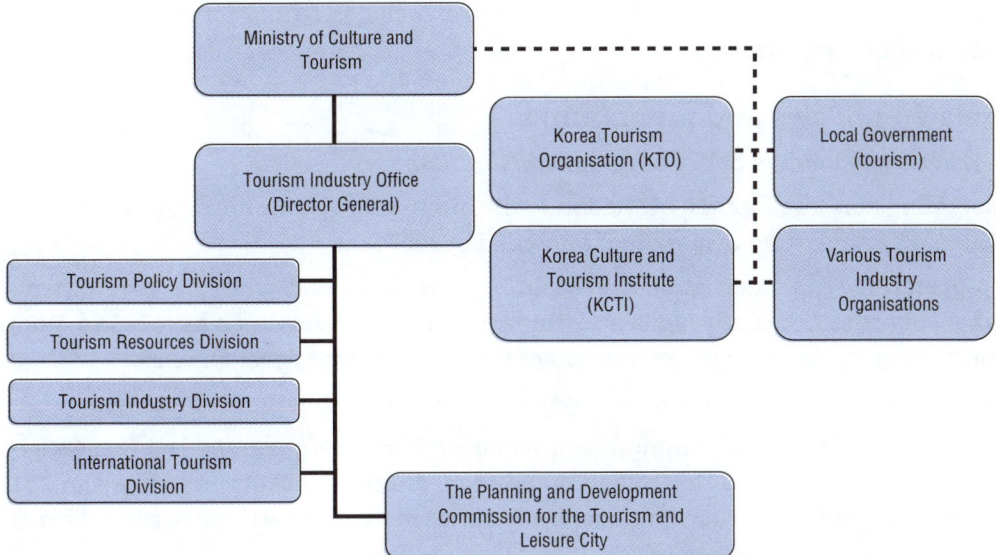

Source: OECD, adapted from Ministry of Culture and Tourism, 2007.

Tourism Industry Office carries out policies under the slogan of "the Tourism Hub of North East Asia" to increase the number of foreign tourists, expand sightseeing opportunities for Koreans, develop a tour and leisure type industrial city, and promote the tourism industry generally for both domestic and international visitors.

The Korea Tourism Organisation (KTO) was established in 1962 as a government organisation to develop Korea's tourism industry. Its main objectives are: *i*) to promote the Korean tourism industry, *ii*) to develop resources for Korean tourism, and *iii*) to conduct training programs for human resources in tourism.

The KTO's seven major functions are: *i*) overseas tourism promotion, *ii*) fostering the convention sector, *iii*) providing tourism information services, *iv*) co-operating with local government and the tourism industry, *v*) promoting the international tourist's satisfaction, *vi*) promoting tourism between North and South Korea, and *vii*) resort development. The KTO has 26 overseas offices and is responsible for overseas marketing.

The Korea Culture and Tourism Institute (KCTI) is affiliated to the ministry and is responsible for researching, consulting and for producing publications related to tourism. The KCTI also sets up information and education networks for collecting, analysing, and distributing information related to tourism policy.

Local governments co-operate with the ministry and at the same time develop their own tourism authorities to market and develop international and domestic visits to their own regions. This decentralised structure has influenced the emergence of local public enterprises and local tourism organisations, an increase in local tourism development, changes in financial operations and greater social diversity.

Tourism budget

In 2007, the budget of the ministry amounted to approximately USD 432 million, of which USD 125 million is allocated to inbound tourism promotion, USD 109 million to fostering the tourism industry, and USD 198 million to the development of tourism zones and programmes. Some of the budget is allocated to KTO mainly for tourism promotion and to local government, primarily for the development of tourist zones. The main source of the budget is the general (national) budget and includes a fund for the promotion and development of tourism.

Tourism related policies and programmes

Korea's key tourism policy developments in 2007 are:

- Marketing Korea as a tourist attraction to the international community, based on Korean Tourism's Brand "Korea, Sparkling" launched in 2007 (Box 3.12).
- Co-operating with international tourism organisations and with the governments of other countries, especially Japan and China (Korea, Japan and China have held a 3-nation conference regularly for the promotion of trilateral tourism development).
- Improving the tourism information system based on information technology.
- Improving the tourist accommodation facilities: BENIKEA (meaning the "Best Night in Korea") was launched as the unified brand of medium-low cost tourist hotels in 2007 to foster medium-low cost accommodation facilities in the industry and to raise the quality of accommodation and service.

- Developing "Tourism and Leisure Cities" as an ideal vehicle to satisfy both the needs of investors and the needs of the market.
- Designating "Best" Cultural Tourism Festivals in Korea and fostering major festivals.

> **Box 3.12. Brand marketing and advertising based on the "Korea, Sparkling" brand launched in 2007**
>
> "Korea, Sparkling" is a strategic brand to distinguish Korea in the international marketplace. The brand was developed from research among 8 000 people in 17 countries, in consultation with a brand specialist over a two-year period, 2005-07. The underlying spirit of "Korea, Sparkling" is an emotional dynamism, which is the fountainhead and energy behind the passion of the Korean people, Korea's colourful personality and its creative culture. It embodies the vitality and enthusiasm that can only be experienced in Korea, and it evokes the powerful emotions and dynamism of Korean people and culture. For the brand to serve its purpose fully, consistent delivery of the values behind the brand through advertising, events, online marketing is and will be carried out. For more information, see *www.tour2korea.com*.

The Korean Wave phenomenon led the way in marketing efforts during 2004-05. This effect was largely influential in drawing over 6 million tourists to Korea during 2005. Korea also economised in its marketing efforts while also maximising their effects by developing various positioning strategies specific to target markets. Japan, China, Singapore, Malaysia, Canada and Australia all had promotional slogans and packages tailored to the characteristics of their respective markets. Various trade shows and events were developed to promote Korean tourism and a large number of journalists and travel agents participated in special promotional tours. New target markets were developed based upon projected demand, such as 30-50 year old Japanese women. In this particular case, such effective tourism marketing resulted in a 64% increase in visitation for that particular demographic segment. New and diverse print, online and audiovisual media were circulated to promote tourism and increase visitors' mobility and understanding of Korean culture during their stay.

Korea-Japan Friendship Year 2005 was held to commemorate the 40th anniversary of the normalisation of diplomatic ties between these two countries. The two countries have since agreed on some 40 exchanges or co-operative projects in the fields of tourism, culture, the arts and sports throughout the year. The two countries' authorities on tourism agreed to hold Visit Korea-Japan Year 2005 and some of the major events included the first performance of the Takarazuka in Seoul, a Korea-Japan Youth Exchange Fiesta, Friendship Concert involving a number of well-known pop singers, Korean Wave 2005 in major cities of Japan, and a KATA/JATA (Korea/Japan Association of Travel Agents) Tourism Forum.

In 2005 also, Korea established the headquarters of the Sustainable Tourism-Eliminating Poverty (ST-EP) Foundation in Seoul. The international foundation's initiative aims to alleviate poverty in the least developed countries by nurturing eco-friendly tourism industries. ST-EP will promote socially, economically and ecologically sustainable tourism, to alleviate poverty and bring jobs to people in developing countries.

> **Box 3.13. Examples of innovation in tourism**
>
> **1. Culture as marketing strategies for inbound tourism**
>
> Korea's international tourism marketing for 2005 was focused on culture, especially pop-culture called "Korean Wave (Hallyu)". This marketing theme strongly influenced inbound tourism, with tourism receipts anticipated to reach USD 5.6 billion for the year. In particular, a television drama named DAEJANGGEUM drew large numbers of fans from abroad who flocked to locations where it was filmed.
>
> Implementation strategies included: Overseas on/off-line promotion and advertisement, the development of differentiated Korean Wave products and attractions, the promotion of unique Korean cultural tourism (featuring well-known Korean pop stars), and the development of a business shopping model for Korean Wave products.
>
> **2. On-line tourism information system**
>
> The Tourism Hub Network (*www.etourkorea.com*) provides seven specialised services including Travel Business, Community, Education, Knowledge, and Shopping. The Tourism Hub Network contributes to higher customer satisfaction by serving user-centred domestic and international tourism information demand. It also contributes directly to the industry by strengthening the network of related affiliates within the tourism industry. The website provides a convenient bundle of services on one website, including information on tourist sites and facilities for booking tourism products.
>
> **3. Temple Stay**
>
> As a further example of innovation in tourism, Temple Stay is a truly unique and special type of accommodation that offers the opportunity for tourists to stay overnight in a Buddhist temple. Major activities in the program include: attending the Buddhist ceremonial service, Seon [Zen] meditation, tea ceremonies that elevate one's meditative efforts, Buddhist meals with traditional bowls, community work around the temple grounds, informative tours around the temple grounds, forest meditation to maximise oneness with nature, and hikes to nearby hermitages.
>
> *Source:* Korean tourism annual report, 2005.

Statistical profile

Table 3.58. **Inbound tourism: International arrivals and receipts**

	Units	2002	2003	2004	2005	2006
Visitors	Thousands	**5 347**	**4 753**	**5 818**	**6 023**	**6 155**
of which:						
Japan	Thousands	2 321	1 803	2 443	2 440	2 339
China	Thousands	539	513	627	710	897
United States	Thousands	459	422	511	531	556
Chinese Taipei	Thousands	137	195	305	351	338
Hong Kong	Thousands	74	78	103	166	143
Tourism receipts	Million USD	5 919	5 343	6 053	5 650	5 295

StatLink http://dx.doi.org/10.1787/155621318683
Sources: Ministry of Culture and Tourism, Annual Statistical Report on Korean Tourism, 2007.

Table 3.59. **Outbound tourism: International departures and expenditure**

	Units	2002	2003	2004	2005	2006
Departures	Thousands	7 123	7 086	8 826	10 080	11 610
Tourism expenditure	Million USD	9 038	8 248	9 856	11 942	13 783

StatLink http://dx.doi.org/10.1787/155663533561
Source: Ministry of Culture and Tourism, Annual Statistical Report on Korean Tourism, 2007.

Table 3.60. **Tourism in the national economy, 2004**

Section		Units	Whole industry	Tourism	Tourism share (%)
Tourism demand	Private consumption expenditure	Billion KRW	400 697	18 750	4.68
	Export	Billion KRW	343 229	9 003	2.62
	Import	Billion KRW	309 366	12 169	3.93
	Government expenditure	Billion KRW	92 383	1 763	1.91
Tourism supply	Value added	Billion KRW	778 446	17 606	2.26
	Employment	Thousands	16 916	852	5.04
	Fixed capital formation	Billion KRW	182 214	8 282	4.54

StatLink http://dx.doi.org/10.1787/155672376422
Source: Ministry of Culture and Tourism, Tourism Satellite Account in 2004.

Table 3.61. **Number of enterprises in tourism**

	2001	2002	2003	2004	2005
Number of enterprises in tourism	**10 031**	**10 736**	**11 034**	**11 421**	**12 480**
of which: Travel agencies	8 077	8 500	8 728	9 036	9 596
Tourist lodging businesses	600	625	664	685	1 104
Casino businesses	13	13	14	14	17
Convention businesses	84	102	123	134	147
Amusement parks	229	225	207	201	234

StatLink http://dx.doi.org/10.1787/155722884140
Source: Ministry of Culture and Tourism, 2007.

Luxembourg

Tourism in the economy

In 2006, there were approximately 2.6 million overnight stays by visitors to Luxembourg. A report by the World Travel and Tourism Council (WTTC) for 2006 estimated the direct and indirect economic importance of the tourism industry at 2.9% of GDP (EUR 0.8 billion) and employment in tourism at 7 000 employees, or 3.9% of the total employed labour force. In 2006, there were 284 accommodation establishments.

Table 3.62 summarises the volume of tourism in Luxembourg in terms of arrivals and total overnight stays. While arrivals increased by 3.3% between 2002 and 2006, there was a decline of 4.1% in total overnight stays in the same period. The main markets for Luxembourg are the Netherlands, Belgium, Germany and France.

Tourism organisation

The Ministry for the Middle Classes, Tourism and Housing is currently setting up Regional Tourism Offices (RTOs), which will bring together a region's main tourism stakeholders in order to ensure better co-ordination of activities and greater professionalism (Figure 3.20). The day-to-day management of RTOs will be entrusted to a director appointed by the Governing Board and approved by the Minister for Tourism. The financial resources of RTOs will include subsidies from the central government and communes, contributions paid by members and any other revenues except for the proceeds of commercial operations.

Figure 3.20. **Organisational chart of tourism bodies in Luxembourg**

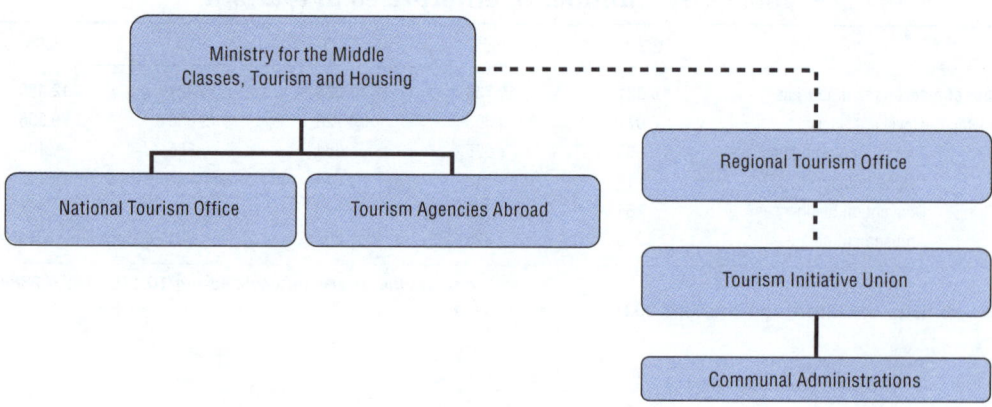

Source: OECD, adapted from Ministry of Tourism, 2007.

Negotiations are under way concerning the scale of apportionment between the share paid by the central government, contributions by communes and the professional sector. Another point that remains to be defined is the allocation of missions and responsibilities between RTOs and Regional Tourism Agreements and their relations with the National Tourist Office.

Tourism budget

The 2007 budget of the Ministry of Tourism is EUR 13.9 million and includes a special fund entitled the "7th Five-year Programme 2003-07 for Tourism Infrastructure" of EUR 7.45 million. The 2007 budget of the National Tourist Office is EUR 3.2 million (including EUR 1.9 million in subsidies from the Ministry of Tourism). The main source of financing for the development of tourism is the general national budget.

Tourism related policies and programmes

For a number of years now, the overall strategic concept for tourism in Luxembourg has been "*Quality of life and quality of tourism*". This reflects the policy choice of envisaging the future of tourism in Luxembourg from a two-fold perspective: the consolidation and qualitative improvement of the living conditions of the population, and a philosophy of tourism products and supply based on the key criteria of quality and sustainability.

Government policy in the field of tourism is based on the needs of the tourism sector, for which multi-year planning has been implemented through seven successive five-year plans that have made it possible to create and improve tourism infrastructure.

There is still good potential for growth in the tourism markets defined by Luxembourg's tourism policy, that is:

- Convention, business and "incentive" tourism.
- Cultural tourism.
- Rural tourism.
- Domestic tourism.

Linkages between tourism and other policies

Given that in 2007 Luxembourg was, for the second time in its history, a European Capital of Culture, the Ministry of Tourism stayed in very close contact with the Ministry of Culture and the 2007 organising committee during the year to ensure that adequate steps were taken to promote tourism with regard to the exceptional cultural offerings available.

In co-operation with the Statistics and Economic Studies Department, the Ministry for Tourism imminently intends to launch a feasibility study with a view to establishing a Tourism Satellite Account system for Luxembourg.

Statistical profile

Table 3.62. **Inbound tourism: International arrivals and nights**

	Unit	2002	2003	2004	2005	2006
Nights	Thousands	**2 469**	**2 541**	**2 514**	**2 465**	**2 414**
Arrivals	Thousands	**885**	**867**	**878**	**913**	**908**
of which:						
The Netherlands	Thousands	254	255	245	232	217
Belgium	Thousands	188	186	186	191	186
Germany	Thousands	113	117	115	124	123
France	Thousands	75	77	84	98	104

StatLink http://dx.doi.org/10.1787/155864876037

Source: STATEC, 2007.

Table 3.63. **International tourism receipts and expenditures**

	Unit	2002	2003	2004	2005	2006
Tourism receipts	Million EUR	2 404	2 994	3 657	3 616	3 620
Tourism expenditure	Million EUR	1 931	2 426	2 924	2 983	3 130

StatLink http://dx.doi.org/10.1787/155868777504

Source: STATEC, 2007.

Table 3.64. **Outbound tourism: International departures**

	Unit	2000	2001	2002	2003	2004
Departures	Millions	263	260	258	273	282

StatLink http://dx.doi.org/10.1787/155876003835

Source: STATEC, 2007.

Table 3.65. **Tourism in the national economy**

	Unit	2002	2003	2004	2005	2006
Number of travel agencies	Establishment	103	103	98	97	. .
Number of hotels, hostels and pensions	Establishment	313	315	297	293	284
Number of camping sites	Establishment	109	107	105	101	100

StatLink http://dx.doi.org/10.1787/155878324485

Source: STATEC, 2007.

Mexico

Tourism in the economy

According to the Tourism Satellite Account for 2005, tourism accounted for the 7.7% of GNP, sustaining about two million jobs. In that same year, the share of domestic tourism consumption was 81.3% of final consumption, with a Gross Value Added of USD 52 878 million. International Tourism Receipts in 2006 were USD 12 177 million or 53% of the value of services exports.

Tourist arrivals (excluding day excursionists) totalled 21.4 million in 2006, some 8.6% more than in 2002, but 2.6% down on 2005. The dominant market for Mexico is the USA, which accounted for 41% of all overnight visitors in 2006.

Tourism organisation

In 2006, the President of Mexico established tourism as a national priority. The Ministry of Tourism is currently designing a major restructuring of the three entities in charge of tourism policy in Mexico (Figure 3.21):

- The Ministry of Tourism is the leading organisation in the Federal Government with a mandate to design, co-ordinate and implement tourism policy. The Ministry registers all tourism services providers, organises and publishes the country's statistics related to tourism, and negotiates international agreements for the promotion of investment and of Mexico's tourism. Moreover, since 2007, the Ministry of Tourism is a full member of both the Economics and Competitiveness Cabinet and of the Infrastructure and Tourism Cabinet within the federal administration.

- The National Fund to Promote Tourism, Fonatur, identifies prospective, large-scale tourism development projects, advises state governments and supports their planning programmes for local tourism development projects, participates in the building of basic infrastructure in tourism destinations, and has the mission of attracting private investment for the development of such tourism destinations.

- The Mexico Tourism Board (see Tourism Budget).

Figure 3.21. **Organisational chart of tourism bodies in Mexico**

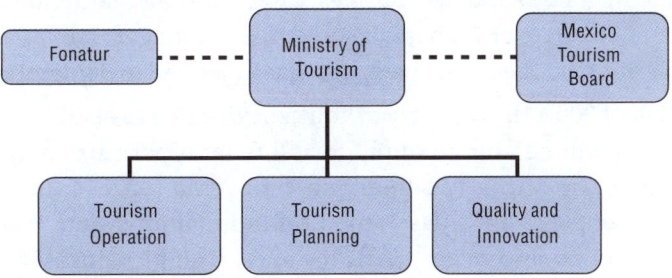

Source: OECD, adapted from Ministry of Tourism, 2007.

Some 26 of the 31 states in the country and the Federal District have included tourism as an important area of government responsibility, including a cabinet-level position within each governor's cabinet. All of the 32 federal entities match federal funds with resources of their own to develop annual investment programmes for the enhancement of local tourism infrastructure.

The Ministry, Fonatur and the Mexican Tourism Board work closely with the 32 federal entities. In 2007, the National Association of Governors set up a Task Force for Tourism.

The new administration has also set up a Tourism Advisory Council that includes participation by the bodies representing the Governors and state-level Tourism Secretaries, in addition to industry chambers.

Tourism budget

The majority of the tourism funds allocated by Congress are for the Ministry of Tourism. The 2007 budget for the Ministry is USD 170 million. In 2007, the Ministry will spend about USD 48 million to encourage states and municipalities to provide matching funds, for a total investment of USD 144 million targeted to improve local tourism infrastructure and the image of tourist destinations.

The Mexican Board (National Tourism Organisation) only receives operational funds. Independent since 1999, it allocates business representatives and encourages their financial contribution – a goal which remains to be fully accomplished. Its promotion campaigns are mainly funded through the "Non-Immigrant Duty" paid by all foreigners upon entering the country, mainly by air. In 2007, it is estimated the Board's budget for promotion will reach USD 115 million. Additionally, a 2% tax is added to the hotel bill of every tourist.

To evaluate the performance of public spending in tourism, both Federal and state governments are engaged in an effort to develop a methodology to measure the return on investment that results from public spending to promote tourism.

Tourism related policies and programmes

The Ministry of Tourism is undertaking the following policies to improve Mexico's position as a destination and to make the country more competitive in the global market:

- Migration and visa policies: the aim is to issue visas worldwide in a maximum of six days.
- Direct Investment: Operate a "Single Window" for all licenses from Federal Ministries to operate tourism projects.
- A culture of permanent training at the workplace.

Several operational and policy changes are currently underway.

Competitiveness

With regard to migration and visa policies, the government announced that as of 1 May 2007, any Mexican Consulate or Embassy should take no longer than twelve days to issue a visa once an application has been received; this was amended in September 2007, to six days.

In the first half of 2007, the Ministry of Tourism was due to establish a new mechanism whereby businesses will be able to apply for all federal permits to operate at a "Single Window" located at the Ministry's headquarters. This represents a major challenge involving Environment, Foreign Relations, Communications and Transport, and other federal ministries bent on improving efficiency and helping businesses.

In the field of transport and with a view to enhancing competitiveness, the Ministry of Tourism supported the growth of low-cost airlines which now represent about 30% of the airline market in the country.

Human resources

The Ministries of Tourism and of Public Education are setting up a large-scale programme targeted at new entrants, particularly the unskilled in the labour market. The objective is to encourage a new culture of permanent training and the long-term commitment of workers to enhance their skills and improve their living conditions as they help to enhance the quality of services in Mexico's tourism destinations.

In terms of education, the Department of Education in the Ministry of Tourism has set as one of its goals in the National Programme of Tourism Training 2007, improving the quality of ministry-led tourism education through training and undergraduate programmes.

Public/private partnerships

The Tourism Advisory Council includes participation by the three Tourism related business chambers operating nationally. The Council is chaired by the President and meets three times a year. Business leaders are encouraged to present their proposals and are also encouraged to work jointly with the Federal and state governments to solve existing roadblocks to tourism development. The Chairs of the Tourism Commissions at both the Senate and Chamber of Deputies also participate in this body.

The Ministry of Tourism and the National Development Bank (NAFIN) are currently designing a new programme that targets small- and medium-sized enterprises in the field of tourism, mainly to provide credit and thus enhance their competitiveness. This is in addition to a programme run with similar purposes by the Ministry of Economics that is to benefit 10 000 business firms until the end of 2012.

To encourage foreign direct investment, the Ministry of Tourism is developing a fast-track mechanism to approve domestic investments at coastal zones. This project was due to become operational in the first half of 2007.

Legislative and regulatory environment

Both the Senate and the Chamber of Deputies are currently engaged in consultations for drafting a new General Tourism Law that will update legal provisions to meet the challenges facing Mexico, as the country strives to enhance its position in the world market.

The Ministry's current participation in two cabinets of the Federal Government is both an unprecedented and a welcome measure. For the long- term, however, it is desirable that the Ministry's weight with regard to decisions made on building roads, regulating economic activities at coastal areas, negotiating international air agreements, designing and implementing migration and visa policies, and many such aspects that are the domain of other Federal agencies but that have a great impact on tourism, become legal attributes of the Ministry of Tourism working in co-ordination with the main agencies responsible for these measures.

Major forms of tourism

The Ministry of Tourism, in co-operation with other Federal entities, State Governments and Municipalities has developed the *Pueblos Mágicos* programme that includes the refurbishing and promotion of 30 towns in the country to develop tourism potential and improve the living standards of their inhabitants. The entities involved in this successful programme spent about USD 144 million in 2007 to improve local tourism infrastructure, public services, road access and redesigning of museums and cultural sites among other activities to improve the image of these tourist destinations. This programme has brought substantial local development to the communities around these towns.

Information technology

Each of three Tourism related Federal entities in Mexico has their own website. The goal is to come up with a first class, state of the art, single Web page that will facilitate travellers and investors to learn of all travel and investment opportunities available in Mexico and, in most cases, to buy the products and services of their choice on-line.

Statistical profile

Table 3.66. **Inbound tourism: International arrivals and receipts**

	Units	2002	2003	2004	2005	2006
Tourists (overnight visitors)	Thousands	19 667	18 665	20 618	21 915	21 353
of which:						
United States[1]	Thousands	..	..	..	8 525	8 765
Canada	Thousands	..	..	..	675	785
Spain	Thousands	..	..	..	203	261
United Kingdom	Thousands	..	..	..	231	260
France	Thousands	..	..	..	160	173
Tourism receipts	Million USD	8 858	9 362	10 796	11 803	12 177

StatLink http://dx.doi.org/10.1787/156103087422
1. This data includes US citizens and residents who cross the border by land.
Sources: Ministry of Tourism, Migration Information System, Banco de México, 2007.

Table 3.67. **Outbound tourism: International departures and expenditure**

	Units	2002	2003	2004	2005	2006
Departures	Thousands	11 948	11 044	12 494	13 305	14 002
Tourism expenditure	Million USD	6 060	6 253	6 959	7 600	8 108

StatLink http://dx.doi.org/10.1787/156107634714
Sources: Ministry of Tourism, Banco de México, 2007.

Table 3.68. **Tourism in the national economy**

	Units	2002	2003	2004	2005	2006
Tourism as % of gross national product	Percentage	8.0	7.9	7.8	7.7	..
Tourism as % of employment[1]	Percentage	5.4	5.4	5.4	..	..
Tourism as % of service exports	Percentage	52.8	56.8	54.9	53.6	53.0
Tourism Satellite Account						
Gross production	Million USD	74 770	69 312	76 159	..	..
Intermediate consumption	Million USD	27 012	25 102	27 697	..	..
Gross value added	Million USD	47 758	44 210	48 461	52 878	..

StatLink http://dx.doi.org/10.1787/156111430101
1. The employment percentage is related to service industries.
Source: Ministry of Tourism, 2007.

The Netherlands

Tourism in the economy

According to the TSA in 2006, the added value of tourism was EUR 13.6 billion, or 2.9% of GDP (Table 3.72). In 2002, TSA data showed that there were some 395 000 employees in the tourism sector, 4.1% of the employed labour force at the time.

In 2006, 10.7 million international visitors arrived in the Netherlands, an increase of 7% on 2005. The average length of stay has decreased a little, while the number of overnight stays grew by 6% to 26.9 million. Domestic tourism in 2006 accounted for 17.8 million domestic holiday trips, 2.9% up from 17.3 million in 2005.

There has been a steady rise in the number of tourism establishments since 2002 in hotels, camp sites and holiday bungalows, although the number of ANVR travel agencies (Dutch Association of Travel Agents and Tour Operators) has declined while tour operator numbers have stagnated.

Tourism organisation

The Ministry of Economic Affairs is responsible for tourism policy in The Netherlands (Figure 3.22). The main focus of tourism policy is to create a competitive business environment for the tourism sector and to attract foreign tourists. International promotion is carried out by the Netherlands Board of Tourism and Conventions (NBTC).

The focus of national tourism policy is international promotion. Provinces and municipalities promote themselves on the domestic market and internationally through the NBTC.

Figure 3.22. **Organisational chart of tourism bodies in the Netherlands**

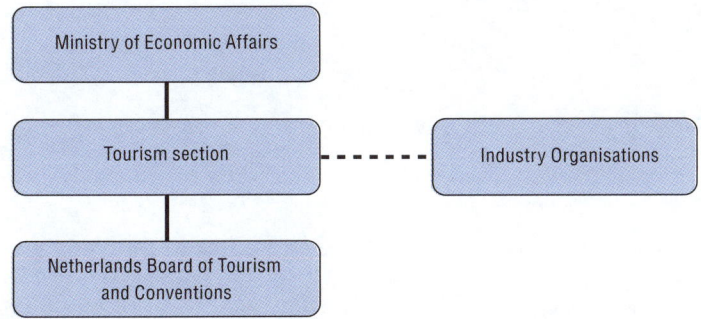

Source: OECD, adapted from Ministry of Economic Affairs, 2007.

Tourism budget

The 2007 budget for the NBTC is EUR 17.3 million. The Ministry of Economic Affairs allocates EUR 1 million annually for investment in the tourism sector's competitiveness. Additional investment in tourism is possible through the European Structural Funds, although most of the investment in tourism in the Netherlands is in fact by the private sector.

Tourism related policies and programmes

Key policies

The main objective of tourism policy during 2004-06 was to attract as many foreign visitors to the Netherlands as possible. The goal was to increase the Netherlands' market share of all incoming tourism in the neighbouring countries of Belgium, Denmark, Germany and the United Kingdom. This policy has been partly successful; incoming tourism rose over the period, but the country's market share has decreased due to a rapid growth in arrivals in Germany and the United Kingdom. These countries have benefited in particular from a growing number of low-cost carrier connections.

A new tourism policy is currently under preparation.

Co-operation with the Tourism Industry, Consumers and Other Stakeholders

The Ministry works in close co-operation with the branch organisations in the design and implementation of policies. Measures towards SMEs are mostly generic. The Dutch government is creating an internationally competitive playing field for SMEs, with improved regulation and the cutting of red tape having been the main focus for the past couple of years.

2006 was the year of the Rembrandt 400 celebration. This was a major public-private partnership event in which national government, municipalities, museums, marketing organisations, the airport and many other stakeholders co-operated. The year was very successful, particularly because of the excellent co-operation between the tourism and the cultural sectors. The organisation of the event is seen as an example of best practice which can be used as a model for forthcoming events.

Statistical profile

Table 3.69. **Inbound tourism: International arrivals and receipts**

	Units	2002	2003	2004	2005	2006
Tourists (overnight visitors)	Thousands	**9 595**	**9 181**	**9 646**	**10 012**	**10 738**
of which:						
Germany	Thousands	2 755	2 804	2 649	2 609	2 812
Unite Kingdom	Thousands	1 951	1 647	1 760	1 853	1 913
United States	Thousands	886	822	900	971	1 047
Belgium	Thousands	705	779	811	917	991
France	Thousands	511	465	510	527	608
Tourism receipts	Million EUR	8 150	8 099	8 306	8 421	9 172

StatLink http://dx.doi.org/10.1787/156112705366
Source: Statistics Netherlands (CBS), 2007.

Table 3.70. **Outbound tourism: International departures and expenditure**

	Units	2002	2003	2004	2005	2006
Departures	Thousands	16 758	16 463	17 173	17 086	16 752
Tourism expenditure	Million EUR	9 730	9 750	10 120	10 260	10 415

StatLink http://dx.doi.org/10.1787/156118624710
Source: Continuous Holiday Survey (CVO), 2007.

Table 3.71. **Employment in tourism in 2002**

	Units	2002 Jobs	2002 Employees
Employment in tourism sector (total)	Thousands	**439**	**395**
of which:			
Accommodations	Thousands	51	47
Restaurants and cafes	Thousands	174	154
Transportation companies	Thousands	60	58
Travel agencies	Thousands	26	25
Cultural institutions	Thousands	33	27
Other recreational companies	Thousands	35	27
Other companies	Thousands	60	57

StatLink http://dx.doi.org/10.1787/156156132440
Source: CBS, Tourism Satellite Account (TSA), 2002.

Table 3.72. **Tourism in the national economy**

	Units	2002	2003	2004	2005	2006
Tourism as % of:						
services exports	Percentage	..	12.9	12.1	11.5	..
gross domestic product	Percentage	3.2	3.1	3.0	3.0	3.0
added value	Percentage	3.1	2.9	2.9	2.9	2.9
employment	Percentage	4.1	4.1	4.1	4.1	4.1

StatLink http://dx.doi.org/10.1787/156186673331
Sources: CBS, Tourism Satellite Account (TSA), 2007.

New Zealand

Tourism in the economy

International tourism makes a major contribution to the New Zealand economy, contributing 18.7% of New Zealand's total export earnings. International tourism receipts reached NZD 8.1 billion in the year ended March 2005 and is forecast to increase by 6.5% per year to 2012, with international visitor arrivals rising by 4% per year. Tourism growth has implications for the physical infrastructure, investment intentions and the skills and talents required of the workforce. All of these need to be of sufficient quality and quantity to support the sector, particularly in peak periods.

Domestic tourists' expenditure reached NZD 9.4 billion in the year ending March 2005, and is forecast to increase by 2.7% per year to 2012. Tourism directly and indirectly contributes NZD 12.3 billion or some 9.0% to New Zealand's GDP, and supports 9.8% of the total workforce (Table 3.76).

Employment in the tourism industry has risen steadily since 2002, by 7.3% in the period to 2005. Tourist arrivals have reached 2.4 million, of which Australia accounts for about 37%. Growth has been steady since 2001, with an increase of some 24% in arrivals in the period 2001-05.

Tourism organisation

The Ministry of Tourism, a ministry within the Ministry of Economic Development, handles national tourism policy which consists of providing core policy advice, including monitoring of Tourism New Zealand (TNZ), the provision of research and statistics, advice and assistance on major events and land and property management of tourism concessions (Figure 3.23). TNZ is the marketing agency responsible for the offshore marketing of New Zealand as a tourism destination, and for capability development of the tourism industry onshore, through, for instance, a national quality assurance scheme.

Figure 3.23. **Organisational chart of tourism bodies in New Zealand**

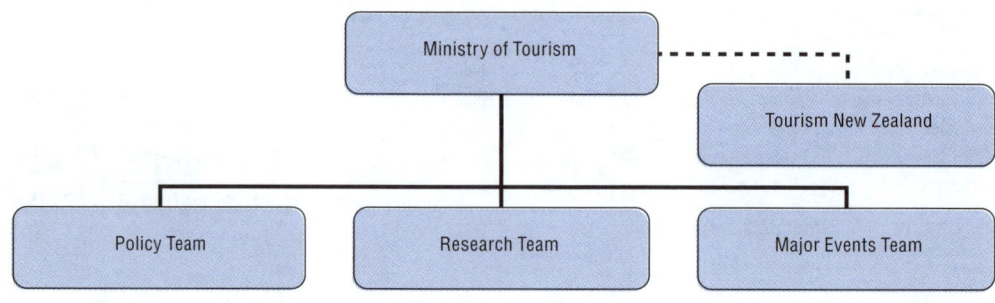

Source: OECD, adapted from Ministry of Tourism, 2007.

There are also 30 Regional Tourism Organisations (RTOs), owned and operated by New Zealand's local and regional governments and supported by the tourism industry, which market New Zealand's regional destinations.

Tourism budget

The budget of the National Tourism Administration is NZD 6.8 million in 2005-06. The budget of Tourism New Zealand is NZD 69 million in 2005-06. The main source of funding for tourism is from consolidated funds, *i.e.* the general budget. The Minister of Tourism allocates a special fund of NZD 2.5 million each year that is available to support initiatives to implement the New Zealand Tourism Strategy 2010. Information on implementation of the Strategy, including funded initiatives, is on the Ministry of Tourism's website.

The Ministry of Tourism provides advice on government's purchase of services from TNZ, and the New Zealand Maori Arts and Crafts Institute. Monitoring and reporting to the Minister on the financial and non-financial performance of Tourism New Zealand is provided annually via the Statement of Intent, the Memorandum of Understanding, the Output Agreement and the Annual Report. Other reporting is carried out quarterly and as required.

Tourism related policies and programmes

Co-operation with the tourism industry, consumers and other stakeholders

The Ministry is currently working in partnership with the Tourism Industry Association New Zealand and Tourism New Zealand to update the New Zealand Tourism Strategy 2010 (NZTS 2010 – see Box 3.14). The Strategy provides a shared vision and direction for the entire New Zealand tourism sector, public and private. Wide-ranging consultation with stakeholders has occurred and a draft of the updated New Zealand Tourism Strategy will be released for stakeholders' comments during the first half of 2007.

Box 3.14. New Zealand Tourism Strategy (NZTS 2010)

The New Zealand Tourism Strategy guides the tourism sector's approach to growth and development. The partnership approach between the public and private sectors applied in the development of the Strategy has been consolidated and enhanced in the implementation process, and there are many examples of where this partnership input has been critical (for example, TNZ working with RTOs and local visitor information offices to improve linkages between destination marketing and management).

Tourism businesses have access to business development assistance through the general business development programmes offered by New Zealand Trade and Enterprise (NZTE), the government's economic development agency. In addition, Maori tourism businesses have received individual mentoring during 2005-06 from the Maori Tourism Facilitation Service, a partnership between public sector agencies – Te Puni Kokiri (the Ministry of Maori Development) and the Ministry of Tourism – and private tourism providers.

The Ministry of Tourism is updating its Approved Destination Status (ADS) system for leisure travel to New Zealand by Chinese visitors to ensure tourism quality and immigration outcomes. Visitors are protected by a range of consumer protection laws and are eligible for state-funded accident compensation coverage while in New Zealand.

> **Box 3.15. Key tourism policy developments**
>
> Key tourism policy developments cover advice on economic, environmental and social policy affecting tourism, including the implementation of programmes to advance the recommendations of the New Zealand Tourism Strategy 2010 and the government's wider objectives as they relate to the sector, including the tourism aspects of major events. It includes the provision and management of tourism research and data to assist in sector decision-making. Further outputs include advice on the government's interests as owner of Tourism New Zealand, the New Zealand Maori Arts and Crafts Institute, and on the government's land and property holdings.

The main areas of intervention and programmes to advance the recommendations of NZTS 2010 are:

- Competitiveness (productivity, innovation, quality, etc.).
    - Qualmark (quality assurance scheme operated by TNZ).
- Sustainable tourism (environmental, economic, social).
    - Sustainable Tourism Charter project (aimed at sustainable business practice).
    - Tourism Planning Toolkit (for local government planning use).
    - Tourism Demand Subsidy Scheme (subsidising infrastructure in small communities with high tourism flows).
- Human resources (skills development, shortage of labour, obstacles in the labour market, immigration and labour, etc.).
    - Tourism and Hospitality Workforce and Skills Strategy 2006.
- Development of an evaluation culture (benchmarking of performance, targets and indicators).
    - Monitoring and evaluation of TNZ.
    - Refinement of marketing performance indicators.
- Legislative and regulatory environment.
    - Enhancement of the Approved Destination Status (ADS) for China (sub-regulatory).
- International and intra-regional activities.
    - Asia Pacific Economic Co-operation (APEC).
    - Australian Standing Committee on Tourism (ASCOT).

Tourism Satellite Account data and analysis

The Tourism Satellite Account in New Zealand is one component of the core tourism dataset, providing economic information for understanding and monitoring the levels and impact of tourism activity in New Zealand. The Tourism Satellite Account in New Zealand is well developed and consistent with the guidelines of the United Nations World Tourism Organisation.

Development of other indicators (employment, sustainability, industry performance)

The Ministry of Tourism is funding the Yield Research Programme, which looks at the development of more comprehensive indicators to measure the performance of the tourism industry and business by considering financial yield, economic yield and sustainable yield. This three year programme assesses yields from different types of travellers, examines public sector investment in tourism firms and benchmarks industry performance.

Tourism Flows Model

The Ministry of Tourism has launched the New Zealand Tourism Flows Model, which is a unique GIS software tool that represents the dynamics of tourism in New Zealand visually. It utilises two surveys from the core tourism dataset, the International Visitor Survey and the Domestic Travel Survey, together with other datasets to build a picture of current and future tourism flows in New Zealand. Users can identify trends and potential capacity constraints.

The purpose of the Tourism Flows Model is to facilitate informed decision-making on where to invest and where to adopt pro-active policy, planning and resource allocation practices. The target audience for this tool is primarily Local Government planners, tourism planners, Regional Tourism Organisations and tourism businesses. The model aims to provide a tool to plan for future growth in tourism to achieve optimum outcomes for New Zealand.

Statistical profile

Table 3.73. **Inbound tourism: International arrivals and receipts**

	Units	2001	2002	2003	2004	2005
Visitors[1]	Thousands	**1 909**	**2 045**	**2 104**	**2 334**	**2 366**
of which:						
Australia	Thousands	632	634	703	857	876
United Kingdom	Thousands	212	237	265	284	307
United States	Thousands	187	205	212	218	215
Japan	Thousands	149	174	151	165	155
Korea	Thousands	87	110	113	114	112
Tourism receipts[1]	Million NZD	6 763	7 093	7 660	7 811	8 067

StatLink http://dx.doi.org/10.1787/156214664686

1. Including nationals residing abroad (year ended March).
Sources: International Visitor Arrival, Tourism Satellite Account, Statistics New Zealand, 2007.

Table 3.74. **Outbound tourism: International departures and expenditure**

	Units	2001	2002	2003	2004	2005
Departures	Thousands	1 287	1 293	1 374	1 730	1 868
Tourism expenditure[1]	Million NZD	..	..	2 741	2 987	..

StatLink http://dx.doi.org/10.1787/156254176576

1. Year ended June.
Sources: External Migration, Survey of Returned Travellers, Statistics New Zealand, 2007.

Table 3.75. **Employment in tourism**

	Units	2002	2003	2004	2005
Total tourism employment[1]	Thousands	164	176	173	176
Directly engaged in tourism	Thousands	98	105	104	105

StatLink http://dx.doi.org/10.1787/156265474487

1. Full-time equivalent, year ended March.
Sources: Tourism Satellite Account, Statistics New Zealand, 2007.

Table 3.76. **Tourism in the national economy**

	Units	2001	2002	2003	2004	2005
Tourism as % of gross domestic product	Percentage	9.9	9.7	9.8	9.5	9.0
Tourism as % of employment	Percentage	..	10.0	10.4	10.0	9.8
Tourism as % of exports	Percentage	16.4	16.2	18.1	19.3	18.7
Total tourism expenditure	Million NZD	15 255	16 095	17 054	17 351	17 483
Domestic tourism share of NZ tourism	Percentage	55.7	55.9	55.1	55.0	53.9
Numbers of enterprises in tourism	Thousands	..	281	295	324	334

StatLink http://dx.doi.org/10.1787/156270474861

Sources: Tourism Satellite Account, Business Demography Studies, Statistics New Zealand, 2007.

Norway

Tourism in the economy

Tourism accounts for 3.1% of GNP and 6.8% of total employment (Table 3.80). Compared to the previous year, tourism employment in 2006 showed a growth of 7% on the previous year.

Total tourism consumption in Norway was NOK 87 billion in 2005, an increase from the previous year of 5%. Domestic tourists consume NOK 43 billion, foreign tourists NOK 27 billion and the business/convention market NOK 17 billion. In 2006, Norwegians took 17.3 million vacation trips, an increase of 4% on 2005. Domestic travel stayed at the same level as the year before, and thus it was holidays abroad that produced the growth (of 12%). In 2006, 69% of Norwegians' holiday trips were domestic. In the period 2002-06, the number of holidays spent abroad rose by 27%, while domestic holidays fell by 7%.

In 2005, there were 12 689 firms in the tourism sector, mostly small enterprises of 1-10 employees. Data on the volume of overnight tourist arrivals show that there has been growth of 27% in the period 2002-06, to a total of 3.9 million. The leading market for Norway is Germany, which accounted for 21% of total bed nights in 2006, followed by Denmark with 13%.

Trip purpose surveys have shown that most tourists travel to Norway to experience unspoilt nature and high environmental standards, followed by the Norwegian culture and way of life. Other important factors that make tourists choose Norway are its quietness and calmness, value for money, safety, well-being and hospitality.

Tourism organisation

The publicly-owned company, Innovation Norway, is Norway's national tourism organisation. Innovation Norway is in charge of the promotion of Norway as a tourism destination abroad and for the development of the tourism sector within Norway's borders. The company has its headquarters in Oslo and regional offices in all 19 counties in Norway, in addition to 31 offices abroad. Some of the offices abroad are co-located with Norwegian embassies. A number of other ministries co-operate with Innovation Norway to promote different Tourism related initiatives within Norway. Additional public funding is provided through these ministries.

Innovation Norway runs a number of tourism projects nationwide in co-operation with regional offices, different national, regional or local organisations and travel destinations.

At local level, most municipalities in Norway operate tourism information offices.

Organisation and links between the national tourism authority and the provinces/regions:

At national level, tourism policy is the responsibility of the Ministry of Trade and Industry (Figure 3.24). Each year a lump sum is proposed by the Ministry and sanctioned by Parliament to promote Norway as a tourist destination and to strengthen the competitiveness of the Norwegian travel and tourism industry.

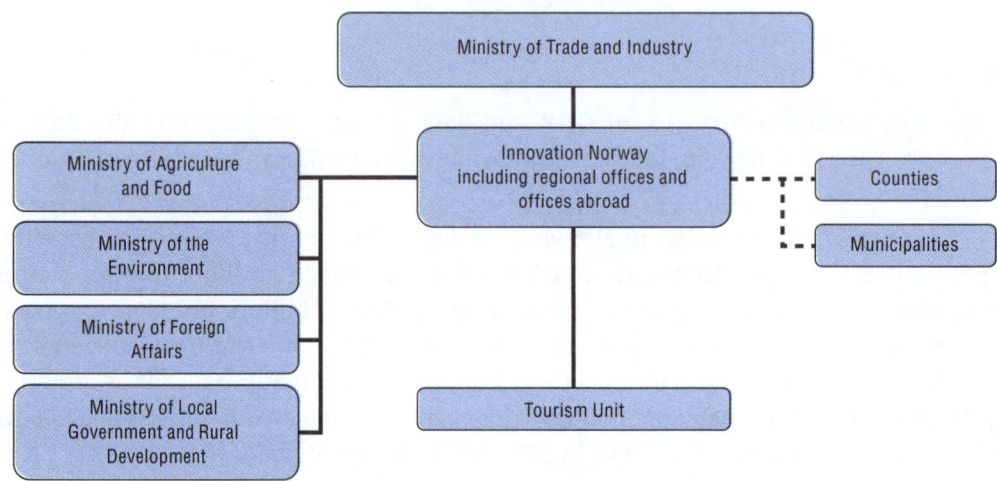

Figure 3.24. **Organisational chart of tourism bodies in Norway**

Source: OECD, adapted from Ministry of Trade and Industry, 2007.

After approval by Parliament of the state budget, the Ministry of Trade and Industry instructs Innovation Norway on the major lines of tourism policy that are to be followed during the coming year. It is left up to Innovation Norway to initiate the action required to put these policies into effect and to instruct their regional offices and offices abroad to follow up on the priorities given by the ministry.

Tourism budget

The main source of funding for tourism promotion and development in Norway is the annual state budget. However, when marketing Norway as a tourism destination abroad, the amount of public funds spent should be matched/co-funded by the travel and tourism industry. In 2006, the amount granted from the state budget was NOK 172.5 million; in 2007, this rose to NOK 200 million.

Innovation Norway's total income in 2006 amounted to NOK 298 million, of which NOK 172 million came from public funds and NOK 126 million from the travel and tourism industry. There are no direct tourism related taxes in Norway.

Tourism related policies and programmes

The Ministry of Trade and Industry is currently working on a National Strategy for the Travel and Tourism Industry. The work is being carried out in close co-operation with the organisations of the tourism industry and the industry itself. The strategy will be published in the fourth quarter of 2007.

In 2005, the ministry launched an Action Plan for the travel and tourism industry focusing on the following topics: Marketing, innovation, raising competence levels, and promoting co-operation. A number of points of action were launched within each field, and an additional NOK 22.5 million granted by the ministry to the follow-up work.

The major points of the Action plan were:

- Produce a new marketing strategy for Norway as a tourist destination abroad (completed).
- Establish a programme for promoting geo-tourism [tourism that sustains or enhances the geographical character of a place] in Norway (completed).
- Establish a programme to establish eco-tourism as a concept adapted to Norwegian conditions (ongoing).
- Establish a programme for strategic research within the field of nature-based tourism (ongoing).
- Revise, update and improve the national tourism portal on the Internet, *www.visitnorway.com* (ongoing).
- Establish publicly-funded projects for the development of new, innovative tourism products with a focus on year-round tourism (ongoing).
- Establish a new programme to promote competence training in the travel and tourism industry (ongoing).
- Study criteria for successful co-operation within the Norwegian travel and tourism industry (completed).
- Establish a programme to stimulate increased co-operation within the travel and tourism industry (ongoing).

Statistical profile

Table 3.77. **Inbound tourism: International arrivals and tourism consumption**

	Units	2002	2003	2004	2005	2006
Tourists (overnight visitors)	Thousands	3 111	3 269	3 628	3 824	3 945
Bed nights in Norway	Thousands	7 275	6 956	7 442	7 651	7 944
of which:						
Germany	Thousands	1 698	1 698	1 649	1 746	1 672
Denmark	Thousands	997	895	1 049	1 065	1 018
Sweden	Thousands	876	763	827	872	867
Netherlands	Thousands	669	715	789	765	769
Britain	Thousands	643	609	677	705	757
Tourism consumption	Million NOK	22 415	22 232	24 846	26 420	..

StatLink http://dx.doi.org/10.1787/156281206100

Source: Ministry of trade and industry, Statistics Norway, 2007.

Table 3.78. **Outbound tourism: International departures**

	Units	2002	2003	2004	2005	2006
Departures	Thousands	1 767	1 749	1 826	1 912	1 942
Tourism expenditure	Billion NOK	39.60	39.41	48.63	56.68	62.38

StatLink http://dx.doi.org/10.1787/156283814135

Source: Ministry of trade and industry, Statistics Norway, 2007.

Table 3.79. **Employment in tourism**

	Units	2001	2002	2003	2004	2005
Employment in tourism (Full time equivalent)	Thousands	**137.6**	**138.7**	**135.1**	**134.0**	**135.1**
of which:						
Hotels and restaurants	Thousands	55.8	55.5	54.1	53.6	53.8
Transport (railways, trams, subway)	Thousands	8.3	8.1	7.5	7.4	7.2
Transport (public buses, taxis)	Thousands	21.1	21.3	20.7	20.6	21.2
Passenger transport at sea, abroad	Thousands	2.1	2.1	2.1	2.0	2.0
Passenger transport at sea, domestic	Thousands	7.4	8.0	8.1	7.6	7.5
Air transport	Thousands	12.8	11.7	11.4	11.3	11.0
Travel agencies, etc.	Thousands	4.9	4.7	4.6	4.4	4.4

StatLink http://dx.doi.org/10.1787/156338783620

Source: Statistics Norway, 2007.

Table 3.80. **Tourism in the national economy**

	Units	2001	2002	2003	2004	2005[1]
Tourism as % of gross national product	Percentage	3.5	3.8	3.5	3.3	3.1
Tourism as % of employment	Percentage	6.9	7	6.9	6.8	6.8
Domestic tourism consumption as % of total final consumption	Percentage	..	..	..	5	5
Domestic tourism consumption as % of households final consumption	Percentage	..	..	..	3.6	3.5
Total tourism consumption in Norway	Million NOK	..	..	..	82 858	87 088
Output in tourism industries	Million NOK	127 263	130 343	130 200	133 592	141 020
Value added in tourism industries	Million NOK	54 210	57 487	56 316	57 879	59 668
Gross fixed capital formation	Million NOK	11 900	10 893	8 313	8 336	..

StatLink http://dx.doi.org/10.1787/156353838071

1. Preliminary data.
Source: Ministry of trade and industry, Statistics Norway, 2007.

Poland

Tourism in the economy

The share of tourism in GDP in 2006 was 6.1%. Foreign tourists' expenditure in Poland in 2006 was estimated at PLN 22.4 billion while domestic tourism expenditure was estimated at PLN 18.9 billion. Expenditure by Poles abroad totalled PLN 6.8 billion, business trips amounted to PLN 13.9 billion, and public expenditures on tourism were estimated at PLN 2.7 billion. The value of the total tourism economy was estimated at PLN 64.7 billion.

In 2006, tourism exports were valued at PLN 22.4 billion, 5.2% of the total value of Polish goods and services exports.

The number of people employed in tourism in 2005 (hotels and restaurants and activities of travel agencies, tour operators, tourist assistance activities) was 225 900, 1.75% of total employment.

Total arrivals from abroad rose by 12% in the period 2002-06, with Germany leading the field as an origin market and accounting for 35% of all arrivals in 2006, followed by Ukraine with 16%.

Tourism organisation

Within central government, tourism has come under the Minister of Sport and Tourism since mid-2007 (Figure 3.24). The tourism administration deals with issues of tourist infrastructure development, market regulation mechanisms, recognition of qualifications of regulated professions (such as tourist guides) and so called regulated activities (such as tour leaders).

In regional government, the voivod is a representative of the government in voivodships (Palatinate regions) in Poland. In 2006, their responsibility in the realm of tourism was transferred to marshal's offices. Tourism also plays an important role in the activities of the organs of regional self-government at all levels (communes, districts and voivodships).

The promotion of tourism in Poland is conducted:

- At the central level, by the Polish Tourist Organisation (PTO).
- At regional level, by Regional Tourist Organisations (RTOs).
- At the local level, by Local Tourist Organisations (LTOs).

Figure 3.25. **Organisational chart of tourism bodies in Poland**

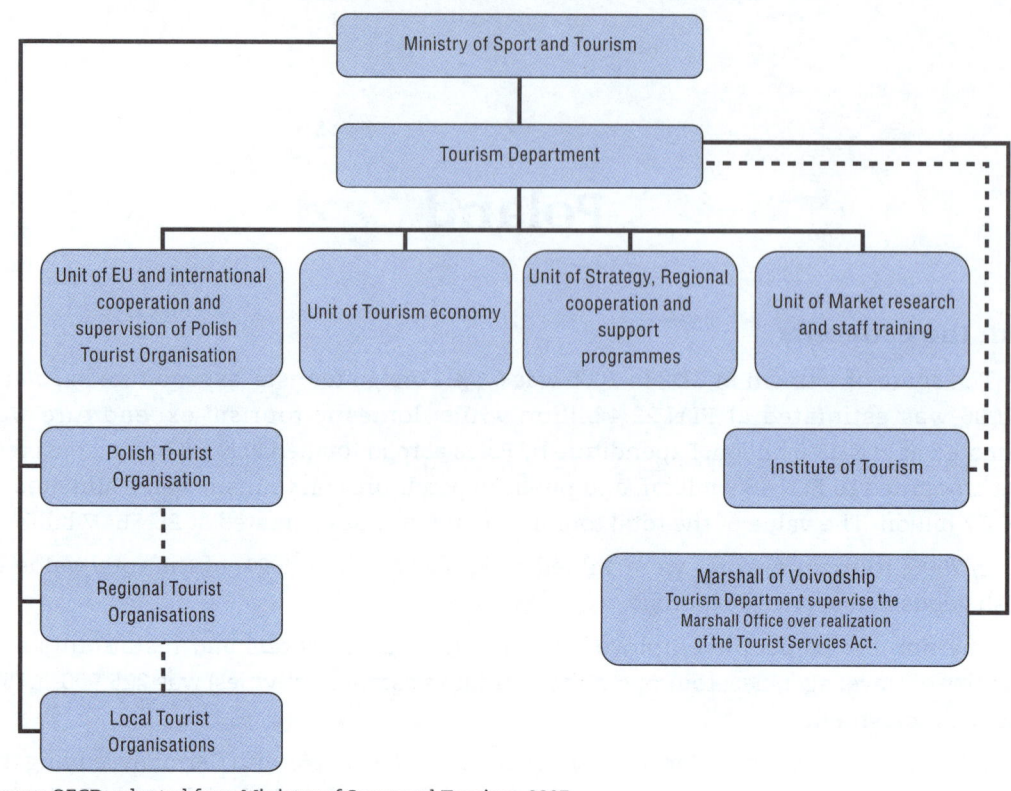

Source: OECD, adapted from Ministry of Sport and Tourism, 2007.

Tourism budget

In 2006, the budget of National Tourism Administration was PLN 46.0 million, including the budget of the National Tourism Organisation which was PLN 38.0 million.

Table 3.81. **Expenditures of local self-government entities budgets for tourism in 2006**

PLN millions

Local self-government of communes	114.4
Local self-government of cities on rights of districts	29.5
Local self-government of districts	3.4
Local self-government of voivodships	13.8
TOTAL	161.1

StatLink ⟶ http://dx.doi.org/10.1787/254631304315
Source: Central Statistical Office.

The total budget for tourism (national, regional and local administrations) in 2006 was PLN 207.1 million.

Tourism related policies and programmes

The government is currently finalising its "Strategy of tourism development in Poland for the years 2007-13". The new strategy assumes that competitive and high quality tourism products will attract foreign and domestic tourists. Healthy lifestyles, new ways of spending free time and other new trends are emphasised strongly in this document, as are the creation of a coherent promotional system in Poland and improvement of tourist information systems. Modernisation of infrastructure and transport in tourism regions is a significant factor, and the new strategy also contains information about the necessity of training professional tourism staff.

At the end of 2006, the Ministry of Economy started a national debate with tourism industry representatives on the changes that are needed in tourism law. The debate was preceded by a survey which showed 60% of respondents have a positive view of the legal institutions created under the Act of 29 August 1997 governing tourist services. However, the view was also held that the law should be reviewed. The results of the survey confirm that the Act should be simplified and that some legal issues should be more precisely defined. In 2007, consultations continued and appropriate changes will be introduced into the current Act by the end of the year.

The EU structural funds for the years 2007-13 offer a great opportunity for Poland to develop its infrastructure and enhance tourism services (Box 3.16).

> **Box 3.16. Key Priorities of "Strategy of tourism development in the years 2007-13"**
>
> - *High quality tourism product*: Creation and development of competitive tourist products; development of tourist infrastructure; supporting tourist entrepreneurship and organisations; development of different types of tourism.
> - *Improving the quality of tourism jobs*: Developing education in the field of tourism; supporting social tourism; training professional tourism staff.
> - *Marketing support*: Improving tourism information and reservation systems; improving marketing.
> - *Shaping tourism space*: Complying with accessibility and sustainability requirements during tourism planning.

At national level, the measures concerning tourism are placed in the *Innovative Economy* Operational Programme – Priority 6: *Polish economy on the international market*. Its objective is to enhance the brand of Poland through the promotion of the country as an attractive destination for tourists and investors, as well as a good place to establish business relations.

Projects connected with tourism will be also backed up in the *Eastern Poland Development* Operational Programme that will be implemented in five regions: lubelski, podkarpacki, podlaski, świetokrzyski and warmińsko-mazurski. Financial support will be provided for joint promotional campaigns of the 5 regions that are aimed at attracting tourists and investors, as well as for projects for the construction and modernisation of fair and convention/conference infrastructure.

Tourism will also be supported from the funds of Operational Programmes of *European Territorial Co-operation*. The support of tourism projects plays an important role especially in the *Poland-Czech Republic* Operational Program and *Poland-Slovakia* Operational Program, as well as within the framework of co-operation with Baltic countries and within three Operational Programmes for Polish and German regions (Länder).

Additionally, *the Infrastructure and Environment* Operational Programme assures support to cultural sites and monuments which are relevant to the further development of tourism. Tourism projects are strongly identified in all sixteen Regional Operational Programmes. These provide support to the construction and modernisation of tourism infrastructure, *e.g.* tourism accommodation establishments, restoration projects, recreational infrastructure, spa infrastructure, tourist information infrastructure, public tourism infrastructure (tourism trails) and tourism promotion.

Linkages between tourism and other policies

The Tourism Department co-operates closely with many Ministries, especially with the Ministry of Regional Development on the subject of structural funds for tourism. In addition, the Department collaborates with the Ministry of National Education on improving education in tourism sector, as well as on support for child and youth tourism. In 2002, the Tourism Department started a successful co-operation with Ministry of Internal Affairs and Administration (the Polish National Police) on a "Tourist Emergency Line", aimed at foreign tourists in Poland needing help in an emergency.

Major forms of tourism

The most popular segments of tourism in Poland are leisure trips (holidays), business, cultural and city tourism. Agri-tourism and eco-tourism are also popular, as well as different kinds of active tourism such as cycling, kayaking, horse-riding and specialised tourism for activities such as bird-watching. One of the most dynamic segments is spa and wellness tourism, as are the fast growing niche products such as visits to post-industrial or post-military sites, and visits for Polish culinary experiences.

Statistical profile

Table 3.82. **Inbound tourism: International arrivals and receipts**

	Units	2002	2003	2004	2005	2006
Tourists (overnight visitors)	Thousands	**13 980**	**13 720**	**14 290**	**15 200**	**15 670**
of which:						
Germany	Thousands	4 160	4 520	5 230	5 570	5 440
Ukraine	Thousands	2 930	2 480	2 340	2 535	2 500
Belarus	Thousands	1 700	1 620	1 460	1 440	1 490
Lithuania	Thousands	840	825	815	830	895
Tourism receipts	Billion PLN	19.1	15.4	21.0	20.3	22.4

StatLink http://dx.doi.org/10.1787/156405840441

Source: Institute of Tourism, 2007.

Table 3.83. **Outbound tourism: International departures and expenditure**

	Units	2002	2003	2004	2005	2006
Departures	Thousands	4 400	3 300	3 800	3 800	4 500
Tourism expenditure	Billion PLN	4.6	4.4	3.7	4.2	6.8

StatLink http://dx.doi.org/10.1787/156411335678

Source: Institute of Tourism, 2007.

Table 3.84. **Employment in tourism**

	Units	2001	2002	2003	2004	2005
Total employment in the tourism sector	Thousands	**226.6**	**219.9**	**222.2**	**222.7**	**225.9**
Hotels and restaurants	Thousands	217.2	210.9	214.3	216.3	219.4
Travel agencies,[1] tour operators and tourist assistance activities	Thousands	9.4	9.0	7.9	6.4	6.5

StatLink http://dx.doi.org/10.1787/156413822654

1. Travel agencies with more than 9 employees.
Source: Central Statistical Office, 2007.

Table 3.85. **Tourism in the national economy**

	Units	2002	2003	2004	2005	2006
Tourism as % of gross domestic product	Percentage	7.3	6.5	6.2	5.7	6.1
Number of enterprises in tourism						
Collective tourism establishments	Establishments	7 050	7 116	6 972	6 723	6 694
Hotels and similar establishments	Establishments	1 478	1 547	2 139	2 200	2 301
Tour operators, travel agencies	Establishments	3 650	3 504	2 839	2 627	2 677

StatLink http://dx.doi.org/10.1787/156428470112

Sources: Institute of Tourism, Data of Central Statistical Office and Department of Tourism, Ministry of Economy, 2007.

Portugal

Tourism in the economy

According to the Portuguese Tourism Satellite Account (PTSA), tourism contributed 4.6% to GDP in 2004, and 4.6% of gross value added. Tourism characteristic activities represented around 88.8 % of that value. Tourism's share of domestic production in that year was 4.2%, while internal tourism consumption represented 9.3% of GDP or around 50% of this aggregate.

The PTSA estimates that employment in tourism-characteristic industries represented around 7.8% of total employment in 2004 (or 8% if full-time equivalent jobs are counted). The activities contributing most to employment in the sector in terms of FTE are restaurants (with 54.5% of total FTE in the TSA characteristic activities), hotels and similar establishments (15.3%) and road passenger transport (9.8%).

The Cross Border Movements survey shows total arrivals of some 22.6 million on 2006, compared with 21.1 million in the two previous years, including day excursionists. Overnight tourists totalled 11.3 million, compared with 10.6 million in the two previous years.

Tourism organisation

As part of a general public administration reform, all centrally-organised tourism bodies are being merged into a single institute, *Turismo de Portugal*. This new organisation brings together the skills bases of the Directorate-General for Tourism (tourist-related regulation of the tourism industry, planning, studies, statistics and licensing), the Portuguese Tourism Institute (support for investment and promotion of tourism), the National Tourism Training Institute (management of the training systems and professional certification in tourism), and the Inspectorate General of Gambling (inspection of gambling and casino activity) (Figure 3.26). The creation of the new institute should reduce administration costs, simplify administrative processes and improve efficiency.

The legislation relating to the configuration, responsibilities and capacities of Portugal's tourism regions is also in the process of revision. This will bring their structures closer to the national organisational model and create a suitable regional model through which to deal with external promotion. In 2007, Portugal will launch another three year cycle of its external tourism promotion model based on public–private partnerships. The objective is to increase efficiency by linking demand and supply more effectively and by means of a more integrated marketing concept.

In the new promotional structure, the Portuguese brand is managed by *Turismo de Portugal*, and the regional brands by the Regional Agencies for Tourism Promotion [*Agências Regionais de Promoção Turística* (ARPT's)]. These latter are non-profit associations of public entities and regional and local tourism companies. There are seven regions: Porto and North, Centre, Lisbon, Alentejo, Algarve, Madeira and Azores.

Figure 3.26. **Organisational chart of tourism bodies in Portugal**

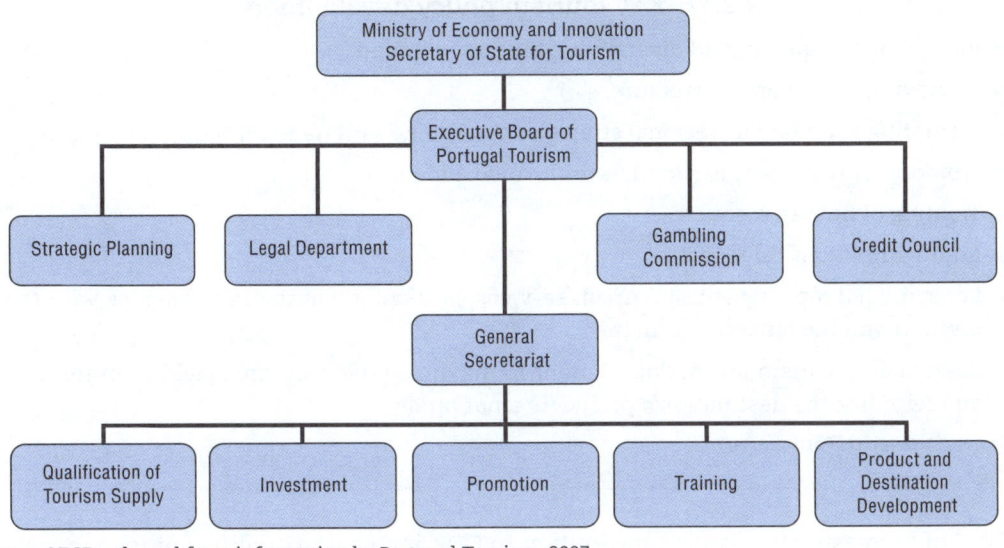

Source: OECD, adapted from information by Portugal Tourism, 2007.

This new structure provides better co-ordination of both national and regional performance within a common strategy and an agreed action plan, and should present a clearer view of the country's destination choices, leading to greater promotional efficiency. The objective is also to achieve greater involvement on the part of the private sector, notably in tourism promotion management and operations, as well as in investment.

Tourism budget

The main sources of income for financing tourism activities are the national budget, gambling/casino taxes, EU programmes and the industry itself (for marketing purposes).

Tourism related policies and programmes

The new tourism management model described above is aimed at providing high quality tourism services to the visitor while simultaneously promoting the preservation of natural resources and respecting the country's cultural values and principles. The implementation of this strategy (Box 3.17) will include a focus on the valorisation of tourism resources, the creation of high quality supply and the pursuit of increased domestic and international demand. It also includes the implementation of autonomous regional strategies integrated with national policies, the stimulation of investment and modernisation, improving the competitive position of tourism companies, and defining a tourism-based law supporting the strategy of a national tourism policy.

Portugal is currently working on a new support program for economic and social development for 2007-13 which will consider new measures for business development and increased competitiveness (quality, training, introduction of information technologies, innovation, etc.). In this support framework, less developed regions, touristic priorities and small and medium-sized companies will be emphasised, and a special focus will be given to supporting business networks and clusters (constitution and development of co-operative networks).

Following the definition of policy options for the sector, a National Strategic Plan for Tourism [*Plano Estratégico Nacional de Turismo (PENT)*] has been developed with the objective

> **Box 3.17. Key tourism policy developments**
>
> - Increasing the quality and diversifying tourism demand.
> - Improving tourism infrastructure.
> - Promoting autonomous regional strategies consistent with national actions and policies.
> - Promoting investment in products with value added.
> - Training of human resources.
> - Improving statistical reporting.
> - Reducing red tape in central tourism services, particularly in the relationships with the investor and the citizen in general.
> - Re-focusing tourism promotion in order to maximise the economic yield from tourism and reinforce the destination's profile internationally.
>
> *Source:* Turismo de Portugal, 2007

by 2015 of increasing tourism's contribution to GDP, increasing qualified employment and accelerating the sustainable growth of the sector. The national objectives for 2007-09 are to achieve an annual growth rate of:

- Hotel receipts +9.2%.
- Hotel nights +4.6%.
- Tourist arrivals +5.8%.

The Plan identified ten key products/market sectors which, due to their characteristics, potential attractiveness and expected growth, should serve as a base for the development of tourism in Portugal, at a national and regional level. These are: sun and sea, golf, the MICE segment, city/short breaks, cultural and landscape touring, nautical tourism, residential tourism, health and well-being, nature tourism, gastronomy and wines.

Portugal has also implemented a Tourism Satellite Account (TSA) for the reference year 2000 and will now publish TSA data on a regular basis. In addition, the country is developing a new methodology to evaluate the weight of each of the main tourism products in the country's tourism earnings. The first main results are expected in 2007.

Statistical profile

Table 3.86. **Inbound tourism: International arrivals and receipts**

	Units	2004	2005	2006
Visitors	Thousands	21 109	21 164	22 572
Tourists (overnight visitors)	Thousands	10 639	10 612	11 282
of which: Spain	Thousands	2 514	2 370	2 497
United Kingdom	Thousands	2 052	2 089	2 254
France	Thousands	1 598	1 560	1 501
Germany	Thousands	1 047	1 075	1 191
Netherlands	Thousands	470	478	515
Tourism receipts		..	..	..

StatLink http://dx.doi.org/10.1787/156440286414
Sources: Statistics Portugal, Crossborder Movements Survey, 2007.

Table 3.87. **Outbound tourism: International departures and expenditure**

	Unit	2004	2005	2006
Departures[1]	Thousands	17 138	18 107	18 376
of which: Visitors with nights	Thousands	3 949	3 993	3 770
Tourism expenditure		..	..	..

StatLink http://dx.doi.org/10.1787/156622662354

1. Including same-day visitors.
Sources: Statistics Portugal, Crossborder Movements Survey, 2007.

Table 3.88. **Number of enterprises and employment in tourism**

	Units	2001	2002	2003	2004
Hotels and restaurants	Establishments	62 082	62 344	65 737	65 628
of which: Hotels	Establishments	3 280	3 153	3 276	3 457
Camp sites and other short-stay accommodation	Establishments	650	789	783	1 107
Restaurants	Establishments	21 664	23 167	23 376	24 476
Bars	Establishments	36 038	34 761	37 783	36 096
Employees	Employees	239 140	229 933	228 941	236 439

StatLink http://dx.doi.org/10.1787/156674415487
Sources: Statistics Portugal, Hotel and Similar Establishments Survey, Structural Business Survey, 2007.

Table 3.89. **Tourism in the national economy**

	Units	2003	2004
Tourism as % of the domestic production (basic prices)	Percentage	4.1	4.2
Internal tourism consumption (purchaser prices)	Billion EUR	12.6	13.4
Tourism characteristic activities as % of total employment	Percentage	7.9	7.8

StatLink http://dx.doi.org/10.1787/156683053313
Sources: Statistics Portugal – The Portuguese Tourism Satellite Account, 2003 and 2004.

Slovak Republic

Tourism in the economy

The share of international tourism receipts in Slovakia's GDP was 2.7% in 2006 and 2.6% in 2005 (Table 3.93). International tourism receipts were EUR 1 207.7 million in 2006, an increase of 24.2% on 2005. International tourism expenditures reached EUR 841.6 million in 2006 compared with EUR 679.8 million in 2005).

The number of tourists (domestic + inbound) increased by 4.5% in 2006 on the previous year, and rose to more than 3.5 million. The number of foreign tourists rose to 1.61 million, an increase of 6.4% year-on-year. The main markets for tourism to Slovakia are the Czech Republic which accounted for 28% of arrivals in 2006, followed by Poland with 14%.

In 2006, 2 490 facilities provided accommodation services in Slovakia (2 446 in 2005), in total offering 48 173 rooms with 124 300 beds. The total number of entrepreneurs in tourism in Slovakia in 2006 was 19 504, a drop of 3.7% on the previous year.

The number of employees in tourism (accommodation establishments, restaurants and catering) was 101 800 in 2006 (90 300 thousand in 2005), equivalent to 4.4% of the employed workforce (4.1% in 2005).

Tourism organisation

Responsibility for tourism in Slovakia rests with the Ministry of Economy (Figure 3.27). On 1 November 2006, the former Tourism Department was transformed into the Tourism Section within the Ministry. The Section consists of three departments: Department of Tourism Policy, Department of Foreign Relations in Tourism and Department of Regional Development in Tourism.

Figure 3.27. **Organisational chart of tourism bodies in the Slovak Republic**

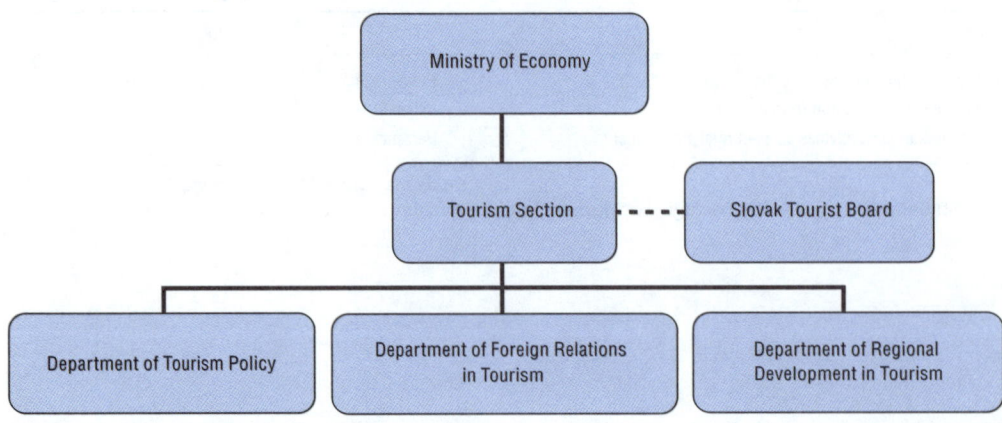

Source: OECD, adapted from Ministry of Economy, 2007.

The promotion of Slovakia as a tourism destination as well as the corresponding marketing activities is the responsibility of the Slovak Tourist Board (STB). The STB was set up by the Ministry of Economy in 1995 as a non-commercial, state-funded organisation. The STB currently has two branch offices in Slovakia and six foreign offices (Germany, the Netherlands, the Czech Republic, Austria, Poland, and the Russian Federation).

As a result of public service reform in 2001, the competencies with respect to tourism were devolved from a local civil service (district and regional offices) to eight self-governing bodies (regional governments) and municipalities. The aim was to strengthen local competencies within the regions and localities which tourists visit, with the municipalities and cities playing the key role in establishing the preconditions for tourism development. The Tourism Section organises regular working meetings with the representatives of these self-governing bodies in charge of tourism. Their purpose is to co-ordinate the development of tourism in particular regions.

Tourism budget

In 2005 the total funding for tourism issues within the government was SKK 262.6 million; this total rose substantially (by 41.4%) to SKK 371.4 million in 2006. EU Structural Funds are also available to the government. In 2005, these totalled SKK 488.1 million, and in 2006 SKK 760.5 million.

Table 3.90. **The financing of tourism, 2005-06**

		2005		2006	
	Unit	State budget	EU structural funds	State budget	EU structural funds
Ministerial tourism budget	Thousands SKK	5 660		1 000	
Tourism development support scheme	Thousands SKK			15 616	
Slovak tourist board	Thousands SKK	103 812		85 616	
Entrepreneurial support in tourism	Thousands SKK	75 510	146 428	80 763	94 223
Tourism infrastructure development	Thousands SKK	45 079	244 047	134 605	504 769
Promotion and tourist information support	Thousands SKK	32 540	97 619	53 842	161 526
Totals	Thousands SKK	**262 601**	**488 094**	**371 442**	**760 518**

StatLink http://dx.doi.org/10.1787/157055637740

Source: Ministry of Economy, 2007.

In recent years, the Slovak Government has taken several measures to support small and medium-sized enterprises. In the field of tourism, the Tourism Development Support Scheme, implemented by the Ministry of Economy in co-operation with the Slovak Guarantee and Development Bank, was funded by the state budget and aimed at stimulating SMEs and enhancing the quality of tourism services. In the period 2004-06, 66 projects were supported within the scheme to a total of SKK 106 million.

Slovakia as a member of the European Union is able to use EU structural funds through the Sectoral Operational Programme Industry and Services for 2004-06 to develop its tourism infrastructure, support business activities in tourism and undertake more sustained marketing campaigns. The programme supported 23 public sector projects to a total of SKK 1 461 billion and 40 private sector projects worth SKK 1 300 billion After joining the European Union, structural funds represent the most significant source of funds for tourism development in Slovakia. The goal is to improve the competitiveness of the tourism industry, improve product quality and overcome qualitative and quantitative shortcomings in tourism services.

Tourism related policies and programmes

In 2005, the government approved the Tourism Development Strategy until 2013. The document lists numerous specific tasks, including: the creation of a national information system for tourism; increasing the volume of state funds for the promotion of Slovakia abroad; preparing an analysis of holidaymakers' trip purposes and targeting tourism marketing towards EU States. Behind the development of the strategy is the need to define a vision for the position and importance of tourism in the national economy within the timeframe of the EU planning period 2007-13.

Following a government policy manifesto in 2006, the Tourism Development Strategy was re-evaluated and revised by the Ministry of Economy and endorsed by the government in May 2007.

In its 2006 policy manifesto, the new government pledged to create conditions for developing the tourism and hotel industry with the objective of increasing tourism's importance in GDP. The government will establish a tourism satellite account in order to quantify tourism's real value and measure accurately its contribution to the economy.

In 2005, the Slovak Tourist Board (STB) launched a new campaign to promote tourism in Slovakia, to build a strong brand and to increase Slovakia's visibility as an attractive tourism destination. The campaign is centred on the slogan "Slovakia: Little Big Country", and uses a butterfly as its logo. During 2005, the Slovak Tourist Board ran a campaign to support domestic tourism and to encourage people to spend their holidays in domestic resorts. The campaign consisted of a motivational TV spot and various social events.

> **Box 3.18. Summary of key tourism policy and strategy issues**
>
> **Tourism strategies**
> - Strengthening the position of the tourism sector in the national economy.
> - Making Slovakia more attractive as a holiday destination.
> - Increasing the volume of tourist visits.
> - Improving the visitor structure by providing better quality services.
> - Supporting the creation of new jobs mainly in regions with a significant tourism potential.
>
> **Tourism policies**
> - Increasing the competitiveness of Slovakia and its sustainable development.
> - Development of employment and of a flexible of labour market.
> - Regional development and development of entrepreneurship.
> - Presentation and promotion of Slovakia as a tourism destination.

In May 2007, the STB launched a new national tourism information portal *www.slovakia.travel*. The portal is available in Slovak, English and German and provides comprehensive information for potential tourists as well as professionals in the tourism sector, including maps of Slovak cities, information on tourist attractions, product packages, photographs of Slovakia, and a calendar of events.

National tourism legislation is harmonised with EU legislation, and the main laws in force are:
- an Act on package tours and conditions of doing business by travel offices and travel agencies (Act No. 281/2001 amended by the Act No. 186/2006); and

- a Decree of the Slovak Ministry of Economy regulating the categorisation of accommodation facilities and their grading classification (No. 419/2001).

Major forms of tourism

The central forms of tourism stipulated in the Tourism Development Strategy until 2013 for which Slovakia has the best conditions and which will need to be supported, developed and qualitatively improved over the coming years are:

- Urban and cultural tourism.
- Spa and health tourism.
- Winter tourism and winter sports.
- Summer tourism and waterside holidays.
- Rural tourism and agro-tourism.

Statistical profile

Table 3.91. **Inbound tourism: International arrivals and receipts**

	Units	2002	2003	2004	2005	2006
Tourists (overnight visitors)	Thousands	**1 399**	**1 387**	**1 401**	**1 515**	**1 612**
of which:						
Czech Republic	Thousands	448	470	419	425	455
Poland	Thousands	267	215	179	198	224
Germany	Thousands	189	176	188	194	190
Hungary	Thousands	88	101	111	122	122
Austria	Thousands	47	51	56	56	61
Tourism receipts	Million USD	724.0	863.0	901.3	1 209.8	1 513.4

StatLink http://dx.doi.org/10.1787/156801021713
Sources: Statistical Office of the Slovak Republic, National Bank of Slovakia, 2007.

Table 3.92. **Outbound tourism: International departures and expenditure**

	Units	2002	2003	2004	2005	2006
Departures[1]	Thousands	..	2 098	1 994	1 951	2 202
Tourism expenditure	Million USD	442.2	572.2	745.1	845.7	1 054.7

StatLink http://dx.doi.org/10.1787/156870881670
1. Including business trips and visits to friends and relatives; excluding same day visits abroad.
Sources: Statistical Office of the Slovak Republic, National Bank of Slovakia, 2007.

Table 3.93. **Tourism in the national economy**

	Unit	2001	2002	2003	2004	2005	2006
Tourism receipts as % of gross domestic product	Percentage	3.1	3.0	2.6	2.2	2.6	2.7
Tourism as % of employment	Percentage	3.4	3.2	3.7	3.9	4.1	4.4
Tourism receipts as % of export of services	Percentage	25.8	26.0	26.3	24.2	27.5	28.0
Enterprises in tourism	Establishments	**17 701**	**17 076**	**18 341**	**19 839**	**20 254**	**19 504**
of which: Hotels	Establishments	855	749	666	710	729	741
Tour operators	Establishments	914	864	770	845	790	786
Travel agencies	Establishments	392	373	317	374	420	425

StatLink http://dx.doi.org/10.1787/157037444016
Sources: Statistical Office of the Slovak Republic, National Bank of Slovakia, 2007.

Spain

Tourism in the economy

Tourism is one of the mainstays of the Spanish economy. It accounts for around 11% of GDP and employment, and contributes substantially to offsetting the trade deficit. With 58.5 million foreign tourists in 2006 (4.5% more than in 2005) and the tourism receipts of close to EUR 40.7 million (5.6% more than in 2005), Spain has consolidated its position as the second-largest destination in the world in terms of tourist arrivals and receipts. Over 1.7 million people work in Spain's tourism sector, the majority (67%) in the hotel sector.

Tourist arrivals increased by 15% in the period 2001-05. The leading markets are the UK (29% of arrivals in 2005), followed by Germany (18%) and France (16%). These three markets therefore accounted for 63% of the total in that year.

Tourism organisation

The distribution of administrative powers in tourism has meant that Autonomous Regions have their own capacities in the promotion and regulation of tourism within their respective territories. This does not bar the State from intervention, however. Government develops and undertakes promotion and marketing of tourism abroad, designs tourism policy and controls the overall co-ordination of tourism sector regulations, in addition to its role in national economic planning in which tourism is a key element (Figure 3.28).

This distribution of powers gives rise to a network of inter-administrative relationships and different instruments of co-operation, whose function is to bring coherence to the action of public authorities in tourism matters. Such integrated action across the various institutional levels, both public and private, depends on co-operation, since there are common interests which have to be appropriately matched and combined in order to ensure maximum possible operational effectiveness.

Key organisations

The designated task of the Ministry of Industry, Tourism and Trade extends to proposing and implementing general measures of industrial, tourism and commercial policies, along with measures in the field of energy and telecommunications and the information society (Figure 3.28).

In tourism, the ministry acts through the offices of the State Secretary for Tourism and Trade, whose remit extends to taking whatever actions are required for the definition, development and implementation of tourism policy, along with any related promotional activities that fall within the sphere of the central government administration.

Figure 3.28. **Organisational chart of tourism bodies in Spain**

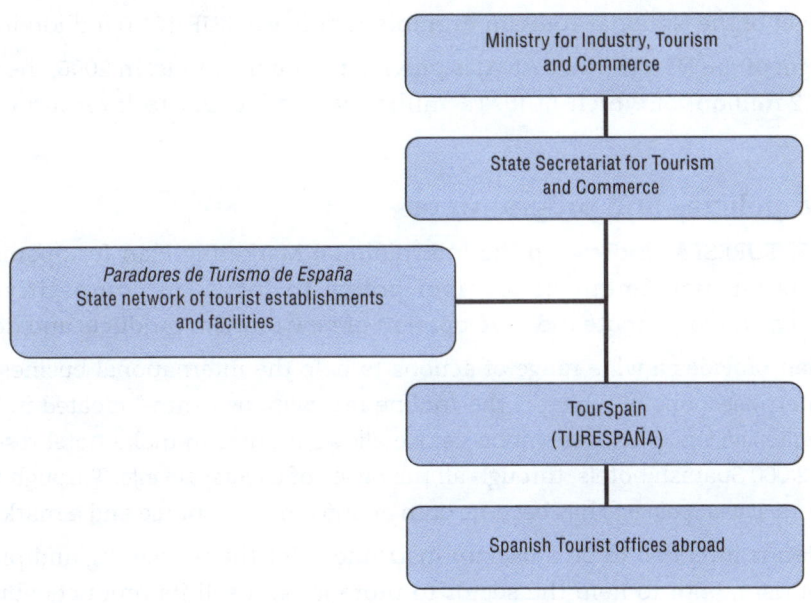

Source: OECD, adapted from Ministry for Industry, Tourism and Commerce, 2007.

The General Secretary of Tourism is the authority who, under the aegis of the Minister and of the Secretary of State has power to act in Tourism related matters which fall within the scope of the Central Government Administration

The General Secretary of Tourism is charged with:

- Defining, proposing, lending impetus to, and co-ordinating government tourism policy.
- Drawing up general plans that serve to foster tourism products; improve the quality and technological innovation in tourist firms and co-operation with the private sector; identify new tourism resources; diagnose and assess factors that affect the supply side of tourism, and design strategies aimed at developing and enhancing tourism products and destinations.
- Liaising with autonomous regions, local authorities, ministries and the tourism sector in general, to draw up the bases for and general planning of tourism sector policy.
- Undertaking research into factors that exert influence on tourism, as well as gathering, compiling and assessing statistics, information and data relating to tourism.
- Defining the Spanish Tourism Institute's strategies.
- Handling institutional tourism relations between the central government administration and international organisations – public and private – as well as international tourism co-operation, in co-ordination with the Ministry of Foreign Affairs.

Paradores de Turismo de España is a State company, coming under the control of the Secretary of State, whose principal function is the management and running of State-owned properties, mostly historic buildings, that have been purpose-adapted for hotel use. It constitutes an enormously successful network of preserved historical buildings that are part of the national archaeological heritage. There are currently 89 Paradores in operation.

The Tourism Studies Institute carries out research required by the tourism sector, and analyses the industry's evolution and trends.

Tourism budget

- The Budget of the National Tourism Administration was EUR 121.0 million in 2006.
- The budget of the NTO (TURESPAÑA) is provided by public funds. In 2006, the budget was EUR 138.2 million, of which EUR 71.6 million was allocated to international tourism promotion.

Tourism related policies and programmes

In 2005, TURESPAÑA drew up the International Marketing Plan for Spanish Tourism prepared as an instrument of tourism policy to focus on competitiveness and sustainability, and to promote the development of new tourism products and destinations.

The Plan provides a wide range of actions to help the international business of Spain's tourism enterprises, one of which is the "online reservations centre" created in 2005 on the website *www.spain.info*. This reservation centre allows tourists to make hotel reservations in more than 2 000 Spanish hotels, through all the pages of *www.spain.info*. Through this project, among others, *www.spain.info* has become both an information source and a market place.

The Plan is intended to be a backup instrument for the marketing and promotion of Spanish tourism, both to help the sector to promote and sell its products abroad and to establish public-policy performance management systems.

Finally, the Plan has been designed as a meeting point and forum for debate, with the participation of regional governments, local authorities and the tourism industry itself, on three levels:

- Access to the analysis and studies carried out.
- Formulation of proposals for the basic plan project.
- Collaboration in the drawing up of the Annual Implementation Plan.

The International Marketing Plan acts in five fields: market research; brand image and communication; product development and marketing; online marketing and managerial excellence. Each Annual Implementation Plan contains a target and indicators for each group of actions which are analysed at the end of the year, in order to design the next year's implementation plan. It also includes activities to promote local tourism drawn up by each regional government, both annually and in the course of the year.

Statistical profile

Table 3.94. **Inbound tourism: International arrivals and receipts**

	Units	2001	2002	2003	2004	2005	2006
Tourists	Thousands	**48 565**	**50 331**	**50 854**	**52 430**	**55 914**	**58 451**
of which:							
United Kingdom	Thousands	13 309	13 846	15 224	15 629	16 090	16 179
Germany	Thousands	10 188	9 575	9 303	9 537	9 918	10 146
France	Thousands	6 791	8 070	7 959	7 736	8 875	9 152
Italy	Thousands	2 436	2 623	2 434	2 801	2 957	3 359
Netherlands	Thousands	2 070	2 342	2 348	2 301	2 435	2 528
Tourism receipts[1]	Million EUR	34 222	33 557	35 047	36 376	38 558	40 710

StatLink http://dx.doi.org/10.1787/157155161113

1. Break in series from 2005 – new methodology.
Sources: Institute of Tourism Studies (IET), Tourist movements on the Borders (FRONTUR), Central Bank of Spain, 2007.

Table 3.95. **Outbound tourism: International departures and expenditure**

	Unit	2004	2005	2006
Departures[1]	Thousands	9 846	10 508	10 678
Tourism expenditure[1]	Million EUR	6 893	7 566	..

StatLink http://dx.doi.org/10.1787/157163374681

1. Break of series from 2005; new methodology; data for previous years are being reviewed.
Sources: Institute of Tourism Studies (IET), Tourist Movements of the Spain (FAMILITUR), 2007.

Table 3.96. **Employment in tourism**

	Units	2001	2002	2003	2004	2005	2006
Tourism (total)	Thousands	**1 522**	**1 572**	**1 622**	**1 676**	**1 759**	**1 846**
of which: Hotels and restaurants	Thousands	1 008	1 048	1 079	1 113	1 172	1 230
Road transport	Thousands	183	183	186	191	196	201
Air transport	Thousands	38	36	38	39	41	42
Travel agencies	Thousands	45	46	48	50	54	58

StatLink http://dx.doi.org/10.1787/157181041767

Sources: Institute of Tourism Studies (IET) and the Ministry of Work and Social Affairs, 2007.

Table 3.97. **Tourism in the national economy**

	Units	2000	2001	2002	2003	2004
Tourism as % of GDP	Percentage	11.6	11.4	11.1	10.9	10.9
Tourism as % of total employment	Percentage	11.3	10.6	10.9	11.1	11.3
Tourism as % of service export	Percentage	63.2	61.3	59.3	59.5	59.8
Domestic tourism as % of final consumption	Percentage	17.0	17.0	16.5	16.4	16.2

StatLink http://dx.doi.org/10.1787/157188353857

Sources: National Statistical Institute (INE), Tourism Satellite Account and Spanish National Accounts, 2007.

Sweden

Tourism in the economy

In Sweden, tourism is gradually becoming more recognised as an important driver for the creation of new jobs, new and growing enterprises and stronger regional development. The now 12-year time series of the Swedish Tourism Satellite Account (TSA) has clearly shown the huge impact of tourism on the economy. In 2006, tourism accounted for almost 3% of GDP.

The number of jobs in tourism over this period has increased by more than 40% (employment growth in the economy as a whole rose by less than 10% in the same period). Foreign tourists' expenditure in Sweden (exports) is now bigger than the export revenue from cars. In 2006 alone, tourism created 16 500 new jobs.

International overnight stays rose by 12% between 2002 and 2006, and the increase in receipts between 2002 and 2006 was 46%.

Tourism organisation

In Sweden, there are two agencies under the Ministry of Enterprise, Energy and Communications responsible for tourism: VisitSweden and the Swedish Agency for Economic and Regional Growth (NUTEK) (Figure 3.29). Since 2006, the Swedish Tourist Authority has been integrated with NUTEK, Sweden's national public agency for economic policy issues. NUTEK promotes enterprise and entrepreneurship within the travel and tourist industry through boosting skills, improving quality and co-operation. NUTEK is responsible for statistics on tourism, and a key task is collecting and disseminating information and knowledge about the development of the tourism and the travel and tourism industry in Sweden.

Figure 3.29. **Organisational chart of tourism bodies in Sweden**

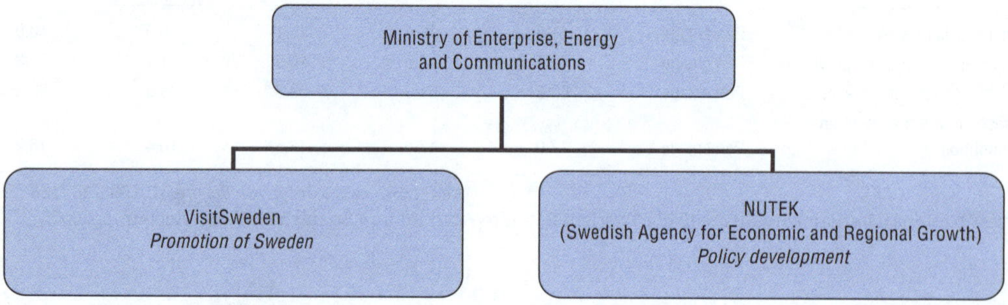

```
        Ministry of Enterprise, Energy
             and Communications
                     |
         _____|_____
        |                         |
   VisitSweden              NUTEK
 Promotion of Sweden   (Swedish Agency for Economic and Regional Growth)
                          Policy development
```

Source: OECD, adapted from NUTEK, 2007.

VisitSweden is a national organisation, responsible for the promotion of Sweden as a business and leisure travel destination. VisitSweden (formerly the Swedish Travel and Tourism Council) is owned equally (50/50) by the Swedish Government and the Swedish tourism industry. The main focus is marketing, information, co-ordination and distribution to the travel trade, media and consumers.

Tourism budget

The 2007 budget for VisitSweden and Nutek is SEK 111.1 million. Between 2002-05, the government allocated special tourism funds to two programmes: SEK 40.5 million was allocated to an innovation programme, and SEK 20 million to a programme for marketing the Swedish mountains. For 2007, the government allocated an extra SEK 10 million for the international marketing of Sweden.

Tourism related policies and programmes

In 2001, a national strategic programme for the development of the travel and tourism industry, prepared by in co-operation with the industry itself, was presented for adoption by the Ministry of Industry, Employment and Communication. This was evaluated in 2006, as a result of which, and in the light of the operational experiences from different stakeholders, a proposal for a new strategy was prepared and presented to the government in mid-March 2007, a response to which is expected shortly.

Co-operation with the tourism industry, consumers and other stakeholders

Co-operation in public/private partnerships and in networks is common for tourism development and in operating different kinds of project initiatives in a destination perspective as well as in thematic business areas. As an example, *Nature's Best* is the first national quality label for ecotourism in the northern hemisphere. It was launched during the UN International Year of Ecotourism in 2002.

Nature's Best is designed to offer the traveller an unforgettable experience in nature. It combines responsible nature conservation with more environmentally friendly ways of travelling that care for cultural heritage, local communities and the environment. *Nature's Best* was developed by travel associations, land owners, nature conservation associations, non profit organisations, public authorities, tourist companies and institutions. More than 30 companies and 20 national associations took part in the process of setting the criteria for *Nature's Best*. *The Swedish Ecotourism Society* is the main organisation responsible for *Nature's Best* and for the certification process.

Linkages between tourism and other policies

- *Transport*: The preparation of a travel planner, Hela Resan, comprising all travel alternatives, makes it possible for the consumer to search for the most suitable way to travel to a tourism destination or identify a tourism company within the country.
- *Education*: With the intention of increasing knowledge and stimulating quality in tourism education, NUTEK has repeatedly initiated surveys on the range of tourism education available. In addition, NUTEK has arranged tourism education conferences in co-operation with the tourism industry and with the organisation for tourism teachers.
- *Trade*: NUTEK has arranged conferences on e-commerce.

Foreign direct investment

There is close co-operation between the government's Invest in Sweden Agency, the national business organisation Swedish Travel, the Tourist Industry Federation and regional stakeholders in order to stimulate and increase foreign investments in Sweden.

3. COUNTRY PROFILES: TOURISM POLICY DEVELOPMENTS AND TRENDS – SWEDEN

Statistical profile

Table 3.98. **Inbound tourism: International nights and receipts**

	Units	2002	2003	2004	2005	2006
Nights in accommodation[1]	Thousands	**9 768**	**9 715**	**9 522**	**10 077**	**10 954**
of which:						
Norway	Thousands	2 541	2 466	2 306	2 464	2 708
Germany	Thousands	1 914	2 013	1 766	1 942	2 127
Denmark	Thousands	1 000	1 024	960	974	1 042
Netherlands	Thousands	541	577	591	558	717
United Kingdom	Thousands	617	593	605	642	640
United States	Thousands	392	365	383	421	412
Tourism receipts	Million SEK	51 592	50 188	53 619	63 236	75 413

StatLink http://dx.doi.org/10.1787/157276220280

1. Nights spent in hotels, holiday youth hostels and camp sites.
Sources: Swedish Agency for Economic and Regional Growth (NUTEK) and Statistics Sweden (SCB), 2007.

Table 3.99. **Outbound: International departures and expenditure**

	Units	2002	2003	2004	2005	2006
Departures	Thousands	12 888	12 649	13 967	12 597	12 591
Tourism expenditure	Billion SEK	70.9	66.6	74.7	80.5	84.9

StatLink http://dx.doi.org/10.1787/157307820467

Sources: Swedish Agency for Economic and Regional Growth (NUTEK) and Statistics Sweden (SCB) and The Riksbank, 2007.

Table 3.100. **Employment in tourism**

	2002	2003	2004	2005[1]	2006[1]
Total	**125 766**	**125 458**	**122 956**	**135 058**	**151 619**
Hotels and restaurants	51 392	50 425	50 150	56 684	65 970
Commerce	26 793	26 678	26 597	29 508	33 739
Transports	18 260	19 287	18 716	17 886	19 695
Travel agencies	10 703	10 404	10 024	10 184	9 911
Culture and leisure	9 338	10 030	9 706	11 313	12 793
Other areas	9 280	8 634	7 763	9 483	9 511

StatLink http://dx.doi.org/10.1787/157257508866

1. Preliminary data.
Sources: Swedish Agency for Economic and Regional Growth (NUTEK) and Statistics Sweden (SCB), 2007.

Table 3.101. **Tourism in the national economy**

	Units	2002	2003	2004	2005[2]	2006[2]
Total tourism consumption in Sweden[1]	Million SEK	171 804	170 989	176 100	194 415	215 502
Total Swedish/domestic consumption[1]	Million SEK	120 206	120 801	122 482	131 179	140 089
Export-foreign consumption in Sweden[1]	Million SEK	51 598	50 188	53 619	63 236	75 413
Added value[1]	Million SEK	57 326	57 204	57 693	63 860	70 278
Tourism as % of gross domestic product	Percentage	2.86	2.76	2.66	2.84	2.94
Employees in tourism	Thousands	126	125	123	135	152

StatLink http://dx.doi.org/10.1787/157273281121

1. Current prices.
2. Preliminary data.
Sources: Swedish Agency for Economic and Regional Growth (NUTEK) and Statistics Sweden (SCB), 2007.

Switzerland

Tourism in the economy

Travel and tourism are among Switzerland's most important economic activities. Tourism is a major industry in terms of job creation. In 2006, the sector accounted for 6.2% of GDP, generating 8.4% of total employment. Tourism also has important positive spill-overs for the national and local economy. It encourages local governments, especially in mountainous areas, to improve infrastructure such as roads, communications services and public transport networks with the help of federal support.

There has been a decline in Tourism related employment in Switzerland (hotels and restaurants) of 11.4% in the period 2001-05 (Table 3.105).

Tourist arrivals rose marginally in the period 2001-06 to reach 7.86 million in 2006, 5.3% above the 2001 figure. International tourism receipts in the same period rose by 16.5%. Switzerland's largest origin market is Germany, which generated 2.1 million tourist arrivals in 2006, slightly down on the 2001 figure (Table 3.103).

Some 80% of tourists say that nature is their main reason for travelling to Switzerland. The government estimates that nature and landscapes generate approximately CHF 2.5 billion (Swiss francs) of "public services" per year.

Tourism organisation

Tourism in Switzerland is primarily a matter for the private sector. The government establishes framework conditions that will allow companies to flourish and provides selective financial aid. Figure 3.30 shows the organisation of tourism in Switzerland for the fields in which government is involved.

Tourism budget

The budget of the National Tourism Administration (NTA) is funded by the Federal State. This budget (Table 3.102) provided CHF 63 million in 2007.

The budget of the National Tourism Organisation is CHF 73 million for the same period, of which CHF 46 million comes from a block grant by the NTA and CHF 27 million from other contributions.

Approximately 10% of the funds appropriated for investment for mountainous regions are allocated for tourism infrastructure needs. There are no specific taxes on tourism at the Confederation level. The Confederation grants a reduced rate of VAT for lodging in all forms of accommodation – set at 3.6% as compared with the normal rate of 7.6%.

The effectiveness of public spending on tourism is measured on an ongoing basis during the implementation of all of the Confederation's promotional programmes. This is required by the Constitution and by the laws governing tourism. On the whole, evaluations

Figure 3.30. **Organisational chart of tourism bodies in Switzerland**

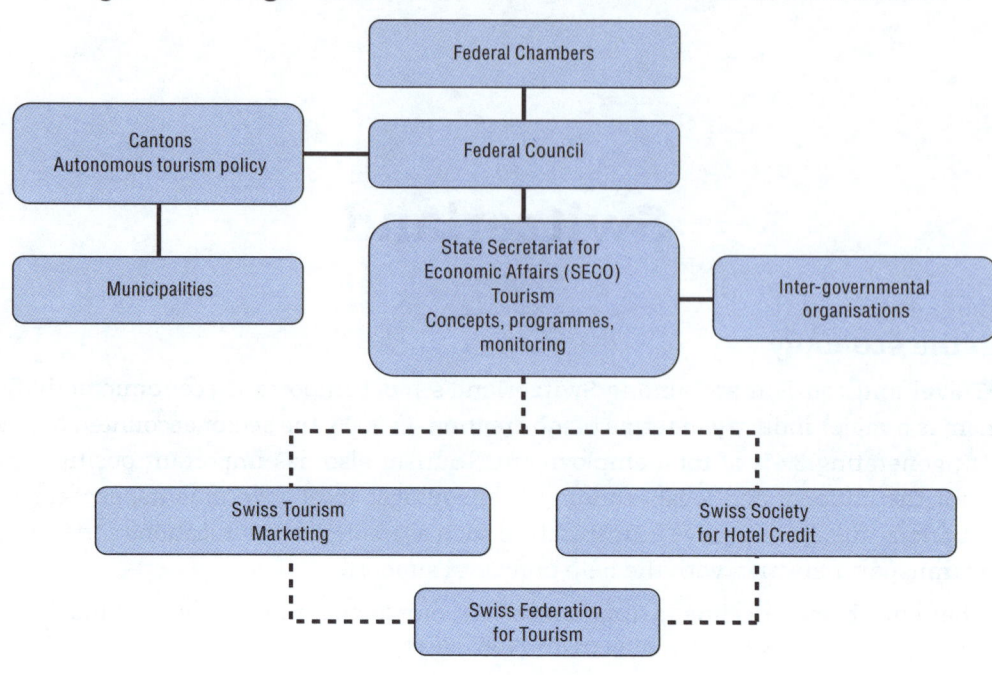

Source: Source: OECD, adapted from State Secretariat for Economic Affairs (SECO), 2007.

Table 3.102. **Budget of the National Tourism Administration (NTA) 2007**
CHF millions

NTA Expenditure items	Units	2007
National Tourism Office NTO	thousands	46 000
Société Suisse de crédit hôtelier	thousands	10 000
Innovation and co operation in the field of tourism	thousands	7 000
Information and documentation	thousands	120
International organisations UNWTO	thousands	375
Total	thousands	**63 495**

StatLink http://dx.doi.org/10.1787/157360227480
Source: State Secretariat for Economic Affairs SECO, 2007.

must be conducted by independent third parties whenever the Parliament decides to allocate appropriations.

Tourism related policies and programmes

New federal tourism policy

The aim of the Swiss Confederation's policy is to create and maintain the most favourable possible framework conditions, which primarily consist of a flourishing economy, well functioning and attractive infrastructure and balanced and sustainable land use. Tourism policy must also highlight the assets of the tourist sites that attract visitors while at the same time modernising and developing them.

It is also important in a developed country to improve tourism productivity, which is below the average for the Swiss economy, by promoting structural change aimed at increasing productivity. The performance of tourism should be similar to that of industry and export services. The Federal Council, which is the Swiss government, submitted to the

Federal Parliament in late February 2007 a tourism development programme for 2008-11 which provides financial assistance worth CHF 186 million to Switzerland Tourism and CHF 21 million for inter-company, inter-industry and inter-regional measures within the Innotour programme, which promotes innovation and co-operation in the field of tourism.

Innotour – A flagship project of Switzerland

The Federal Act of 10 October 1997 promoting innovation and co-operation in the field of tourism (Innotour) was developed with a view to adapting tourism supply to the new structures of the world market. The challenges of globalisation called for a programme of renovation of the existing supply. Innotour is aimed at raising the innovation rate and using tourism resources more effectively through co-operation. The measures concern the following fields:

- *The creation of business opportunities*: An important aspect of Innotour consists of helping companies to take advantage of new business opportunities in Switzerland and abroad in an inter-company rather than an individual context. These opportunities involve new products, facilities and channels of distribution. The national information and reservation system, Switzerland Destination Management (SDM), is a good example of this.
- *Improvement of existing structures*: Quality is a major facet of promotion, which still needs to be consolidated through appropriate projects.
- *Structures of destinations*: Destinations also need an inter-company strategy covering a number of branches. Innotour has contributed over the past four years to the implementation of new destination management concepts, as in the canton of Grisons. However, the strategic renewal of tourist sites is only in its early stages.
- *Training and upgrading*: The qualification initiative has had a concrete impact in an area where other measures, such as the Vocational Training Act, were ineffective. Innotour supports the organisations responsible for tourism in developing new training concepts.
- *Databases for tourism development*: Innotour develops databases of major importance for tourism, for example, the *tourism forecasts* and the *benchmark* report, which are aimed at monitoring tourism developments closely in order to inform policy changes as necessary.

Approximately 80% of funds have been allocated to specific fields of innovation, such as "quality", "designing destinations", "information and reservation systems", "tourism in harmony with nature" and "self-catering accommodations". The projects supported by "Innotour II" represent a total cost of CHF 80 million, of which CHF 19 million comes from the Innotour programme (at the end of 2006), which means that the degree of self-financing of projects is over 75%.

Co-operation with the tourism industry, consumers and other market stakeholders

The Swiss Federal State delegates most of its measures for promoting tourism to "public law corporations". These organisations are given a legal mission and perform their functions under "service mandates". They have an independent legal personality that enables them to admit interested members of the operational sector concerned who contribute financially. These organisations are genuine vertical and horizontal co-operation platforms that operate on the basis of the principles of public-private partnership.

The National Tourism Office (Switzerland Tourism) organises the "Swiss Vacation Day", which makes it possible to co-ordinate short- and medium-term promotional programmes with stakeholders in the economy dependent on tourism. The Swiss Society for Hotel Credit

(SGH) co-operates with commercial banks to provide alternative financing for accommodation projects in tourist regions. The Confederation also supports the Swiss Tourism Federation, which provides information and consultation services to the sector. Local and cantonal governments are members of its organisations, which allows them to co-ordinate their initiatives with the Federal State at the operational rather than the policy level.

Statistical profile

Table 3.103. **Inbound tourism: International arrivals and receipts**

	Units	2001	2002	2003	2004[1]	2005	2006
Tourists	Thousands	**7 468**	**6 880**	**6 541**	..	**7 229**	**7 863**
of which:							
Germany	Thousands	2 189	1 961	1 890	..	2 007	2 107
United Kingdom	Thousands	662	620	613	..	709	785
United States	Thousands	827	689	598	..	657	726
France	Thousands	503	489	489	..	543	586
Italy	Thousands	440	430	435	..	461	499
Tourism receipts	Million CHF	11 448	11 286	11 613	11 941	12 549	13 334

StatLink http://dx.doi.org/10.1787/157327564173

1. Break of series.
Sources: Secretary of State for the Economy; Federal Statistical Office, 2007.

Table 3.104. **Outbound tourism: International departures and expenditure**

	Units	2001	2002	2003	2004	2005	2006
Departures[1]	Thousands	..	..	16 283	..	..	..
Tourism expenditure	Million CHF	8 691	8 546	9 268	10 080	11 056	12 384

StatLink http://dx.doi.org/10.1787/157342687132

1. Includes private trips with nights.
Sources: Secretary of State for the Economy; Federal Statistical Office, 2007.

Table 3.105. **Employment in hotels and restaurants**

	Units	2001	2002	2003	2004	2005
Total	Thousands	**163**	**161**	**152**	**149**	**145**
Men	Thousands	86	86	83	80	77
Women	Thousands	77	75	70	69	67

StatLink http://dx.doi.org/10.1787/157355253073

Source: Secretariat of State for Economic Affairs, 2007.

Turkey

Tourism in the economy

In 2004, tourism contributed some 5.3% to Turkish GDP, and accounted for 66% of the value of services exports and 24% of the value of goods exports. In all three measures, the relative importance of tourism declined in the period 2002-04.

International arrivals in 2006 were, at 19.8 million, 6.2% down on 2005 (which had been a record year, recording 21.1 million arrivals, 20.6% above the level recorded in 2004). In 2006, 59% of foreign visitors came from OECD countries (60.3% in 2005), with 5.6 million or 28.3% coming from Eastern Europe. The leading origin market for Turkey in 2006 was Germany, which contributed 19% of total arrivals, followed by the Russian Federation with 9.4% and the UK with 8.5%.

International tourism receipts in 2006 were USD 16 851 million (7.2% down on the previous year), of which USD 4.3 million was spent by Turkish citizens resident abroad but returning to visit their homeland.

Tourism organisation

In order for the *Tourism Strategy of Turkey 2023* (Box 3.19) to be carried out, the correct institutional arrangements are crucial. The roles and responsibilities of inter and intra-organisational actors in Turkey are as follows.

> **Box 3.19. Tourism Strategy of Turkey – 2023**
>
> The *Tourism Strategy of Turkey – 2023* is intended to improve the management and implementation of strategic planning efforts as to boost co-operation between the public and private sector tourism operators on the basis of good "governance". The Strategy and Action Plan were prepared with a participatory planning perspective and have the primary objective of guiding the travel and tourism industry at the level of both production management and implementation, by means of a "road map" for the industry's future.
>
> The study on which the Strategy is based proposes a variety of long term actions in areas such as Planning, Investment, Organisation, Domestic Tourism, Research and Development (R&D), Services, Strengthening Transportation and Infrastructure, Promotion and Marketing, Education, Branding at City Level, Diversification of Tourism Areas and Improvement of Destinations.

The National Tourism Council is a guiding and decision making body for determining policies, and realising the implementation of the Turkish tourism strategy (Figure 3.31). This body, managed by a board of executives, consists of 15-20 members, qualified to

Figure 3.31. **Organisational chart of tourism bodies in Turkey**

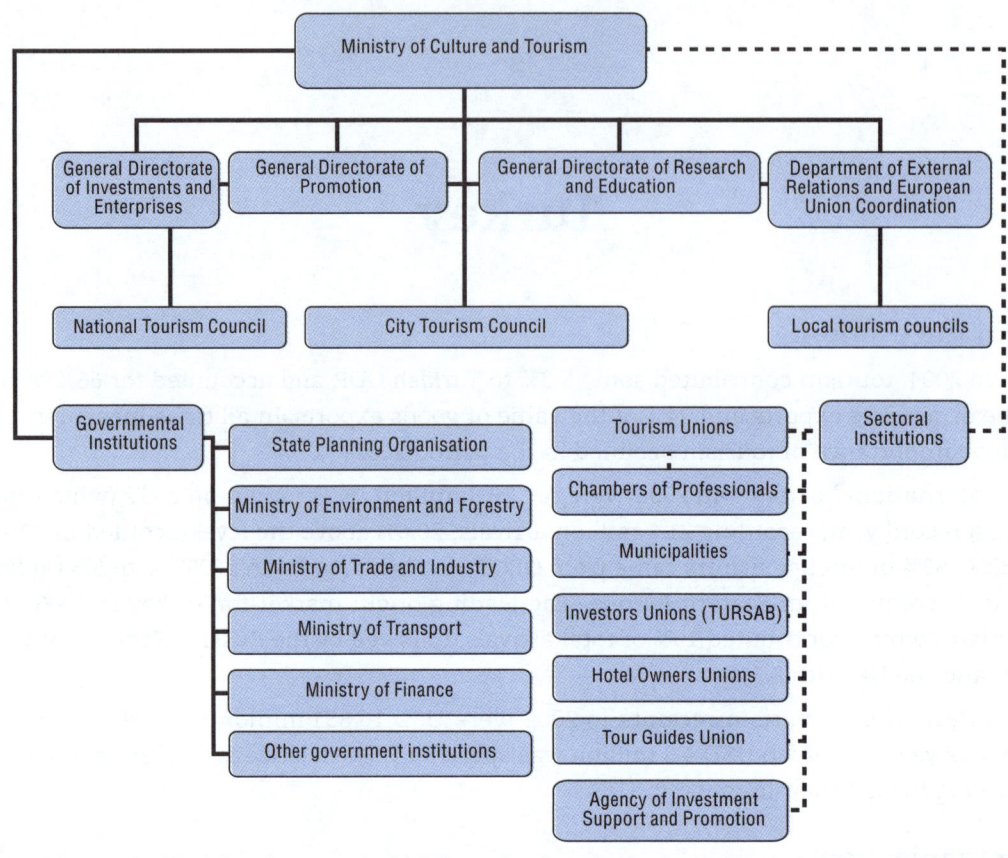

Note: This organisational chart is prepared with information from the document "*Tourism Strategy of Turkey – 2023*".
Source: OECD, adapted from Ministry of Culture and Tourism, 2007.

represent all shareholders in the industry. It is composed of delegations from the Ministry of Culture and Tourism, the State Planning Organisation and a group of representatives from the tourism industry. The Council's duties are as follows:

- Creating national, regional and local brands and co-ordinating efforts to market tourism centres.
- Making all necessary arrangements to ensure that the positive impacts of tourism are received by all, in line with the development of domestic tourism.
- Setting out the minimum quality standards applicable to accommodation facilities, products and labour in the travel and tourism industry.
- Diversifying the tourism product.
- Supporting business enterprises through in-service training.
- Carrying out research and compiling and preparing data for use by the Ministry of Culture and Tourism in the policy-making process.
- Measuring and monitoring the consistency of tourism policies and informing the Ministry of Culture and Tourism of the results.
- Making suggestions to guide the Ministry in crisis management.

The State Planning Organisation takes full responsibility and plays an active role in the industry's development by being a member of the National Tourism Council. The Ministry of Culture and Tourism has a regulatory role in tourism and is responsible for the planning, implementation, documentation and orientation of tourism education. The Ministry is thus the main regulatory, supervisory and directing body.

The General Directorate of Promotion (GDoP) within the Ministry, operates 36 offices worldwide and carries out marketing and advertising activities. The GDoP's role, based on market trend assessments and a detailed knowledge of the tourism product, is to carry out strategic marketing activities. It has defined the main points for its activities in the future, which will be based on: funding, market identification, market research, goal setting, marketing and promotion, measuring the effectiveness of marketing initiatives and encouraging year-round tourism.

The State Planning Organisation takes full responsibility and plays an active role in the industry's development by being a member of the National Tourism Council.

The Ministry of Culture and Tourism plays a regulatory role in tourism and is responsible for the planning, implementation, documentation and orientation of tourism education. The Ministry is thus the main regulatory, supervisory and directing body.

The General Directorate of Promotion (GDoP) within the Ministry operates 36 offices worldwide and carries out marketing and advertising activities. The GDoP's role, based on market trend assessments and a detailed knowledge of the tourism product, is to carry out strategic marketing activities. It has defined the main points for its activities in the future, which will be based on: funding, market identification, market research, goal setting, marketing and promotion, measuring the effectiveness of marketing initiatives and encouraging year-round tourism.

Tourism related policies and programmes

The Mediterranean-Aegean Tourism Infrastructure Coastal Management Project

This project is already being implemented by the Ministry of Culture and Tourism, in order to resolve the infrastructure problems of the Mediterranean and Aegean coasts where tourism potential is very high. To achieve this, it is crucial to secure user contribution funding, which will be realised through infrastructure unions to be formed by local governments and users, and by the creation of suitable institutions and legal arrangements. The Ministry of Culture and Tourism will pursue improvements to infrastructure in areas with substantial tourism potential in close co-operation with local governments.

Tourism centres, and culture and tourism preservation and development regions

Areas deemed important for tourism development are designated as "tourism centres" and "culture and tourism preservation and development regions" by the Law for the Encouragement of Tourism, and receive financial incentives for infrastructure purposes.

Health and thermal tourism

Each of the ancient Troy, Aphrodisian and Phrygian settlements will be developed into regional destinations with thermal facilities and cultural themes. These will be integrated into other alternative tourism types.

Mediator role

The General Directorate of Investments and Enterprises of the Ministry of Culture and Tourism and the 36 Culture and Information Offices abroad, receive complaints from both inbound and outbound travellers. The Ministry carries out investigations, in co-operation with the Ministry of Industry and Trade and the local authorities, in those establishments that are the subject of complaints (for example hotels, restaurants, shops, etc.), on completion of which the Ministry informs the traveller and seeks a resolution of the dispute.

In 1999 and 2000, data on tourism receipts and expenditures were provided by the Central Bank of the Republic of Turkey; but since then they have been measured by a "foreign visitors questionnaire" conducted jointly by the Ministry of Tourism and the State Institution of Statistics. Data on visitor arrivals are provided by the Passport Police and passed monthly to the tourism authorities.

Statistical profile

Table 3.106. **Inbound tourism: International arrivals and receipts**

	Units	2001	2002	2003	2004	2005	2006
Visitors	Thousands	**11 619**	**13 256**	**14 030**	**17 517**	**21 124**	**19 820**
of which:							
Germany	Thousands	2 884	3 482	3 332	3 984	4 244	3 762
Belgium	Thousands	310	314	308	427	504	460
France	Thousands	524	523	471	549	701	658
Netherlands	Thousands	633	873	940	1 191	1 254	998
United Kingdom	Thousands	846	1 038	1 091	1 388	1 758	1 679
Tourism receipts	Million USD	10 067	11 901	13 203	15 888	18 153	16 851

StatLink http://dx.doi.org/10.1787/157361736883
Sources: Ministry of Culture and Tourism, International Monetary Fund, Turkish Statistical Institute (TURKSTAT), 2007.

Table 3.107. **Outbound tourism: Residents departures and expenditure**

	Unit	2001	2002	2003	2004	2005	2006
Departures	Thousands	4 856	5 131	5 928	7 299	8 246	8 275
Tourism expenditure	Million USD	1 738	1 881	2 113	2 524	2 870	2 742

StatLink http://dx.doi.org/10.1787/152081330125
Sources: Ministry of Culture and Tourism, International Monetary Fund, Turkish Statistical Institute (TURKSTAT), 2007.

Table 3.108. **Tourism in the national economy**

	Units	2002	2003	2004	2005	2006
Tourism as % of gross domestic product	Percentage	6.5	5.5	5.3	..	..
Tourism as % of goods exports	Percentage	29.7	25.8	23.7	..	..
Tourism as % of services exports	Percentage	80.4	69.2	66.1	..	..
Gross domestic product	Million USD	183 888	240 376	301 950	360 876	399 673
Exports of goods	Million USD	40 124	51 206	67 001	..	..
Exports of services	Million USD	14 802	19 086	24 047	..	..
Hotels and similar establishments						
Number of rooms	Rooms	189 528	201 510	206 214	230 605	241 032[1]
Number of bed-places	Bed-places	393 718	418 177	428 589	481 704	506 522[1]
Occupancy rate	Percentage	48.7	46.9	50.1	52.4	47.3
Average length of stay	Nights	3.3	3.3	3.3	3.2	2.9

StatLink http://dx.doi.org/10.1787/152100806213
1. Preliminary data.
Source: Ministry of Culture and Tourism, 2007.

United Kindom

Tourism in the economy

In 2005, the UK tourism industry was estimated to have generated GBP 85 billion for the UK economy, with 80% coming from the domestic tourism market. 2003 data suggest that tourism contributes 3.3% to national gross value added.

In 2006, overseas residents made an estimated 32 million visits to the UK, generating expenditure of approximately GBP 15 billion.

In 2004, there were 1.4 million people directly employed in tourism (44% in restaurants, bars and canteens and 16% in tourist accommodation) with more employed indirectly, equal to 5% of all employment in the UK. In 2004 also, there were an estimated 180 000 businesses in tourism industries.

International tourist arrivals in the UK grew by 31% between 2001 and the 2005 total of 30.0 million, while expenditure by tourists in the UK reached GBP 14.2 billion in 2005, 26% higher than in 2001. The largest origin markets for the UK are the USA which contributed 11.5% of total arrivals in 2005, Germany (11.1%) and France (11.0%).

Tourism organisation

The National Tourism Administration for the UK is the Tourism Division of the Department for Culture, Media and Sport (DCMS), a central department of the UK Government (Figure 3.32). DCMS is responsible for Tourism related diplomatic relations and membership of international organisations such as the UN World Tourism Organisation and EU Tourism Advisory Committee. It also directly funds VisitBritain, which is the UK's national tourist office, marketing England to the British (through EnjoyEngland) and the UK to the world.

Figure 3.32. **Organisational chart of tourism bodies in the United Kingdom**

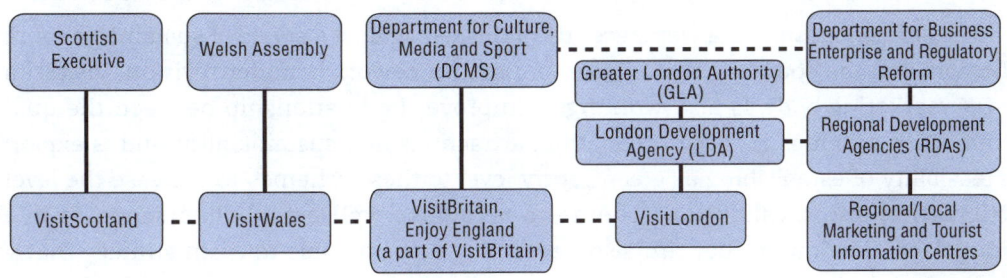

Source: OECD, adapted from Department for Culture, Media and Sport, 2007.

Apart from national marketing, tourism is devolved to the regions. Funding and the direction of policy are the responsibilities of the Scottish Parliament and the Welsh Assembly, which fund VisitScotland and VisitWales respectively to carry out functions analogous to those of VisitBritain at national level (including the marketing of Scotland and Wales to the British and the world). There is a considerable amount of activity at regional and local level. Local authorities and Regional Development Agencies are responsible for marketing their areas, and for providing Tourist Information Centres at key destinations.

Tourism budget

UK public spending on tourism is as follows:

- A grant of GBP 50 million per annum is made by DCMS to VisitBritain, of which, approximately GBP 35 million is for the international marketing of the whole of the UK, and the balance for domestic tourism work.
- A grant of GBP 38 million per annum is made by the devolved Scottish Executive.
- A grant of GBP 22 million per annum is made by the devolved Welsh Assembly.
- An estimated GBP 50 million is available in aggregate each year for Tourism related issues from the nine Regional Development Agencies (which are responsible for tourism in the English regions) The RDAs in turn receive their funding from a range of central government departments.
- An estimated GBP 120 million is spent on tourism by local authorities (funded by a combination of local taxes, and central funding).

In terms of the performance of public spending on tourism, in 2005, VisitBritain was estimated to have delivered a return on investment of 44:1 for its overseas marketing and 20:1 for domestic marketing.

Tourism related policies and programmes

DCMS is responsible for overall UK tourism policy (Box 3.20). The main areas of support and intervention are the following:

Competitiveness: The main target of the National Tourism Administration is to raise the value of the tourism sector to GBP 100 billon, per year by 2010 (that is, the sum of the turnovers of all businesses in this sector). The UK has national quality assessment schemes run by VisitBritain, VisitScotland and VisitWales in the public sector, and by the AA (Automobile Association) in the private sector. Non-statutory in nature, these schemes have common grading criteria. The UK Government's target is to raise the proportion of businesses which participate in the schemes from the present 50%, to over 90% by 2016.

Sustainable Tourism: Data were recently published against a series of sustainable tourism indicators and the country's sustainable tourism framework is under revision. VisitBritain, the UK marketing body, is also working to improve the relationship between the quality accreditation schemes for accommodation, attractions and sustainability, and is exploring the feasibility of establishing a "green" entry level to these schemes to increase the level of participation and a validation scheme to recognise well-established schemes in the marketplace. In addition they are also developing a sustainable tourism strategy that will support the position of Britain as a premier sustainable destination through a shared agenda across the UK tourism industry, promote the take-up of best practice and encourage responsible tourists to enjoy products offered by sustainable tourism businesses.

> **Box 3.20. Key tourism policy developments**
>
> - DCMS has recently published a comprehensive strategy for Tourism and the London 2012 Olympic and Paralympic Games.
> - The Strategy's action plan for the six years between 2007 and 2013 includes:
>   - The framework under which DCMS, its partners VisitBritain and Visit London, and the industry will market the UK at home and overseas.
>   - A cross-UK public/private sector marketing campaign starting at the Beijing handover, with all 180 000 UK tourism businesses given the chance to get involved.
>   - Plans to make the most of the Cultural Olympiad right across the nation.
>   - New initiatives in product quality (the hotel "Star" schemes): with more money for London and national work which will benefit the whole of the UK.
>   - Skills work alongside the National (Tourism) Skills Strategy.
>   - Plans for real changes in the industry's response to disability issues.

Human Resources: There are considerable issues of staff retention and training within the UK tourism sector, particularly in customer service, management/leadership and chef skills. In terms of the labour market, recruitment is often very short term with the employment of large numbers of students and international workers. Also, over a third of the workforce is under 25. The Government is working to address this as a priority through People 1st – the sector skills council for hospitality, leisure, travel and tourism. This is an employer organisation which is funded by Government, the private sector and through commercial activity.

Legislative and Regulatory Environment: The UK Government works to ensure that the impact of national and EU regulation on tourism businesses is at an appropriate level, whilst ensuring that they adhere to key health, safety and security standards.

Domestic/Inbound/Outbound Tourism: The UK is keen to encourage both international and domestic tourism and hence marketing is carried out to domestic consumers through EnjoyEngland, VisitScotland and VisitWales, and to international consumers through VisitBritain.

International and Intra-Regional Activities: The UK's international tourism promotion agency VisitBritain has an extensive network of international offices in all parts of the world. The UK is a member of the EU Tourism Advisory Committee and UN World Tourism Organisation.

Dialogue with the tourism industry: The UK Government maintains a close and regular dialogue with the tourism industry: through the national tourism body VisitBritain, through representative organisations including the DCMS-supported public/private partnership, the Tourism Alliance, and with individual businesses. VisitBritain works closely with the industry on joint marketing and other projects, as does the London-only body, Visit London (which is jointly funded by the city of London, DCMS and tourist businesses).

Statistics: The key publicly-funded measure of inbound tourism is the International Passenger Survey, and of domestic turnover the UK Tourism Survey. Consolidated data from these inform policy in accordance with Satellite Accounting principles. Central measures of productivity are also maintained (Value Added per Labour Unit).

Major forms of tourism

20% of UK tourism turnover comes from inbound business. In the international market, the UK specialises to a certain extent in heritage tourism, particularly London with its established and world-famous range of attractions. London is using the opportunity of the 2012 Olympic Games to build on this World City status and attract a younger and more diverse range of visitors, alongside the increasingly important business tourism offer. Efforts are also being made to improve London's performance as a gateway to the rest of the UK.

The domestic market – accounting for 80% of the UK's tourism business – encompasses longer holidays by UK citizens, short-breaks and day trips. With businesses widely dispersed across the UK, the domestic offer includes country houses, castles, historic towns and exceptional countryside.

Statistical profile

Table 3.109. **Inbound tourism: International arrivals and receipts**

	Units	2001	2002	2003	2004	2005
Visitors	Thousands	22 835	24 180	24 715	27 755	29 970
of which:						
United States	Thousands	3 580	3 611	3 346	3 616	3 438
France	Thousands	2 852	3 077	3 073	3 254	3 324
Germany	Thousands	2 309	2 556	2 611	2 968	3 294
Ireland	Thousands	2 039	2 439	2 488	2 578	2 806
Netherlands	Thousands	1 411	1 419	1 549	1 620	1 786
Tourism receipts	Million GBP	11 306	11 737	11 855	13 047	14 248

StatLink http://dx.doi.org/10.1787/152128562088
Source: International Passenger Survey, 2007.

Table 3.110. **Outbound tourism: International departures and expenditure**

	Units	2001	2002	2003	2004	2005
Departures	Thousands	58 281	59 377	61 424	64 194	66 441
Tourism expenditure	Million GBP	25 332	26 962	28 550	30 285	32 154

StatLink http://dx.doi.org/10.1787/152138027463
Source: International Passenger Survey, 2007.

Table 3.111. **Employment in tourism**

	Units	2000	2001	2002	2003	2004
Employment in tourism	Thousands	1 332	1 353	1 367	1 398	1 420
of which:						
Hotels and other tourist accommodation	Thousands	230	227	222	226	230
Restaurants/bars/canteens	Thousands	556	567	587	610	618
Transport	Thousands	132	135	133	134	132
Travel agents/tour operators	Thousands	135	145	139	138	147
Recreation services	Thousands	73	73	78	80	83
Rest of the economy	Thousands	205	208	208	210	211

StatLink http://dx.doi.org/10.1787/152183008046
Source: Department for Culture, Media and Sport, 2007.

Table 3.112. **Tourism in the national economy**

	Units	2000	2001	2002	2003	2004[1]	2005
Total tourism consumption	Billion GBP	**89.6**	**88.3**	**90.1**	**91.6**	..	**104.5**
Tourism consumption on UK trips	Billion GBP	74.9	72.9	73.7	74.2	..	85
Tourism as % of gross value added (GVA)	Percentage	**3.8**	**3.6**	**3.5**	**3.3**	..	..
Tourism GVA estimate	Billion GBP	32	31.5	32.2	32.7	..	..
Tourism's share of national GVA	Percentage	3.8	3.6	3.5	3.3	..	..

StatLink ⟶ http://dx.doi.org/10.1787/152203547002

1. A total 2004 figure is unavailable due to a problem with estimates of domestic overnight tourism from the UK Tourism Survey.

Source: Department for Culture, Media and Sport, UK Tourism Satellite Account, 2007.

United States

Tourism in the economy

United States' travel and tourism industries are major contributors to US GDP, accounting for 2.6% of value-added in the US economy (Table 3.116). In a USD 13 trillion economy, travel and tourism are of paramount importance. The industry contributed more to the economy than the insurance industry or than public utilities, and more than twice as much as either agriculture, the automotive or the oil and gas industries. Travel and Tourism related exports now account for 26% of all US services exports and 7% of all goods and services exports.

2006 was a record year for the US travel and tourism industry – America's leading services exporter. According to the Travel and Tourism Satellite Accounts (TTSAs), the industry generated USD 1.2 trillion in sales in 2006 (international and domestic tourism combined); in constant (2000) prices, real direct output for each sub-sector of the industry was the highest ever recorded. In 2006, real direct tourism output was 3% up on 2005 at more than USD 587 billion.

Travel and tourism is one of the USA's largest employers, with one out of every sixteen Americans employed in travel and tourism businesses, of which 94% are classified as small businesses. In aggregate, more people are employed by travel and Tourism related industries than are employed in each of the following sectors: construction, the business and financial industries, agriculture, education, and healthcare.

International tourist arrivals reached 49.2 million in 2005, just 4.9% ahead of 2001 but representing a recovery nonetheless from the slump of 2002 and 2003. The largest origin markets are Canada and Mexico (accounting for 30% and 26% of all arrivals respectively in 2005), followed by the UK, Japan and Germany. International travellers spent USD 81.7 billion in 2006, almost 5% above the previous record set in 2000.

Tourism organisation

The United States does not have a minister of tourism. Although, the Secretary of Commerce serves in this capacity, he also has responsibility for the numerous other agencies that comprise the US Department of Commerce (Figure 3.33). A majority of the work performed for this sector comes from the Office of Travel and Tourism Industries (OTTI), which is an Office reporting to the International Trade Administration within the Department of Commerce. OTTI has three main functions: research, policy and outreach. The outreach section includes overseeing the United States' international marketing programme (see the tourism budget section below), as well as serving as a liaison to the US Commerce Service, a sister agency with the Department of Commerce that oversees the domestic and international operations of offices that focus on assisting US businesses

Figure 3.33. **Organisational chart of tourism bodies in the United States**

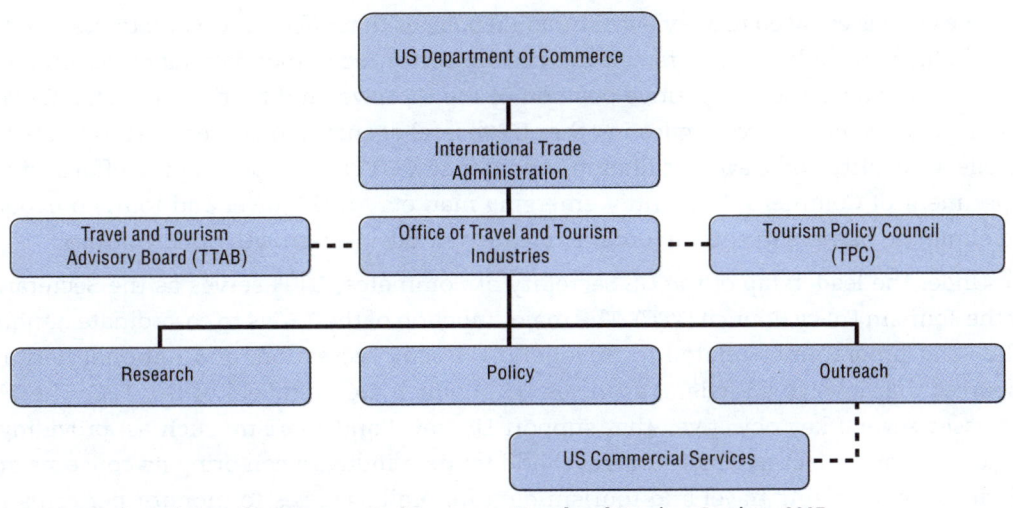

Source: OECD, adapted from US Department of Commerce Travel and Tourism Services, 2007.

exports. Staff working for the US Commerce Service focus part-time on travel and tourism exports both in the USA and abroad.

The Travel and Tourism Advisory Board is a committee comprising 15 private sector travel executives who provide advice and guidance to the Secretary of Commerce related to the US promotional campaigns for 2005-08. This committee will be disbanded if Congress does not allocate additional funds for tourism promotion administered by the Department of Commerce.

The Tourism Policy Council is an inter-agency committee established by law for the purpose of ensuring that the nation's tourism interests are considered in Federal decision-making. Its major function is to co-ordinate national policies and programmes relating to international travel and tourism, recreation, and national heritage resources that involve federal agencies.

Tourism budget

- The US Department of Commerce, Office of Travel and Tourism Industries (OTTI) serves as the national tourism office for the United States. It obtains its funds from a congressional appropriation to the Department of Commerce and the funds are then allocated to OTTI. In addition, OTTI sells research reports and data to generate additional revenue to run its operation, along with inter-agency agreements that also generate funds for the Office.

- The US Congress appropriated funds for a matching co-operative grant of USD 4 million in FY 2007, and in FY 2006 Congress provided marketing funds of USD 9.8 million to promote travel to the United States. The United Kingdom and Japan were selected as the markets for the promotion campaign. In FY 2005, Congress provided USD 6 million to promote travel to the United States and the United Kingdom was chosen for this campaign.

- In addition to the money allocated to OTTI for tourism promotion, there are also funds for nine research programmes and other operational programmes, excluding salaries and benefits. The OTTI's operational budget for FY 2007 was USD 2 million from all sources (appropriated funds and sales of research data). In FY 2006, the OTTI's operational budget was USD 1.7 million, and in FY 2005 it was USD 2.2 million.

Tourism related policies and programmes

The OTTI is engaged in a review of national policies that affect travel and tourism to the United States. Included in this review are private sector recommendations on government policies to enhance the competitive position of the US travel and tourism industry. OTTI is working closely with its colleagues in other US federal agencies to address issues related to travellers' security and travel facilitation. Additionally, OTTI is supporting the efforts of the Department of Commerce to identify emerging markets for US travel and tourism exports and eliminate barriers to entry in order to create new business growth opportunities.

Under the leadership of the US Secretary of Commerce, OTTI serves as the Secretariat for the Tourism Policy Council (TPC). The major function of the TPC is to co-ordinate national policy and programmes related to travel and tourism, recreation, and national heritage resources that involve US federal agencies, 18 of which are members of the TPC. The TPC addresses several key objectives that support US travel and tourism, such as: providing a single point of contact to which the travel and tourism industry can bring its concerns and priorities; synthesising travel and tourism data from all agencies to monitor performance and competitiveness most effectively; and engaging inter-agency commitment at senior level on policies and issues which have an impact on the travel and tourism industry.

In order to demonstrate the value of travel and tourism to the US economy, the Office provides funding to the US Department of Commerce Bureau of Economic Analysis. This funding is used to produce quarterly Travel and Tourism Satellite Accounts (TTSAs) data. The information produced by the TTSAs includes direct and indirect travel and Tourism related output, direct and indirect travel and Tourism related employment, and total US travel and Tourism related sales/expenditures. Additionally, the annual TTSAs data provide the US travel and tourism industry with output and employment data for 26 individual industries; the value-added contribution of travel and tourism to the US economy; the supply of, and demand for, travel and tourism commodities; and disaggregated demand data of household, businesses, government, and non-resident demand for US travel and Tourism related goods and services.

Statistical profile

Table 3.113. **Inbound tourism: International arrivals and receipts**

	Units	2001	2002	2003	2004	2005
Tourists (overnight visitors)	Thousands	**46 927**	**43 581**	**41 218**	**46 085**	**49 206**
of which:						
Canada[1]	Thousands	13 527	13 024	12 666	13 857	14 862
Mexico[1]	Thousands	11 567	11 440	10 526	11 907	12 665
United Kingdom	Thousands	4 097	3 817	3 936	4 303	4 345
Japan	Thousands	4 083	3 627	3 170	3 748	3 884
Germany	Thousands	1 314	1 190	1 180	1 320	1 416
Tourism receipts	Million USD	71 893	66 605	64 348	74 547	81 680

StatLink http://dx.doi.org/10.1787/152250647010

1. Estimates provided by the respective countries.
Sources: US Department of Commerce, Office of Travel and Tourism Industries, Bureau of Economic Analysis, Statistics Canada (Canada); Banco de Mexico/Secretaria de Turismo (Mexico), 2007.

Table 3.114. **Outbound tourism: International departures and expenditure**

	Units	2001	2002	2003	2004	2005
Departures	Thousands	59 442	58 066	56 250	61 809	63 503
Tourism expenditure	Million USD	60 200	58 715	57 444	65 750	69 175

StatLink http://dx.doi.org/10.1787/152265101006

Sources: US Department of Commerce, Office of Travel and Tourism Industries, Bureau of Economic Analysis, Statistics Canada (Canada); Banco de Mexico/Secretaria de Turismo (Mexico), 2007.

Table 3.115. **Employment in tourism**

	Units	2001	2002	2003	2004	2005
All tourism industries	Thousands	**8 291**	**8 023**	**7 968**	**8 123**	**8 239**
of which:						
Traveller accommodation	Thousands	1 687	1 628	1 624	1 634	1 659
Transport	Thousands	2 262	2 061	1 939	1 947	1 949
Food services and drinking places	Thousands	2 155	2 193	2 271	2 353	2 415
Recreation, entertainment, shopping	Thousands	1 841	1 798	1 787	1 842	1 863

StatLink http://dx.doi.org/10.1787/152315807614

Sources: US Department of Commerce, Office of Travel and Tourism Industries from the Bureau of Economic Analysis, 2007.

Table 3.116. **Tourism in the national economy**

	Units	2001	2002	2003	2004	2005
United States	Million USD	10 127 976	10 469 601	10 960 770	11 712 462	12 455 835
Travel and tourism value added	Million USD	266 010	268 573	283 617	302 649	..
Tourism as % of GDP (value added)	Percentage	2.6	2.6	2.6	2.6	..

StatLink http://dx.doi.org/10.1787/152328465501

Note: There is a 2-year lag for travel and tourism value-added data; therefore, 2005 data are not yet available.
Sources: US Department of Commerce, Office of Travel and Tourism Industries from the Bureau of Economic Analysis, 2007.

OECD Non-member Economies

Romania

Tourism in the economy

In 2006, the tourism industry accounted for 4.8% of Romanian GDP, taking into account the direct and indirect impact of the sector on the economy. In the same year, 5.8% of the workforce at national level was employed in tourism (Table 3.119).

Visitor arrivals, including day excursionists, rose by 26% in the period 2002-06, while the number of stay-over tourists rose in the same period by 38%. European markets dominate tourism to Romania, providing 82% of all visitors in 2005, followed by the Americas with 8.5% and Asia with 8.4%. The main overseas origins for Romania are Germany, Italy and France, although no one country accounts for more than 14% of tourist arrivals.

Tourism organisation

Romania, a member of the European Union (EU) since January 2007, has 41 counties and one municipality (Bucharest) performing administrative functions, organised into eight "development regions" in order to co-ordinate regional development more effectively in the context of accession to the EU. Local administrations have their own tourism departments, and virtually every county has its own tourist office for information and promotion, although tourism policy is still centralised (Figure 3.34).

In April 2007, the Romanian government was restructured and responsibility for tourism was passed to the Ministry of SMEs, Trade, Tourism and Liberal Professions. The ministry is responsible for drawing up and implementing national tourism policy and also for promoting Romania as a tourism destination, evaluating and protecting the national tourism heritage, issuing accommodation and tourism licenses, controlling the quality of tourism services and developing tourism infrastructure. Two other institutions – the National Institute for Research and Development in Tourism (INCDT) and the National Centre for Tourism Education (CNIT) – come under this ministry.

Tourism budget

The Romanian government has allocated EUR 325 million for the development and modernisation of the country's tourism infrastructure. For tourism promotion, the annual budget was approximately EUR 4 million in the period 2001-05, but for 2006, for the first time, a budget of over EUR 19 million was allocated for promotional campaigns, promotional materials and partnership programmes.

Figure 3.34. **Organisational chart of tourism bodies in Romania**

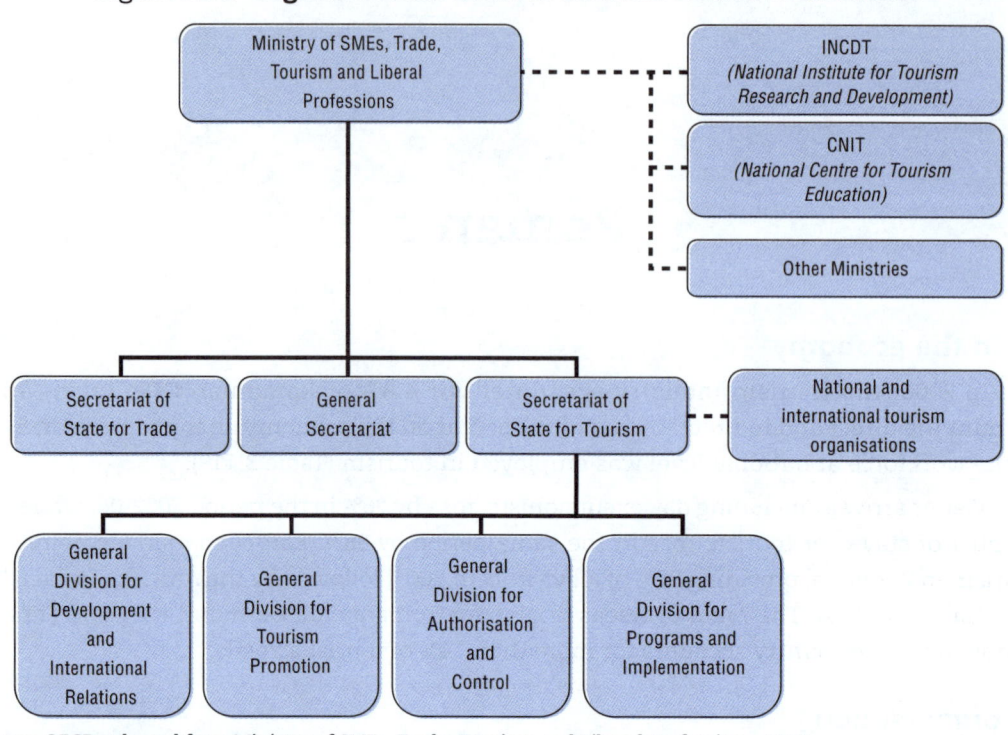

Source: OECD, adapted from Ministry of SMEs, Trade, Tourism and Liberal Professions, 2007.

Tourism related policies and programmes

Programmes developed recently by the National Tourism Authority include:

- "Blue Flag programme": the international recognition of quality for Romanian Black Sea beaches; eight beaches achieved this status.
- Social programmes developed for tourists with low incomes: "A week on the Black Sea Coast" (in co-operation with the National Association of Travel Agencies); "A holiday in the country" (developed in co-operation with the National Association for the Rural, Ecological and Cultural Tourism); "A week of rejuvenation in the spas" (developed together with the National Organisation of Spas).

Box 3.21 summarises some of the recent policy initiatives in the country, and Box 3.22 gives details of innovative measures taken within the tourism field.

Romania is very active in the field of international tourism co-operation, and takes an active part in the activities of the EU Tourism Advisory Committee. It has been a member of UNWTO since 1975, of the Black Sea Economic Co-operation (BSEC) since 1992, and of the Central European Initiative since 1996, and is also a member of "The Danube" Organisation, and the European Travel Commission. Romania achieved observer status in the OECD Tourism Committee in 2006.

A Protocol of Co-operation between the Romanian and Chinese authorities was concluded in June 2004 and Romania received "approved destination status (ADS)" in China – an encouraging step given the potential of outbound tourism from China. Romania has concluded bilateral co-operation agreements in the field of tourism with 38 states: 15 from Europe, 15 from Asia, 4 from Africa and 4 from Latin America. Romania is part of a trilateral tourism agreement with Bulgaria and Turkey.

> **Box 3.21. Key tourism policy developments**
>
> - National tourism policy starts from the premise that Romania has the potential to become a year-round tourism destination, given the diversity of the country's tourism attractions which include:
>   - ❖ **Sun and winter tourism** continue to be major forms of mass tourism in Romania.
>   - ❖ **Cultural tourism and eco-tourism (geo-tourism)** have huge growth potential due to the country's rich national heritage. In 2007, Sibiu was the European capital of culture, together with Luxembourg. City-breaks were given an impetus as well, mainly due to the increase in the number of low-cost carriers serving the country.
>   - ❖ **Spa tourism** is one of the most important forms of specialised tourism in Romania. The main reasons for the development of such products include satisfying the demands of an ageing European population, the opportunity to increase the average length of stay of tourists, and the economic potential.
>   - ❖ **MICE tourism** (Meetings, Incentives, Conferences and Exhibitions) represents another important form of specialised tourism, and the most important source of revenues. In Romania there are almost 900 conference centres, with almost 100 000 seats.
>   - ❖ **Rural tourism** is important from the social perspective, as almost half of the Romanian population lives in the rural areas. The value of the rural tourism products could be enhanced with closer linkages to gastronomy, wine and handicrafts.
> - Travel and tourism is also seen as a sector that can provide jobs for the country's vast rural population.
> - The objectives set in tourism policy can be achieved by upgrading and individualising each component of the product, by increasing the quality of tourism services, by training the workforce in order to provide the industry with skilled professionals and managers, and by drawing up special tourism programmes and efficient strategies.

Linkages between tourism and other policies

Taxation

The Ministry of SMEs, Trade, Tourism and Liberal Professions is aware of the private sector's needs and is mobilising further domestic resources in order to facilitate community driven tourism programmes and SMEs programmes. The Romanian taxation system is competitive: corporate taxation and income tax are both set at 16%, Romania having adopted a flat tax regime. The current level of VAT of 9% for hotels and Bed and Breakfast accommodation is an incentive for the industry in comparison with the general rate of 19%. Nevertheless, there is a need for a stronger co-operation with the Ministry of Economy and Finance, in the field of the tourism taxation.

Transport

Co-operation with the Ministry of Transport is very intense, especially in the field of identifying infrastructure development priorities.

Education

The development of human resources is a government priority following the adoption of the Lisbon Strategy. Although there is a National Centre for Tourism Education (CNIT) under the Ministry of SMEs, Trade, Tourism and Liberal Professions, there is a strong need

> Box 3.22. **Examples of innovation in tourism**
>
> - The organisation of international events (*e.g.* FIA GT Bucharest, Romanian Grand Prix of Mamaia, Transilvania International Film Festival, etc.), as well as initiatives like sand sculptures, city tours, etc.
> - The development of team-building practices in regions such as the Danube Delta (bird and animal watching) or in regions where activity-based tourism can be practiced (*e.g.* cave diving, paragliding, parachuting and paintballing).
> - The development of artificial snow tracks and ice rinks (including on the Black Sea Coast).
> - Funicular railways (gondolas) on the Black Sea Coast and in the mountains.
> - The opening of the first ice hotel in Romania, and of the first ice church, in a region with huge development potential (the mountaineous region of Fagaras, crossed by the highest road of Europe – Transfagarasan).
> - The introduction of business class trains with full on-board facilities, including wireless Internet access.
> - The use of the Global Distribution Systems on a large scale, and the use of modern promotional techniques.
> - The establishment of the first low-cost charter flight company in 2005, followed by the continuous development of the low-cost carriers, which spurs the city-breaks market.
> - The use of the old (but secure) means of transport to visit regions that are difficult to reach by car or other modern means – Travel by Mocanita (a narrow gauge train/railway) on picturesques routes, the possibility of using the old Royal Train for special events, etc.

for the improvement of the tourism educational system, in order to develop the management and marketing skills of employers and employees. Alongside education needs, there is also a strong need to motivate employees of the travel and tourism industry, as it is difficult to attract skilled professionals to a sector with low levels of motivation and a high degree of seasonality.

Foreign direct investment

Using the statistical data of the Romanian Agency for Foreign Investment as a source, the tourism sector accounts for around 2% of the total FDI inflows at national level, reflecting a generally low level of productivity in the sector.

Other co-operation issues

As trade and tourism are organised under the same Ministry, under a Secretary of State for Trade and a Secretary of State for Tourism, the departments exchange information of common interest. At the central administration level, the ministry co-operates with other governmental departments such as the Ministry of Foreign Affairs (for international events, the visa system and promotion), the Ministry of Labour, Family and Equal Opportunities (since Romania's travel and tourism industry is already an important source of jobs), the Ministry of Economy and Finance (as priorities in its strategy for 2005-08, rural and health tourism were chosen among 16 sectors), the Ministry of Agriculture and Rural Development (for countryside, culinary and wine tourism, as well as natural and national reserves), the Ministry of Public Health (for issues related to wellness and spa tourism and future projects in this area, which are under debate), and the Ministry of Environment and Sustainable Development (for eco- and geo-tourism matters).

Statistical profile

Table 3.117. **Inbound tourism: International arrivals and receipts**

	Units	2002	2003	2004	2005	2006
Visitors	Thousands	**4 794**	**5 595**	**6 600**	**5 839**	**6 037**
Tourists	Thousands	**999**	**1 105**	**1 359**	**1 430**	**1 380**
of which:						
Germany	Thousands	135	154	173	192	190
Italy	Thousands	140	161	201	195	183
France	Thousands	84	93	110	115	110
United States	Thousands	58	67	95	99	98
Hungary	Thousands	63	81	100	90	81
Tourism receipts	Million EUR	392	396	406	845	1 034

StatLink http://dx.doi.org/10.1787/156721067108

Sources: National Institute of Statistics, National Bank of Romania, 2007.

Table 3.118. **Outbound tourism: International departures and expenditure**

	Units	2001	2002	2003	2004	2005	2006
Departures	Thousands	6 408	5 757	6 497	6 972	7 140	8 906
Tourism expenditure	Million EUR	402	416	423	434	750	1 035[1]

StatLink http://dx.doi.org/10.1787/156728657535

1. Provisional data.
Sources: National Institute of Statistics, National Bank of Romania, 2007.

Table 3.119. **Tourism in the national economy**

	Units	2002	2003	2004	2005	2006
Tourism as % of gross domestic product (direct impact)	Percentage	1.92	1.88	1.86	1.85	1.92
Tourism as % of gross domestic product (direct and indirect impact)	Percentage	4.58	4.71	4.66	4.63	4.81
Tourism as % of employment (direct impact)	Percentage	3.00	3.07	3.07	3.05	3.15
Tourism as % of employment (direct and indirect impact)	Percentage	5.52	5.58	5.58	5.55	5.75
Tourism as % of services exports	Percentage	14.2	14.8	13.9	20.7	18.6

StatLink http://dx.doi.org/10.1787/156774545575

Sources: World Travel and Tourism Council (Romania country special report), National Institute of Statistics, National Bank of Romania, 2007.

South Africa

Tourism in the economy

In 2006, almost 8.4 million foreign nationals visited South Africa. This was easily the highest number of arrivals South Africa has ever experienced, and it represented a 13.9% increase over the previous year (2005). The global average growth was 4.5% over this period.

Tourism has been recognised at the highest possible level for its significant impact on the economy. The industry's contribution to the GDP has increased from 4.6% in 1993 to 8.3% in 2006. South Africa is now looking to increase its GDP contribution to 12% by 2014. Tourism brings in over ZAR 66 billion (South African Rand) per annum to the economy and contributes over half a million jobs.

Tourism organisation

The National Tourism Administration (Department of Environmental Affairs and Tourism) engages national tourism authorities and provinces on key issues affecting the development of tourism in South Africa (Figure 3.35).

Figure 3.35. **Organisational chart of tourism bodies in South Africa**

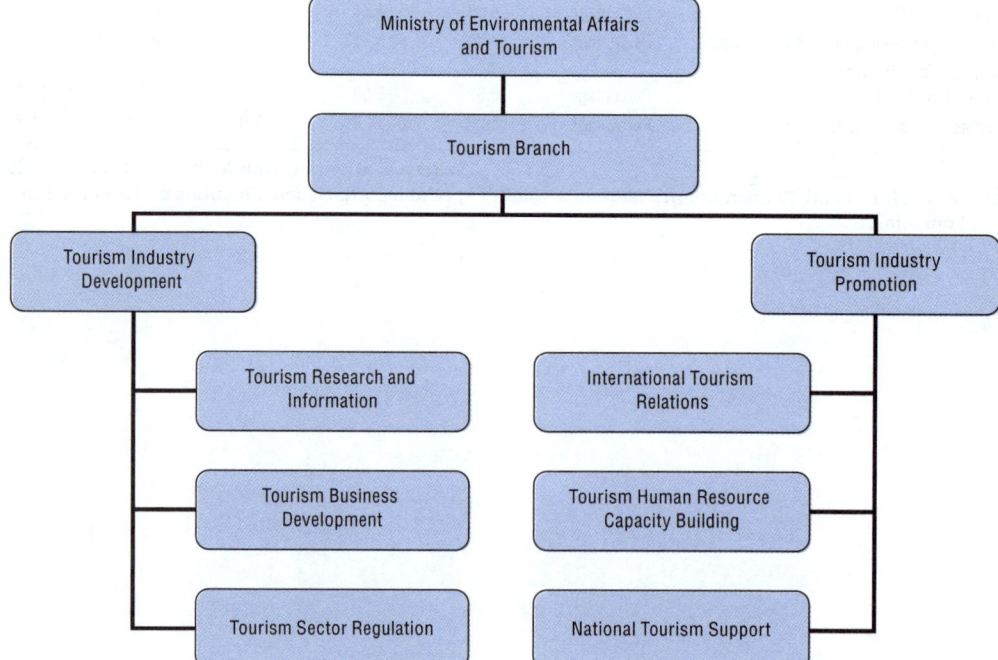

Source: OECD, adapted from Department of Environmental Affairs and Tourism, 2007.

Tourism budget

The budget of the National Tourism Administration/Organisation is ZAR 556.8 million.

Tourism related policies and programmes

To gain competitiveness in tourism, research, quality assurance, training and development initiatives are fully supported by all tourism stakeholders. At a national level research is conducted by the Department of Environmental Affairs and Tourism (DEAT) with South African Tourism (marketing arm), the nine tourism provinces also conduct their own research to meet their unique needs. These various researches promote innovative ways of managing and monitoring tourism trends and strategies. The Tourism Grading Council is responsible for grading tourism products to ensure that they meet a certain set standards to ensure sustainable competitiveness.

Tourism supports the triple bottom effect of tourism in all its strategies and programmes, and Agenda 21 on sustainable development is fully supported and implemented. The 2010 FIFA Soccer World Cup is an initiative that South Africa aims to utilise to promote sustainable tourism through the Greening of South Africa for 2010 and beyond. South Africa's efforts therefore will go well beyond showcasing South Africa as a soccer nation, and into a whole range of legacy projects that support sustainable tourism.

South Africa has acknowledged the challenges the nation faces in human resources in many sectors including tourism. An Accelerated and Shared Growth Initiative of South Africa (ASGISA) and Joint Initiative for Priority of Skills in Acquisition (JIPSA) were launched by the country to accelerate economic growth. Tourism stakeholders gathered in Johannesburg in October 2006 to develop strategies to address skills shortages in the tourism industry to gain competitiveness. The tourism stakeholders committed to working together to address the skills challenge in tourism, taking small-, medium- and micro-enterprises (SMMEs) as a critical component of the sector.

The National Tourism Administration (DEAT) develops and regulates the South African tourism environment. The development of legislative policies is done through a transparent and consultative manner where input and comments from all stakeholders and the general public is taken seriously.

South African Tourism is responsible for developing and implementing marketing strategies for domestic inbound and outbound tourism to encourage South Africans to travel in their own country. A *Sho't Left* campaign (*sho't left* is local slang in the South African taxi industry, meaning that if a person says "sho't left", it means they intend to alight at the next corner) is the initiative that promotes domestic tourism in South Africa.

At a regional level in the Southern African Development Community (SADC), through the Regional Tourism Organisation of Southern Africa (RETOSA), South Africa interacts with other member States on issues of regional development and co-operation. A strategy to involve all SADC member states as a part of the 2010 Soccer World Cup is underway. At international level South Africa engages with other countries at a bilateral and multilateral level (UNWTO, OECD, Africa Travel Association, etc.) to develop tourism, co-operation, learn best practices and drive the Africa development agenda.

Gender mainstreaming is viewed as key to tourism development and poverty alleviation. The role played by women in the tourism sector is significant and gender mainstreaming is considered seriously in the tourism sector as all programmes and projects are measured amongst other issues on gender mainstreaming.

Support exists for SMMEs in tourism, which receive assistance in setting up, financing, managing their enterprises as well as with training in financial administration, business administration, human resources and general understanding of the whole hospitality industry, and of the economic, social, environmental and competitiveness arenas to gain sustainability in tourism.

Transport

Tourism has engaged the transport sector to ensure that all transport policies developed take the needs of tourism into consideration. The result has been the development of a joint aviation strategy that is also tourism driven. Tourism now also sits in bilateral air services negotiations with the Transport Department and relevant airlines.

Education

On education, tourism engages with the Tourism Hospitality Sport Education and Training Authority on developing the skills of workers in the sector, increasing the levels of investment in education and training in the tourism and hospitality sector, encouraging employers in the sector to train their employees, providing opportunities for work experience and employing new staff, encouraging workers to participate in training programmes and improving the employment prospects of disadvantaged people. Tourism also interacts with schools and universities on the inclusion of hospitality studies in the curriculum. The challenges of skills shortages are being addressed with all tourism stakeholders.

Issues of Trade and Foreign Direct Investment are led by the Department of Trade and Industry (DTI). Tourism co-operates with the DTI on a number of initiatives and investment missions (*e.g.* The Gulf Co-operation Council Tourism and Trade road shows will be undertaken with the DTI and tourism stakeholders in February 2007 to attract Foreign Direct Investment and create trade linkages).

Statistical profile

Table 3.120. **Inbound tourism: International arrivals and receipts**

	Units	2002	2003	2004	2005	2006
Visitors	Thousands	**6 550**	**6 640**	**6 815**	**7 518**	**8 464**
of which:						
Lesotho	Thousands	1 163	1 291	1 480	1 669	1 920
Swaziland	Thousands	789	809	853	912	993
Zimbabwe	Thousands	613	569	558	783	990
Mozambique	Thousands	580	475	406	649	926
United Kingdom	Thousands	449	463	463	477	495
Tourism receipts	Million USD	3 695	6 533	7 380	8 448	8 967

StatLink http://dx.doi.org/10.1787/157101214882

Source: South African Tourism (SAT), 2007.

Table 3.121. **Outbound tourism: International departures and expenditure**

	Unit	2001	2002	2003	2004	2005
Departures	Thousands	3 794	..	..	..	..
Tourism expenditure	Million USD	2 251	3 654	4 237	4 811	5 230

StatLink http://dx.doi.org/10.1787/157122112846

Source: South African Tourism (SAT), UNWTO, 2007.

Table 3.122. **Tourism in the national economy**

	Units	2001	2002	2003	2004	2005
Tourism as % of:						
Government expenditure	Percentage	0.52	0.52	0.53	0.54	0.54
Capital investment	Percentage	14.74	14.41	14.41	14.4	14.4
Exports	Percentage	12.19	13.2	16.31	14.88	14.65
Employment (direct impacts only)	Percentage	3.08	3.53	3.51	3.3	3.35
Employment (direct and indirect impacts)	Percentage	6.79	7.55	7.55	7.26	7.42
Gross domestic product (direct impacts only)	Percentage	3.07	3.5	3.48	3.27	3.32
Gross domestic product (direct and indirect impacts)	Percentage	7.53	8.27	8.28	7.98	8.15

StatLink http://dx.doi.org/10.1787/157122426611

Source: Travel and Tourism Accounts, 2007.

ANNEX 3.A1

Annex Table 3.A1. **National tourism administration and related websites**

OECD member countries		
Australia	Department of Industry, Tourism and Resources	www.industry.gov.au
	Australian Bureau of Statistics	www.abs.gov.au
	Australian Tourism Export Council	www.atec.net.au
	Ecotourism Australia	www.ecotourism.org.au
	Quality Tourism	www.qualitytourism.com.au
	Tourism and Transport Forum	www.ttf.org.au
	Tourism Australia	www.tourism.australia.com
Austria	Federal Ministry of Economics and Labour	www.bmwa.gv.at
	Austrian Federal Economic Chamber	www.wko.at
	Austrian National Tourist Office	www.austria.info
	Statistics Austria	www.statistik.at
	Tourism Studies	www.studien.at
Belgium	Ministry for Administrative Affairs, Foreign Policy, Media and Tourism of the Flemish region	www.flanders.be
	Ministry of Agriculture, Rural affairs, Environment and Tourism of the Walloon region Commissariat Général au Tourisme	www.commissariat.tourisme.wallonie.be
	Tourism Promotion Office of Flanders	www.visitflanders.com
	Tourism Promotion Office of Walloon and Brussels	www.opt.be
Canada	Federal Ministry of Industry	www.ic.gc.ca
	Canadian Tourism Commission	www.canadatourism.com
Czech Republic	Ministry for Regional Development	www.mmr.cz
	Czech National Tourism Board	www.czechtourism.com
	Czech Statistical Office	www.czso.cz
Denmark	Ministry of Economic and Business Affairs	www.oem.dk
	Official tourism website of Denmark	www.visitdenmark.com
Finland	Ministry of Trade and Industry	www.ktm.fi
	Finnish Tourist Board	www.mek.fi
France	Ministry of Economy, Finance and Employment	www.minefe.gouv.fr
	Official Tourism website of France	www.tourisme.gouv.fr
	French government tourist office	www.franceguide.com
Germany	Federal Ministry of Economics and Technology	www.bmwi.bund.de
	Official tourism website of Germany	www.germany-tourism.de
Greece	Ministry of Tourism	www.mintour.gr
	Greek National Tourism Organisation	www.gnto.gr
	Organisation of Tourism Education and Training	www.otek.edu.gr
	Tourism Development Co.	www.tourism-development.gr
Hungary	Ministry of Local Government and Regional Development	www.meh.hu
	Official tourism website of Hungary	www.hungary.com

Annex Table 3.A1. **National tourism administration and related websites** (cont.)

Country	Organisation	Website
Iceland	Ministry of Communications	http//eng.samgonguraduneyti.is
	Central Bank of Iceland	www.sedlanbanki.is
	Icelandic Tourist Board	www.visiticeland.com
	Statistics Iceland	www.statice.is
Ireland	Department of Art, Sport and Tourism	www.dast.gov.ie
	Irish Tourist Industry Confederation	www.itic.ie
	National Tourism Development Authority	www.failteireland.ie
	Tourism Ireland	www.tourismireland.com
Italy	Presidency of the Council of Ministers	www.governo.it
	Italian National Tourism Board	www.enit.it
Japan	Ministry of Land, Infrastructure and Transport	www.mlit.go.jp
	Japan National Tourist Organisation	www.jnto.go.jp
Korea	Ministry of Culture and Tourism	www.mct.go.kr
	Korea Association of Travel Agents	www.kata.or.kr
	Korea Culture and Tourism Institute	www.kcti.re.kr
	Korea Tourism Organisation	www.knto.or.kr
	Main tourism websites	www.etourkorea.com
		www.tour2korea.com
	Tourism Knowledge Information System	www.tour.go.kr
Luxembourg	Ministry for the Middle Classes, Tourism and Housing	www.mdt.public.lu
Mexico	Ministry of Tourism	www.sectur.gob.mx
Netherlands	Ministry of Economic Affairs	www.minez.nl
	Netherlands Board of Tourism and Conventions	www.holland.com
New Zealand	Ministry of Tourism	www.tourism.govt.nz
	New Zealand's official tourism dataset	www.tourismresearch.govt.nz
	Statistics New Zealand	www.stats.govt.nz
	Tourism Industry Association	www.tianz.org.nz
	Tourism New Zealand	www.newzealand.com
	Tourism New Zealand's corporate website	www.tourismnewzealand.com
Norway	Ministry of Trade and Industry	www.regjeringen.no
	Official travel guide to Norway	www.visitnorway.com
Poland	Ministry of Sport and Tourism	www.msport.gov.pl
	Central Statistical Office	www.stat.gov.pl
	Institute of Tourism	www.intur.com.pl
	Polish Tourist Organisation	www.pot.gov.pl
Portugal	Ministry of Economy and Innovation	www.min-economia.pt
	Turismo de Portugal	www.turismodeportugal.pt
Slovak Republic	Ministry of Economy	www.economy.gov.sk
	Slovak Tourist Board	www.slovakiatourism.sk
	Statistical Office of the Slovak Republic	www.statistics.sk
Spain	Ministry for Industry, Tourism and Commerce	www.mityc.es
	Official tourism website of Spain	www.tourspain.es
	Turismo 2020	www.turismo2020.es
Sweden	Ministry of Enterprise, Energy and Communications	www.sweden.gov.se
	Agency for Economic and Regional Growth	www.nutek.se
Switzerland	State Secretariat for Economic Affairs	www.seco.admin.ch
	Swiss National Tourism Board	www.myswitzerland.com
Turkey	Ministry of Culture and Tourism	www.kultur.gov.tr
	Official tourism website of Turkey	www.tourismturkey.org
United Kingdom	Department for Culture, Media and Sport	www.culture.gov.uk
	Official tourism website of Britain	www.visitbritain.com
	Official tourism website of England	www.enjoyengland.com
	Official tourism website of London	www.visitlondon.com
	Official tourism website of Scotland	www.visitscotland.com
	Official tourism website of Wales	www.visitwales.com
United States	Department of Commerce	www.commerce.gov
	Office of Travel and Tourism Industries	www.tinet.ita.doc.gov

Annex Table 3.A1. **National tourism administration and related websites** (cont.)

	OECD non-member countries	
Romania	Ministry of SMEs, Trade, Tourism and Liberal Professions	*www.mimmctpl.ro*
	Official tourism website of Romania	*www.romaniatravel.com*
South Africa	Department of Environmental Affairs and Tourism	*www.deat.gov.za*
	Official tourism website of South Africa	*www.southafrica.net*
	Statistics South Africa	*www.statssa.gov.za*
	Tourism Business Council of South Africa	*www.tbcsa.travel*

OECD PUBLICATIONS, 2, rue André-Pascal, 75775 PARIS CEDEX 16
PRINTED IN FRANCE
(85 2008 01 1 P) ISBN 978-92-64-03967-4 – No. 55891 2008